Property

Elizabeth Mallicoat

P9-DXN-459

**AMERICAN SCHOOL OF NEEDLEWORK**
PRESENTS

# THE GREAT GRANNY CROCHET BOOK

President: Jean Leinhauser
Art Director: Louise O'Donnell
Editorial Directors: Barbara A. Retzke and Mary Thomas
Designer/Editor: Anis Duncan
Operations: Irmgard Barnes

Photography by Stemo Photography Inc., Northbrook, IL
Roderick A. Stemo, President
James E. Zorn, Photographer

**Columbia House**

Published by Columbia House, a Division of CBS Inc.,
1211 Avenue of the Americas, New York, New York 10036

# CONTENTS

Copyright © 1979 by American School of Needlework, Inc.
Published simultaneously in Canada. Protected under Berne and other international copyright conventions. All rights reserved.

This volume may not be reproduced in part or in whole in any form without permission from the publisher.

ISBN-0-930748-10-7
Library of Congress Catalog Card Number: 78-73380
Printed in the United States of America

Published by Columbia House, a Division of CBS Inc.
1211 Avenue of the Americas, New York, New York 10036

*We have made every effort to ensure the accuracy and completeness of the instructions in this book. We cannot, however, be responsible for human error, typographical mistakes or variations in individual work.*

# Introduction

Nobody knows whose grandmother first thriftily crocheted her leftover bits of yarn into squares from which to fashion a colorful, warm afghan. But the design of the now classic ''granny square'' afghan follows the tradition set by American pioneer women, who made use of every available scrap of fabric to create useful and beautiful patchwork quilts. In fact, in Europe the technique of making granny squares is called ''American crochet.''

The popularity of the granny square is based on a firm foundation: granny squares are quick and easy to make and easily portable—they can be made in waiting rooms of doctors or dentists; while attending meetings; and even traveling in a car, plane or bus.

No longer is the granny humble, appearing only on chilly evenings. Today the granny is used to make fashionable wearables, delightful toys, charming baby clothes, and decorative household items. The variety of granny squares has expanded; now we have not only granny squares, but granny triangles, hexagons, octagons, rectangles—and granny circles!

For this book, we've gathered a collection of diversified designs, all based on the original granny square, and all easy enough to be made by an inexperienced crocheter.

We hope you enjoy our collection of granny patterns as much as we enjoyed designing them for you.

*Jean Leinhauser*

President
American School of Needlework, Inc.

# ACKNOWLEDGMENTS

Several designs in this book were originally created by us for American Thread, and copyrighted by them. It is with their kind permission that we are able to include them in this book.

To ensure the accuracy and clarity of our instructions, all of the garments and projects in this book were tested by a group of dedicated, hard-working women who have willingly given up many evenings, weekends and hours of sleep to make the designs which we have photographed.

We express our appreciation to these pattern testers:

*Jan Corbally, Evanston, IL*
*Judy Demain, Highland Park, IL*
*Eleanor Denner, Buffalo Grove, IL*
*Gina Fiocchi, Riverwoods, IL*
*Kim Hubal, Evanston, IL*
*Tina Judah, Glenview, IL*
*Sandy Kimble, Wheeling, IL*
*Joan Kokaska, Wildwood, IL*
*Sandy Levitt, Buffalo Grove, IL*
*Barbara Luoma, Mundelein, IL*
*Margaret Miller, Chicago, IL*
*Elizabeth Mitzen, Glenview, IL*
*Janet Nelson, Wilmette, IL*
*Patty Rankin, Des Plaines, IL*
*Cindy Raymond, Vernon Hills, IL*
*Kathie Schroeder, Tucson, AZ*
*Helen Smith, Evanston, IL*

We also acknowledge our thanks and appreciation to the following contributing designers:

*Eleanor Denner, Buffalo Grove, IL*
*Anis Duncan, Northbrook, IL*
*Doris England, Des Plaines, IL*
*Kim Hubal, Evanston, IL*
*Jean Leinhauser, Glenview, IL*
*Barbara Luoma, Mundelein, IL*
*Barbara A. Retzke, Libertyville, IL*
*Kathie Schroeder, Tucson, AZ*
*Mary Thomas, Libertyville, IL*

# Granny's Recipe

Making a granny motif is easy, even if you're a beginning crocheter. Following is the "recipe" for a basic granny square. The ingredients needed for practice are a few yards each of several different colors of worsted weight yarn, and a size H aluminum crochet hook.

This pattern lets you practice the basic techniques of granny squares, but when making a specific project in this book or any other source, follow the *exact* instructions given, as there are slight differences in working methods of different motifs.

## BASIC GRANNY SQUARE

Make a sl knot on hook with first color, leaving a 3″ end. Ch 4, join with a sl st to form a ring *(Fig 1)*.

**Rnd 1:** [On this round, you will be working *into* the ring. As you do this, also work over the 3″ end left after making the sl knot; this keeps down the number of yarn ends to be run in after the square is completed.] Ch 3 *(Fig 2)*, 2 dc in ring *(Fig 3* shows first dc being worked in ring); (ch 2, 3 dc in ring) 3 times; ch 2, join in 3rd ch of beg ch-3 with a sl st *(Fig 4)*. [The side of the work now facing you is called the *right side* of the work.] Finish off first color.

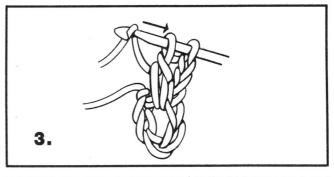

3.

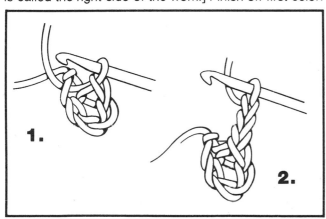

1.

2.

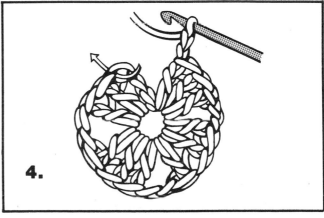

4.

**Rnd 2:** Make a sl knot on hook with 2nd color; with right side of work facing you, join 2nd color with a sl st in any ch-2 sp (these are corner sps); ch 3, 2 dc in same sp (Fig 5 shows first dc being worked in sp); ch 2, 3 dc again in same sp; * in next ch-2 sp, work (3 dc, ch 2, 3 dc); rep from * twice, join with a sl st in 3rd ch of beg ch-3. Finish off 2nd color. Look at your work; you should now have a perfect square.

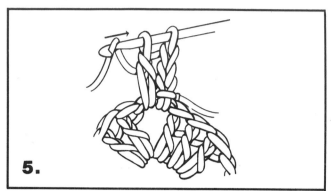

**5.**

**Rnd 3:** With right side of work facing you, join 3rd color as before in any ch-2 corner sp; (ch 3, 2 dc, ch 2, 3 dc) all in same sp; between next two 3-dc groups (Fig 6), work 3 dc for side; * (3 dc, ch 2, 3 dc) all in next ch-2 sp for corner; 3 dc between next two 3-dc groups for side; rep from * twice, join with a sl st in 3rd ch of beg ch-3. Finish off 3rd color.

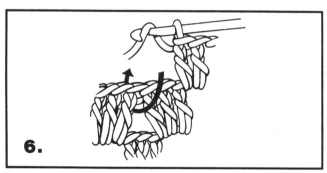

**6.**

**Rnd 4:** With right side of work facing you, join 4th color as before in any ch-2 corner sp; (ch 3, 2 dc, ch 2, 3 dc) all in same sp; * (3 dc between next two 3-dc groups) twice for side; (3 dc, ch 2, 3 dc) all in next ch-2 sp for corner; rep from * twice; (3 dc between next two 3-dc groups) twice for side; join with a sl st in 3rd ch of beg ch-3. Finish off 4th color. Weave in all loose yarn ends, trim them off.

**Notes:** You now have a 4-rnd square; work any additional desired rnds as for Rnd 4, working one more side group of 3 dcs on every additional rnd.

Unless a pattern specifies that you must *turn* your work before each new rnd, always work with the right side facing you.

When a pattern calls for working 2 or more rnds of the same color in succession, work to end of rnd, join, but do not finish off. Sl st in tops of each of next 2 dcs and into corner sp; work next rnd as specified.

When making grannys, you'll have lots of yarn ends to weave in (do this securely). Make it a practice to weave these in as you finish each square, unless the pattern says not to.

# SYMBOLS AND ABBREVIATIONS

The following abbreviations and symbols are used in our patterns:

## ABBREVIATIONS

| | | | |
|---|---|---|---|
| beg | begin(ning) | rnd(s) | round(s) |
| ch(s) | chain(s) | sc | single crochet(s) |
| dc | double crochet(s) | sk | skip |
| dec | decrease | sl | slip |
| hdc | half double crochet(s) | sp(s) | space(s) |
| inc | increase | sl st | slip stitch |
| lp(s) | loop(s) | st(s) | stitch(es) |
| patt | pattern | Tch | turning chain |
| rem | remain(ing) | tog | together |
| rep | repeat | tr | triple crochet |
| | | YO | yarn over |

## SYMBOLS

( ) Parentheses are used to enclose instructions which should be worked the exact number of times specified immediately following the parentheses, such as: (inc in next st, hdc in each of next 2 sts) 6 times.

[ ] Brackets (and/or parentheses) are used to provide additional information to clarify the instructions preceding the brackets, such as: 2 hdc in next st [inc made] or ch 2 (counts as one hdc).

= The number after an equal sign indicates the number of sts you should have when the row/rnd immediately preceding the equal sign has been completed.

† A pair of daggers is used to identify a portion of instructions in a row/rnd that will be repeated again later in the same row/rnd, or sometimes referred to later in the patt.

* An asterisk is used to mark the beg of a portion of instructions which will be worked more than once; thus, "rep from * twice" means after working the instructions once, repeat the instructions following the asterisk twice more (3 times in all).

# GAUGE

It is essential that you achieve the gauge—the number of sts and rows per inch, or the size of the square—exactly as given in a project. If you don't get the exact gauge, your garments will not fit correctly, and you may not have sufficient yarn to complete the project.

Before beginning a project, refer to the specified gauge and make a gauge swatch or square using the hook and yarn specified. If the test piece is *smaller* than specified in the gauge note, make another using a *larger* size hook; if the test piece is *larger* than specified, try again with a *smaller* size hook. Keep trying until you find a hook that gives you the correct size. Often you won't achieve gauge with the size hook recommended; do not hesitate to change hook sizes to obtain the correct gauge.

# Chapter 1

# Granny's Cozy Covers

The granny square made its debut as an afghan or bedcovering, and in this traditional form is still a favorite. But new shapes for the motifs and striking new color combinations have made the granny afghan a contemporary decorating accessory.

Included in this chapter are eight afghans, each in a different mood. In *Snowfire,* bright red against stark white creates a dramatic accent; *Bridal Rose* is a delicate, feminine confection; *Geometrics* is striking and sophisticated. *Calico Granny* has a country look, achieved by combining ombre yarn with solid solors; *Popcorn Diamonds* is reminiscent of the lovely Aran fisherman designs, and *Emerald Isle* hints of the green landscape of Ireland. *Starburst* utilizes both color and texture for its design impact, and of course the *Traditional Granny,* made in bedspread size, is a colorful reminder of where it all began.

# CALICO GRANNY

*designed by Jean Leinhauser*

**SIZE: Approx 44″ wide × 67″ long**
**MATERIALS: Dawn Sayelle\* Knitting Worsted Size: three 4-oz skeins White (Color A); five 4-oz skeins Grass Green (Color B); six 3½ oz skeins Tiger Lily (Color C); aluminum crochet hook size I (or size required for gauge).**
**GAUGE: One 10-rnd square = 10½″**

## INSTRUCTIONS

GRANNY SQUARE (make 24)
**Note:** All rnds are worked on right side. With Color A, ch 5, join with a sl st to form a ring.

**Rnd 1:** Ch 3, 2 dc in ring; (ch 2, 3 dc in ring) 3 times; ch 2, join with a sl st in top of beg ch-3.

**Rnd 2:** Sl st in each of next 2 dc and into next ch-2 sp; ch 3, work (2 dc, ch 2, 3 dc) all in same sp; * in next ch-2 sp work (3 dc, ch 2, 3 dc); rep from * twice, join with a sl st in top of beg ch-3. You have now made 4 corners with ch-2 sp at each corner.

**Rnd 3:** Sl st in each of next 2 dc and into corner sp; ch 3, work (2 dc, ch 2, 3 dc) all in same sp; * work 3 dc between next two 3-dc groups, (3 dc, ch 2, 3 dc) in next corner sp; rep from * twice, 3 dc between next two 3-dc groups, join as before.

**Rnd 4:** Sl st in each of next 2 dc and into corner sp; ch 3, (2 dc, ch 2, 3 dc) in same sp; * work 3 dc between each pair of 3-dc groups along side; in next corner sp work (3 dc, ch 2, 3 dc); rep from * twice, work 3 dc between each pair of 3-dc groups along last side, join as before. Finish off, weave in yarn ends.

**Rnd 5:** Join Color B with a sl st in any corner sp; ch 3, (2 dc, ch 2, 3 dc) in same sp; * 3 dc between each pair of 3-dc groups along side; in next corner sp work (3 dc, ch 2, 3 dc); rep from * twice, work 3 dc between each pair of 3-dc groups along last side, join as before. Finish off, weave in yarn ends.

**Rnd 6:** With Color C, work as for Rnd 5 but do not finish off yarn.

**Rnd 7:** Sl st in each of next 2 dc and into corner sp; ch 3, (2 dc, ch 2, 3 dc) in same sp; * 3 dc between each pair of 3-dc groups along side; in next corner sp work (3 dc, ch 2, 3 dc); rep from * twice, work 3 dc between each pair of 3-dc groups along last side, join as before.

**Rnd 8:** Rep Rnd 7; finish off Color C, weave in yarn ends.

**Rnd 9:** With Color B, rep Rnd 5 but do not finish off.

**Rnd 10:** Rep Rnd 7. Finish off, weave in yarn ends.

*ASSEMBLING*

Afghan is 4 squares wide by 6 squares long. Squares for the afghan in our photo were joined with Color B, using Method 3 (see joining methods in Chapter 8). Beg with a sl st in one ch of one corner and end with a sl st in one ch of next corner.

*EDGING*

With right side facing, join Color B with a sl st in ch-2 sp of square at upper right-hand corner.

**Rnd 1:** Ch 3, work (2 dc, ch 2, 3 dc) all in same corner sp; * work 3 dc between each pair of 3-dc groups along side *and* in each joining; in corner sp work (3 dc, ch 2, 3 dc); rep from * twice, work 3 dc between each pair of 3-dc groups along last side, join with a sl st in top of beg ch-3.

**Rnd 2:** Sl st into each of next 2 dc and into corner sp; continue in same manner as Rnd 1. Finish off, weave in yarn ends. Lightly steam joinings if desired.

# SNOWFIRE

*designed by Jean Leinhauser*

**SIZE: Approx 54″ wide × 73″ long**
**MATERIALS: Dawn Sayelle\* Knitting Worsted Size in 4-oz skeins, 9 skeins Flame and 8 skeins White; aluminum crochet hook size G (or size required for gauge).**
**GAUGE: One square = 7¼ ″**

## INSTRUCTIONS

*SQUARE (make 70)*
With White, ch 6, join with a sl st to form a ring.

**Rnd 1:** Ch 3, 15 dc in ring, join with a sl st in top of beg ch-3.

**Rnd 2:** Ch 5, dc in same place as sl st; * sk next dc, work (dc, ch 2, dc) all in next dc; rep from * 6 times; sk last dc, join with a sl st in 3rd ch of bcg ch 5.

**Rnd 3:** Sl st into beg sp; in same sp, work (ch 3, dc, ch 3, 2 dc); * work (2 dc, ch 3, 2 dc) all in next ch-2 sp; rep from * 6 times, join with a sl st in top of beg ch-3.

**Rnd 4:** Sl st in next dc and into next ch-3 sp; in same sp, work (ch 3, 2 dc, ch 3, 3 dc); * work (3 dc, ch 3, 3 dc) in next ch-3 sp; rep from * 6 times, join with a sl st in top of beg ch.

**Rnd 5:** Sl st in each of next 2 dc and into ch-3 sp; in same sp, work (ch 3, 3 dc, ch 2, 4 dc); * work (4 dc, ch 2, 4 dc) in next ch-3 sp; rep from * 6 times, join with a sl st in top of beg ch. Finish off White.

**Rnd 6:** Join Flame with a sl st in any ch-2 sp. [**Note:** For this rnd only, work in *sps* between dcs, not in the dcs. When instructions say work in sp or sps, it means those *between* the dcs; when a ch-2 sp is meant, it is so specified.] * Sc in next sp, hdc in next sp, dc in each of next 5 sps; work (2 dc, ch 3, 2 dc) all in next ch-2 sp for corner; dc in each of next 5 sps, hdc in next sp, sc in next sp, sl st in next ch-2 sp; rep from * 3 times, working last sl st into first sl st of rnd.

**Rnd 7:** Ch 1, sc in next sc, sc in next hdc, sc in next dc; * dc in each of next 6 dc; work (2 dc, ch 3, 2 dc) in corner sp; dc in each of next 6 dc; sc in each of next 7 sts [these are: dc, hdc, sc, sl st, sc, hdc, dc]; rep from * 3 times, ending last rep by working sc in each of last 3 sts; join with a sl st in beg ch-1.

**Rnd 8:** Ch 1, sc in each st around, working 3 sc in each corner ch-3 sp; join with a sl st in beg ch-1. Finish off, weave in yarn ends.

Place square right side down on a padded ironing surface; lightly steam press so that square lays flat.

### ASSEMBLING

Afghan is 7 squares wide by 10 squares long. Squares for the afghan in our photo were joined with Flame using Method 3 (see joining methods in Chapter 8). Beg with a sl st in center sc of one corner sp and work in each st across, ending in center sc of next corner sp.

### EDGING

With right side of afghan facing you, join Flame with a sl st in back lp of center sc in upper right-hand corner; work 3 sc in same st; sc in back lp of each st around, working 3 sc in center st of each rem corner, ending by joining with a sl st in beg sc. Finish off, weave in yarn ends.

Place afghan right side down on padded surface; lightly steam press each joining and each outer edge.

(Shown in color on page 69.)

# BRIDAL ROSE

*designed by Jean Leinhauser*

This afghan is an adaptation of the traditional Irish Crochet rose motif which enjoyed worldwide popularity during the mid-1800's. Done then with the finest threads, the art was taught in convents, and items for export sale were made at home by Irish women to support their families during the disastrous years of the potato famine. Our updated version, a tribute to those dedicated women who put their needlework skills to good use during a time of national calamity, would make a lovely gift for a new bride or an anniversary present for a not-quite-so-new one.

**SIZE: Approx 53″ wide × 68″ long**

**MATERIALS: Dawn Wintuk\* Sport Yarn in 2-oz skeins, 24 skeins White; aluminum crochet hook size E (or size required for gauge).**

**GAUGE: One square = 7½″**

## INSTRUCTIONS

SQUARE *(make 63)*
Ch 6, join with a sl st to form a ring.

**Rnd 1:** Ch 3 (counts as first dc), 11 dc in ring, join with a sl st in top of beg ch-3 = 12 dc.

**Rnd 2:** Ch 2, hdc in sl st; work 2 hdc in each dc around = 24 hdc (counting beg ch-2 as first hdc). Join with a sl st in top of beg ch.

**Rnd 3:** Ch 1, sc in same st as sl st; * ch 5, sk 2 hdc, sc in next hdc; rep from * 6 times, ending ch 5, join with a sl st in first sc of rnd = 8 ch lps made.

**Rnd 4:** * In next ch-5 lp, work a petal of (sc, hdc, 5 dc, hdc, sc); rep from * 7 times, join with a sl st in first sc = 8 petals made.

**Rnd 5:** * Ch 5; holding first petal forward and working behind it, sc around next sc made in Rnd 3, inserting hook from back to front to back *(Fig 1)*; rep from * 6 times, ch 5, do **not** join = 8 lps made.

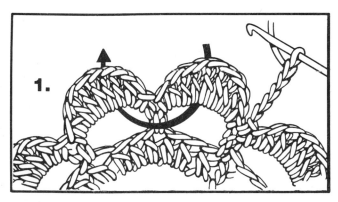

**1.**

**Rnd 6:** Holding each petal forward and working behind it, * into next lp, work a petal of (sc, hdc, 7dc, hdc, sc); rep from * 7 times, join with a sl st in first sc.

**Rnd 7:** * Ch 7, holding petal forward and working behind it, sc around next sc made in Rnd 5; rep from * 6 times, ch 7, do **not** join = 8 lps.

**Rnd 8:** * Into next lp, work petal of (sc, hdc, 9 dc, hdc, sc); rep from * 7 times, join with a sl st in first sc. Flower center is now completed.

**Rnd 9:** Ch 7, * in 5th dc of next petal work (dc, ch 4, dc) for corner; ch 4, dc between next 2 petals; ch 4, sc in 5th dc of next petal; ch 4, dc between this and next petal; ch 4; rep from * twice. In 5th dc of next petal work (dc, ch 4, dc); ch 4, dc between next 2 petals; ch 4, sc in 5th dc of next petal; ch 4, join with a sl st in 3rd ch of beg ch.

**Rnd 10:** Sl st into next ch-4 sp, ch 3, 3 dc in same sp, ch 1; * in corner sp work (2 dc, ch 3, 2 dc); ch 1, 4 dc in next sp; work (ch 1, 3 dc in next sp) twice; ch 1, 4 dc in next sp; ch 1, rep from * twice. In corner sp work (2 dc, ch 3, 2 dc); ch 1, 4 dc in next sp; work (ch 1, 3 dc in next sp) twice; ch 1, join with a sl st in top of beg ch.

**Rnd 11:** Sl st into each of next 3 dc and into ch-1 sp; sl st into each of next 2 dc and into corner sp; in **same** sp work (ch 3, dc, ch 3, 2 dc), ch 1; * sk next 2 dc of corner sp, dc in each of next 4 dc, ch 1; work (dc in each of next 3 dc, ch 1) twice; dc in each of next 4 dc, ch 1; work (2 dc, ch 3, 2 dc) all in next corner sp; ch 1; rep from * twice. Sk next 2 dc of corner sp, dc in each of next 4 dc, ch 1; (dc in each of next 3 dc, ch 1) twice; dc in sl st at top of ch-3 and in each sl st at top of next 3 dc, ch 1, join with a sl st in top of beg ch-3.

**Rnd 12:** Sl st in next dc and into corner sp; in **same** sp work (ch 3, 2 dc, ch 3, 3 dc), ch 1; * sk next 2 dc of corner sp, dc in each of next 4 dc, ch 1; work (dc in each of next 3 dc, ch 1) twice; dc in each of next 4 dc, ch 1; work (3 dc, ch 3, 3 dc) all in next corner sp, ch 1; rep from * twice. Sk next 2 dc of corner sp; dc in each of next 4 dc, ch 1; work (dc in each of next 3 dc, ch 1) twice; dc in each of next 4 dc, ch 1, join with a sl st in top of beg ch-3.

**Rnd 13:** Sl st in each of next 2 dc and into corner sp; in **same** sp work (ch 3, 2 dc, ch 3, 3 dc); * sk next 3 dc of corner sp, dc in each of next 4 dc, ch 1; work (dc in each of next 3 dc, ch 1) twice; dc in each of next 4 dc, ch 2; work (3 dc, ch 3, 3 dc) all in next corner sp, ch 2, rep from * twice. Sk next 3 dc of corner sp, dc in each of next 4 dc, ch 1; work (dc in each of next 3 dc, ch 1) twice; dc in each of next 4 dc, ch 2; join with a sl st in top of beg ch-3. Finish off, weave in yarn ends.

### ASSEMBLING

Afghan is 7 squares wide by 9 squares long. Squares for the afghan in our photo were joined using Method 4 (see joining methods in Chapter 8). Beg in one corner, work in each st across, ending in next corner.

### EDGING

With right side of afghan facing, join yarn with a sl st in any corner sp.

**Rnd 1:** Ch 5, sc in same sp; * ch 5, sc in next sp; rep from * around, being sure to count the corner sp on each side of every joining as a sp (2 sps at each joining); and working (sc, ch 5, sc) in all of rem 3 outer corner sps, join with a sl st in first sc of rnd.

**Rnd 2:** In corner sp work petal of (sc, hdc, 5 dc, hdc, sc); work same petal in each ch-5 sp and in each corner around, join with a sl st in first sc of rnd. Finish off, weave in yarn ends.

# POPCORN DIAMONDS

*designed by Jean Leinhauser*

**SIZE: Approx 51¼″ × 61½″ before fringing**

**MATERIALS: Dawn Sayelle\* Knitting Worsted Size in 4-oz skeins, 20 skeins Fisherman; aluminum crochet hook size I (or size required for gauge).**

**GAUGE: One square = 10¼″**

## INSTRUCTIONS

*POPCORN DIAMOND SQUARE (make 30)*

Ch 8, join with a sl st to form a ring.

**Rnd 1:** Ch 3, make a popcorn (abbreviated PC) as follows: [Ch 1, 5 dc in ring; drop lp from hook, insert hook in ch-1 before 5-dc group, hook dropped lp and draw through—see Fig 1]. * Dc in ring, make a PC as before; rep from * 6 times join with á sl st in top of beg ch-3 = 8 PC made.

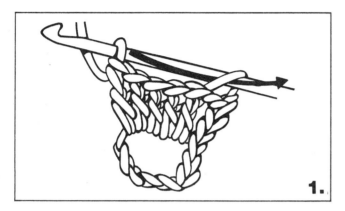

**1.**

**Rnd 2:** Ch 3; holding back on hook last lp of each dc, work 2 dc in same place as joining; YO and draw through all 3 lps now on hook [beg cluster made], ch 2; holding back last lp of each dc as before, work 3 dc in same place as beg cluster; YO and draw through all 4 lps now·on hook [3-dc cluster made]. You have now completed first corner of square. * Ch 1, sk next PC; 3 dc in next dc [for side], ch 1, sk next PC; make (3-dc cluster, ch 2, 3-dc cluster) all in next dc for corner; rep from * twice, ch 1, sk next PC, 3 dc in next dc for last side, ch 1, join with a sl st in top of beg ch-3.

**Rnd 3:** Sl st into ch-2 sp, ch 3; in same sp work (beg cluster, ch 2, 3-dc cluster) for corner; * ch 1, 2 dc in next sp, dc in each dc along side, 2 dc in next sp, ch 1; in next ch-2 sp work (3-dc cluster, ch 2, 3-dc cluster); rep from * twice, ch 1, 2 dc in next sp, dc in each dc along last side, 2 dc in next sp, ch 1, join as before.

**Rnd 4:** Rep Rnd 3; at end of rnd, you should have 7 dc along each side and 2 dc worked in each ch-1 sp: a total of 11 dc between corners.

**Rnd 5:** Sl st into ch-2 sp, ch 3; in same sp work (beg cluster, ch 2, 3-dc cluster) for corner; * ch 1, 2 dc in next sp, dc in each of next 5 dc, ch 1, PC in next dc, dc in each of next 5 dc, 2 dc, 2 dc in next sp, ch 1; in next ch-2 sp work (3-dc cluster, ch 2, 3-dc cluster) for corner; rep from * twice, ch 1, 2 dc in next sp, dc in each of next 5 dc, ch 1, PC in next dc, dc in each of next 5 dc, 2 dc in next sp, ch 1; join with a sl st in top of beg ch-3.

**Rnd 6:** Sl st into ch-2 sp, work beg corner as before; * ch 1, dc in next sp, dc in each of next 5 dc, ch 1, PC in next dc, dc in next dc, dc in ch at back of next PC, dc in next dc; ch 1, PC in next dc, dc in each of next 5 dc, dc in next sp, ch 1, work corner as before; rep from * 3 times, but at end of last rep, do not work corner, join with a sl st in top of beg ch-3.

**Rnd 7:** Sl st into ch-2 sp, work beg corner as before; * ch 1, 2 dc in next sp, dc in each of next 4 dc, ch 1, PC in next dc; work (dc in next dc, dc in ch at back of next PC, dc in next dc, ch 1, PC in next dc) twice; dc in each of next 4 dc, 2 dc in next sp, ch 1, work corner as before; rep from * 3 times, ending in same manner as Rnd 6.

**Rnd 8:** Sl st into ch-2 sp, work beg corner as before; * ch 1, dc in next sp, dc in each of next 4 dc, ch 1, PC in next dc; work (dc in next dc, dc in ch at back of next PC, dc in next dc, ch 1, PC in next dc) 3 times; dc in each of next 4 dc, dc in next sp, ch 1, work corner as before; rep from * 3 times, ending in same manner as before.

**Rnd 9:** Sl st into ch-2 sp, work beg corner as before; * ch 1, 2 dc in next sp, dc in each of next 3 dc, ch 1, PC in next dc; work (dc in next dc, dc in ch at back of next PC, dc in next dc, ch 1, PC in next dc) 4 times, dc in each of next 3 dc, 2 dc in next sp, ch 1, work corner as before; rep from * 3 times, ending in same manner as before. You should have 5 PC along each side; finish off, weave in yarn ends.

**Note:** Measure first square to be sure it conforms to gauge.

### ASSEMBLING

Afghan is 5 squares wide by 6 squares long. The squares for the afghan in our photo were joined by using Method 1 (see joining methods in Chapter 8). Beg in ch-2 corner sp, work in first corner cluster, in ch-1 sp, each dc, in ch at top of each PC along side, in ch-1 sp, corner cluster and end in next ch-2 corner sp.

### EDGING

With right side of afghan facing, join yarn with a sl st in upper right-hand corner sp.

**Rnd 1:** Work 3 sc in same sp, * sc in top of corner cluster, in first ch-1 sp, through both lps of each dc and in ch at top of each PC along side of square, in last ch-1 sp, through both lps of corner cluster, and in joining; rep from * to next corner, work 3 sc in corner; continue around in same manner, working 3 sc in each corner, join with a sl st in beg sc of rnd.

**Rnd 2:** Ch 1, 3 sc in next sc, * sc in each st to next corner, work 3 sc in center st of corner; rep from * twice, sc in each st to beg corner, join with a sl st in beg ch-1. Finish off, weave in yarn ends.

### FINISHING

**Fringe:** Following Fringe Instructions in Chapter 8, make triple knot fringe. Cut strands 18″ long; using 10 strands for each knot, tie 36 knots evenly spaced across each short end.

# STARBURST

*designed by Mary Thomas*

**SIZE:** Approx 45″ × 65″

**MATERIALS:** Worsted weight yarn, 48 oz green, 12 oz ecru; aluminum crochet hook size I (or size required for gauge).

**GAUGE:** One motif = 5″ square

## INSTRUCTIONS

*BASIC MOTIF*

**Rnd 1:** Ch 6, join with a sl st to form ring. Make a beg popcorn (abbreviated beg PC). [**To do this:** ch 3, work 3 dc in ring, drop lp from hook; insert hook in top of beg ch-3, hook dropped lp and draw through; ch 1]. * Ch 3, make a PC [**To do this:** work 4 dc in ring, drop lp from hook; insert hook in first dc, hook dropped lp and draw through; ch 1]. Rep from * twice, ch 3, join with a sl st in ch-1 sp at top of beg PC.

**Rnd 2:** Sl st into ch-3 sp; work (beg PC, ch 3, PC) in **same** sp; * ch 3, work (PC, ch 3, PC) in next sp; rep from * twice, ch 3, join with a sl st as before.

**Rnd 3:** Sl st into ch-3 sp, work (ch 3, 3 dc, ch 2, 4 dc) in **same** sp; * 4 hdc in next sp, work (4 dc, ch 2, 4 dc) in next sp; rep from * twice, 4 hdc in last sp, join with a sl st in top of beg ch-3.

**Rnd 4:** Ch 3, dc in each of next 3 sts; * in ch-2 sp work (2 dc, ch 2, 2 dc); dc in each of next 12 sts; rep from * 3 times ending last rep by working dc in each of last 8 sts, join with a sl st in top of beg ch-3. Finish off.

Following Basic Motif instructions, make motifs as follows:

**MOTIF A (make 52)**
Rnds 1, 2, 3 and 4: Green

**MOTIF B (make 21)**
Rnd 1: Ecru
Rnd 2: Green
Rnd 3: Ecru
Rnd 4: Green

**MOTIF C (make 16)**
Rnd 1: Ecru
Rnds 2, 3, and 4: Green

**MOTIF D (make 28)**
Rnd 1: Green
Rnd 2: Ecru
Rnds 3 and 4: Green

**Note:** You will have a total of 117 motifs which will be assembled and joined in position shown on chart in Fig 1.

| B | B | C | D | A | D | C | B | B |
|---|---|---|---|---|---|---|---|---|
| B | C | D | A | A | A | D | C | B |
| C | D | A | A | A | A | A | D | C |
| D | A | A | A | D | A | A | A | D |
| A | A | A | D | B | D | A | A | A |
| A | A | D | B | C | B | D | A | A |
| A | D | B | C | B | C | B | D | A |
| A | A | D | B | C | B | D | A | A |
| A | A | A | D | B | D | A | A | A |
| D | A | A | A | D | A | A | A | D |
| B | D | A | A | A | A | A | D | C |
| B | C | D | A | A | A | D | C | B |
| B | B | C | D | A | D | C | B | B |

**1.**

*ASSEMBLING*

Afghan is 9 motifs wide by 13 motifs long. Motifs for the afghan in our photo were joined with green using Method 5 (see joining methods in Chapter 8). Beg in one ch st of ch-2 corner sp and end in one ch st of next ch-2 corner sp.

*EDGING*

With right side facing, join green with a sl st in any dc along outer edge; sc in same st, in each dc and in each ch st around [there are 2 ch sts at each joining and in each of four outer corners]; join with a sl st in first sc of rnd. Finish off, weave in yarn ends.

# GEOMETRICS

*designed by Barbara Retzke*

**SIZE: Approx 48″ × 63″**

**MATERIALS: Worsted weight yarn, 6 oz lt blue, 9 oz med blue, 12 oz dk blue, 23 oz white; aluminum crochet hook size H (or size required for gauge).**

**GAUGE: One square = 4½″**

## INSTRUCTIONS

**Note:** Throughout patt, each rnd/row is worked on right side.

*GRANNY SQUARE (make 48)*

With lt blue, ch 4, join with a sl st to form a ring.

**Rnd 1:** Ch 3, 2 dc in ring; ch 2, work (3 dc in ring, ch 2) 3 times, join with a sl st in top of beg ch-3. Finish off.

**Rnd 2:** Join white with a sl st in any ch-2 sp, work a **beg double group** in same sp as follows: ch 3 [counts as first dc], 2 dc, ch 2, 3 dc. Ch 1, * work a double group of (3 dc, ch 2, 3 dc) in next sp, ch 1; rep from * twice, join with a sl st in top of beg ch. Finish off.

**Rnd 3:** Join med blue with a sl st in any ch-2 sp, work a beg double group in same sp; * ch 1, 3 dc in next sp; ch 1, double group in next sp; rep from * twice, ch 1, 3 dc in next sp; ch 1, join with a sl st in top of beg ch. Finish off.

**Rnd 4:** Join white with a sl st in any ch-2 sp, work a beg double group in same sp; * ch 1, work (3 dc in next sp, ch 1) twice; double group in next sp; rep from * twice, ch 1; work (3 dc in next sp, ch 1) twice, join with a sl st in top of beg ch. Finish off.

*HEXAGON (make 35)*

With lt blue, ch 20.

**Rnd 1:** In 4th ch from hook work (2 dc, ch 2, 3 dc, ch 2, 3 dc); ch 1, sk 3 chs; work (3 dc in next ch, ch 1, sk 3 chs) 3 times; in last ch work (3 dc, ch 2, 3 dc, ch 2, 3 dc). Now work on other side of foundation ch as follows: ch 1, sk next 3 chs; work (3 dc in next ch, ch 1, sk 3 chs) 3 times, join with a sl st in 3rd ch of starting ch = 12 3-dc groups. Finish off.

**Rnd 2:** Join white with a sl st in ch-2 sp between first two 3-dc groups of Rnd 1, work a **beg double group** in same sp as follows: ch 3, 2 dc, ch 2, 3 dc. Ch 1, work a double group of (3 dc, ch 2, 3 dc) in next sp, ch 1; † work (3 dc in sp between next 2 groups, ch 1) four times†; work (double group in next sp, ch 1) twice; rep from † to †, join with a sl st in top of beg ch-3. Finish off.

**Rnd 3:** Join med blue with a sl st in sp between 2 double groups, work a beg double group in same sp; † ch 2, sc in next sp, ch 2 †; work (3 dc in next sp, ch 1) 4 times, 3 dc in next sp; rep from † to †, work double group in next sp, rep from † to †; work (3 dc in next sp, ch 1) 4 times, 3 dc in next sp, join with a sl st in top of beg ch. Finish off.

**Rnd 4:** Join white with a sl st in ch-2 sp of beg group, work a beg double group in same sp; † ch 1, 3 dc in next sp; ch 1, double group in next sp; work (ch 1, 3 dc in next sp) 4 times; ch 1, double group in next sp; ch 1, 3 dc in next sp †; ch 1, double group in next sp, rep from † to †, ch 1; join with a sl st in top of beg ch. Finish off.

**Rnd 5:** Join dk blue with a sl st in ch-2 sp of beg group, work a beg double group in same sp; work (ch 1, 3 dc in next sp) 11 times, ch 1; double group in next sp, ch 1; work (3 dc in next sp, ch 1) 11 times, join with a sl st in top of beg ch. Finish off.

*HEXAGON HALF (make 10)*

With lt blue, ch 20.

**Row 1:** Dc in 4th ch from hook, ch 2, 3 dc in same st; work (ch 1, sk 3 chs, 3 dc in next ch) 3 times, ch 1, sk 3 chs; in last ch work (3 dc, ch 2, 2 dc). Finish off.

**Row 2:** Join white with a sl st in 3rd ch of starting ch; ch 4, work (3 dc, ch 2, 3 dc) in next sp; work (ch 1, 3 dc in next sp) 4 times; ch 1, (3 dc, ch 2, 3 dc) in next sp; ch 1, dc in last dc. Finish off.

**Row 3:** Join med blue with a sl st in beg ch-4 sp, ch 3, 2 dc in same sp; ch 2, sc in next sp; ch 2, work (3 dc in next sp, ch 1) 4 times; 3 dc in next sp, ch 2; sc in next sp, ch 2; 3 dc in last sp. Finish off.

**Row 4:** Join white with a sl st in top of beg ch-3, ch 3, 2 dc in same st; ch 1, 3 dc in next sp, ch 1; (3 dc, ch 2, 3 dc) in next sp, work (ch 1, 3 dc in next sp) 4 times; ch 1, (3 dc, ch 2, 3 dc) in next sp; ch 1, 3 dc in next sp; ch 1, 3 dc in last dc. Finish off.

**Row 5:** Join dk blue with a sl st in top of beg ch-3, ch 3, 2 dc in same st; ch 1, work (3 dc in next sp, ch 1) 11 times, 3 dc in last dc. Finish off.

*ASSEMBLING AND JOINING*

Assemble hexagons and squares in positions shown on chart in Fig 1. To join, hold 2 hexagons with right sides tog; you will be working across the five 3-dc groups at long edge. Thread dk blue into tapestry needle; carefully matching each dc and each ch-1, sew with overcast st in **outer lps only** of each st across (Joining Method 5 in Chapter 8). First join 7 hexagons to form a row, then join one hexagon half at each end of row. Join squares (one at a time) to hexagon row using dk blue; with right sides of square and hexagon tog, you will be working across the four 3-dc groups along short edge. Beg in one ch st at one corner of square; after you have joined one ch st in 2nd corner of square, fold work so right side of square and right side of next hexagon are tog and continue joining across ending in one ch st of 3rd corner of square. Join rem squares across row in same manner. On first and last rows of squares (each short end of afghan), secure squares by joining into **both** chs in first and 3rd corners.

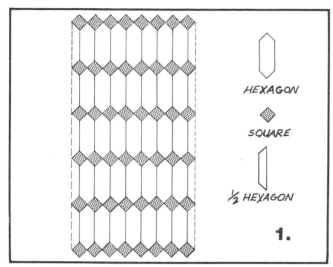

HEXAGON

SQUARE

½ HEXAGON

**1.**

*FINISHING*

**Edging:** Hold afghan with right side facing and long edge across top; join dk blue with a sl st in ch-2 sp of first square in upper right-hand corner. Across edge of hexagon work * 3 dc in first row of hexagon, sk next row; 3 dc in next row, sk next row; 3 dc in next row, work (3 dc in next ch-3 sp) 4 times; work (3 dc in next row, sk next row) twice; work 3 dc in last row of hexagon, then work 3 dc in ch-2 sp of square. Rep from * 3 times, work across last hexagon as before, sl st into ch-2 sp of last square; finish off, weave in yarn ends. Work other long edge in same manner.

**Tassels:** Follow Tassel Instructions in Chapter 8, make a total of 16 tassels. Cut strands of dk blue yarn 14″ long; use 12 strands to make each tassel; attach one in each ch-2 sp of squares at both short ends of afghan. With wrong side facing, steam lightly at all joinings.

*(Shown in color on the book jacket.)*

# TRADITIONAL GRANNY

*designed by Jean Leinhauser*

| SIZES: | SMALL (Twin) | LARGE (Full) |
|---|---|---|
| Approx size before fringing | 60"x94" | 88"x94" |

**MATERIALS:** Worsted weight yarn: 3(4) oz each Red, Blue, Yellow, Green, Orange, Brown, Pink, White and 5(7) oz matching ombre for each of the eight solid colors; 52(76) oz Black; aluminum crochet hook size G (or size required for gauge).

**Materials Note:** The numbers in parentheses are for the large size.

**GAUGE:** One Granny Square = 5½"

## GRANNY SQUARE INSTRUCTIONS

**Note:** All rnds are worked on right side.

**Rnd 1:** With solid color, ch 4, join with a sl st to form a ring. Ch 3, work 2 dc in ring; * ch 2, work 3 dc in ring; rep from * twice, ch 2; join with a sl st in top of beg ch-3, do not finish off.

**Rnd 2:** Sl st in each of next 2 dc, sl st into ch-2 sp; ch 3, work (2 dc, ch 2, 3 dc) all in same sp [for corner]; * in next ch-2 sp work (3 dc, ch 2, 3 dc) for corner; rep from * twice, join with a sl st in top of beg ch-3. Finish off.

**Rnd 3:** Join black with a sl st in any corner ch-2 sp; ch 3, work (2 dc, ch 2, 3 dc) in same sp, work 3 dc between two 3-dc groups at side; * work (3 dc, ch 2, 3 dc) in next corner sp, 3 dc between 3-dc groups at side; rep from * twice, join with a sl st in top of beg ch-3. Finish off.

**Rnd 4:** Join ombre with a sl st in any corner sp; ch 3, work (2 dc, ch 2, 3 dc) in same sp, 3 dc between each group along side; * work (3 dc, ch 2, 3 dc) in next corner sp, 3 dc between each group along side; rep from * twice, join with a sl st in top of beg ch-3; do not finish off.

**Rnd 5:** Sl st in each of next 2 dc and into ch-2 sp; work around in same manner as Rnd 4. Finish off ombre.

**Rnd 6:** Join black with a sl st in any corner sp; work around in same manner as Rnd 4. Finish off black.

## AFGHAN INSTRUCTIONS

Following Granny Square Instructions, make 20 each of the following 8 squares (160 squares total) for Small Size; make 30 each (240 squares total) for Large Size.
**Note:** Use black for Rnd 3 and Rnd 6 of **every** square.

### Square R
Rnds 1 and 2: Red
Rnds 4 and 5: Red Ombre

### Square B
Rnds 1 and 2: Blue
Rnds 4 and 5: Blue Ombre

### Square O
Rnds 1 and 2: Orange
Rnds 4 and 5: Orange Ombre

### Square G
Rnds 1 and 2: Green
Rnds 4 and 5: Green Ombre

### Square Y
Rnds 1 and 2: Yellow
Rnds 4 and 5: Yellow Ombre

### Square P
Rnds 1 and 2: Pink
Rnds 4 and 5: Pink Ombre

### Square Br
Rnds 1 and 2: Brown
Rnds 4 and 5: Brown Ombre

### Square W
Rnds 1 and 2: White
Rnds 4 and 5: Red/White/Blue Ombre

*ASSEMBLING*

For Small Size, assemble 16 rows of squares with 10 squares in each row; for Large Size, assemble 16 rows of squares with 15 squares in each row as shown in Fig 1. Squares for the afghan in our photo were joined with black, using Method 5 (see joining methods in Chapter 8). Beg in one corner st and work across, ending in next corner st.

**TRADITIONAL GRANNY BEDSPREAD CHART**

| LARGE SIZE | | | | | | | | | | | | | | |
|---|---|---|---|---|---|---|---|---|---|---|---|---|---|---|
| **SMALL SIZE** | | | | | | | | | | | | | | |
| R | Y | B | P | O | Br | G | W | Y | R | P | O | Br | G | W |
| B | P | O | Br | G | W | Y | R | P | B | Br | G | W | Y | R |
| O | Br | G | W | Y | R | P | B | Br | O | W | Y | R | P | B |
| G | W | Y | R | P | B | Br | O | W | G | R | P | B | Br | O |
| Y | R | P | B | Br | O | W | G | R | Y | B | Br | O | W | G |
| P | B | Br | O | W | G | R | Y | B | P | O | W | G | R | Y |
| Br | O | W | G | R | Y | B | P | O | Br | G | R | Y | B | P |
| W | G | R | Y | B | P | O | Br | G | W | Y | B | P | O | Br |
| R | Y | B | P | O | Br | G | W | Y | R | P | O | Br | G | W |
| B | P | O | Br | G | W | Y | R | P | B | Br | G | W | Y | R |
| O | Br | G | W | Y | R | P | B | Br | O | W | Y | R | P | B |
| G | W | Y | R | P | B | Br | O | W | G | R | P | B | Br | O |
| Y | R | P | B | Br | O | W | G | R | Y | B | Br | O | W | G |
| P | B | Br | O | W | G | R | Y | B | P | O | W | G | R | Y |
| Br | O | W | G | R | Y | B | P | O | Br | G | R | Y | B | P |
| W | G | R | Y | B | P | O | Br | G | W | Y | B | P | O | Br |

**1.**

*EDGING*

**Rnd 1:** Join black with a sl st in ch-2 sp at any corner, ch 3, work (2 dc, ch 2, 3 dc) in same sp for corner. * Work (3 dc between each pair of 3-dc groups) 5 times, † ch 1; 3 dc in joining, ch 1; work (3 dc between each pair of 3-dc groups) 5 times †; rep from † to † to next corner sp. Work (3 dc, ch 2, 3 dc) in corner sp. Rep from * to beg corner sp, join with a sl st in top of beg ch-3, do not finish off.

**Rnd 2:** Sl st into each of next 2 dc and into ch-2 sp, ch 3, work (2 dc, ch 2, 3 dc) in same sp; work 3 dc between each pair of 3-dc groups across to next corner; * in corner sp work (3 dc, ch 2, 3 dc), work 3 dc between each pair of 3-dc groups across to next corner; rep from * to beg corner sp, join with a sl st in top of beg ch-3. Finish off.

*FINISHING*

**Fringe:** Following Fringe Instructions in Chapter 8, make single knot fringe. Cut 16″ strands of black for Small Size or 20″ strands of black for Large Size. Using 5 strands for each knot, tie one knot in each outer corner sp and in each sp between 3-dc groups along two long ends and one short end of afghan.

*(Shown in color on page 67.)*

# EMERALD ISLE

*designed by Jean Leinhauser*

**SIZE: Approx 48″ wide × 60″ long before fringing**

**MATERIALS: Dawn Sayelle\* Knitting Worsted Size, eight 3½-oz skeins Shaded Greens, five 4-oz skeins Nile Green, two 4-oz skeins White; aluminum crochet hook size H (or size required for gauge).**

**GAUGE: One square = 12″**

## INSTRUCTIONS

*GRANNY SQUARE (make 20)*

**Note:** All rnds are worked on right side; do not turn at end of rnd. With Nile Green, ch 4, join with a sl st to form a ring.

**Rnd 1:** Ch 3, work 2 dc in ring; ch 2, * work 3 dc in ring, ch 2; rep from * twice, join with a sl st in top of beg ch-3.

**Rnd 2:** Sl st in each of next 2 dc and into next ch-2 sp; ch 3, in **same** sp work (2 dc, ch 2, 3 dc); * work (3 dc, ch 2, 3 dc) in next ch-2 sp; rep from * twice, join with a sl st in top of beg ch-3. Finish off.

**Rnd 3:** Join Shaded Greens with a sl st in any ch-2 sp; ch 3, work (2 dc, ch 2, 3 dc) in same sp [for corner]; * work 3 dc between next two 3-dc groups [for side], work (3 dc, ch 2, 3 dc) all in next ch-2 sp for corner; rep from * twice, work 3 dc between next two 3-dc groups for last side, join with a sl st in top of beg ch-3.

**Rnd 4:** Sl st in each of next 2 dc and into next ch-2 sp; ch 3, work (2 dc, ch 2, 3 dc) in same sp; * work 3 dc in each sp between 3-dc groups along side; work (3 dc, ch 2, 3 dc) in next corner sp; rep from * twice, work 3 dc in each sp between 3-dc groups along side, join with a sl st in top of beg ch-3.

**Rnds 5 through 10:** Rep Rnd 4 six times. Finish off.

**Rnd 11:** Join Nile Green with a sl st in any corner sp; ch 3, work (2 dc, ch 2, 3 dc) in same sp; * work 3 dc in each sp between 3-dc groups along side; work (3 dc, ch 2, 3 dc) in next corner sp; rep from * twice, work 3 dc in each sp between 3-dc groups along last side, join with a sl st in top of beg ch-3. Finish off.

**Rnd 12:** With White, rep Rnd 11.

**Rnd 13:** With Nile Green, rep Rnd 11. Weave in all yarn ends.

### ASSEMBLING

Afghan is 4 squares wide and 5 squares long. Squares for afghan in our photo were joined with Nile Green using Method 5 (see joining methods in Chapter 8).

### FINISHING

**Fringe:** Following Fringe Instructions in Chapter 8, make single knot fringe. Cut 10″ strands of Nile Green; using 5 strands for each knot, tie one knot in each corner sp and in each sp between 3-dc groups along both short ends of afghan.

# Chapter 2

# Picture Afghans

Pictures made out of granny squares?

We wouldn't have thought it possible—but then Anis Duncan, our staff designer, began experimenting and created a new kind of two-color diagonal granny square that's fun to make and permits shaping of the pictorial motifs.

Fitting the squares together is a bit like working a jigsaw puzzle, and becomes exciting as you see the picture grow as you add each square.

This chapter includes ten designs by Anis—for adults and for children. The smaller, child size afghans can also be used as rugs or as wall hangings.

## GENERAL INSTRUCTIONS

Granny squares, quick and easy to make—some with one color and some with two colors—are joined to form the pictures in these afghans. All squares are the same size (2 rnds each) and made with the same gauge (1 square = 2¼ "). Instructions are given for one-color squares, two-color squares (a different color used for each rnd), and diagonal two-color squares (colors create 2 triangles within a square).

One-color and diagonal two-color squares are used for each afghan; however, **My Home Town** afghan requires all three types of squares.

There is a chart for each afghan, and each individual pattern contains instructions for working the details (flower stems, eyes, beaks, etc.) which complete the picture after the squares have been joined. Instructions for joining and using the chart also appear.

# GRANNY SQUARES
## ONE-COLOR GRANNY SQUARE

Ch 4, join with a sl st to form a ring. **Rnd 1 (wrong side):** Ch 3, 2 dc in ring *(Fig 1)*; ch 2, work (3 dc in ring, ch 2) 3 times, join with a sl st in top of beg ch-3 *(Fig 2)*. Turn work. **Rnd 2 (right side):** Sk joining st, sl st in next ch st; sl st into ch-2 sp, ch 3; 2 dc in same sp, ch 1, * work (3 dc, ch 2, 3 dc) all in next ch-2 sp for corner, ch 1; rep from * twice; in beg corner sp, work 3 dc *(Fig 3)*; ch 2, join with a sl st in top of beg ch-3. Finish off, leaving approx 8″ sewing length for joining.

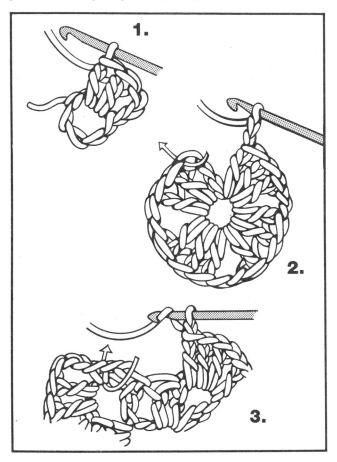

## TWO-COLOR GRANNY SQUARE

With center color, ch 4, join with a sl st to form a ring. **Rnd 1 (wrong side):** Ch 3, 2 dc in ring; ch 2, work (3 dc in ring, ch 2) 3 times, join with a sl st in top of beg ch-3. Finish off center color; turn work. **Rnd 2 (right side):** Join second color with a sl st in any ch-2 sp; ch 3, 2 dc in same sp; ch 1, * work (3 dc, ch 2, 3 dc) all in next ch-2 sp for corner, ch 1; rep from * twice, work 3 dc in beg corner sp, ch 2, join with a sl st in top of beg ch-3. Finish off, leaving approx 8″ sewing length for joining.

## DIAGONAL TWO-COLOR GRANNY SQUARE

**Note:** Individual patterns list two colors for Diagonal Squares; instructions below refer to "color A" and "color B." When making squares, either color listed in pattern can be "A" and the other "B"; however, when joining be sure to match colors of adjacent squares to form pictures.

With color A, ch 4, join with a sl st to form a ring. **Rnd 1 (wrong side):** Ch 3, 2 dc in ring; ch 2, 3 dc in ring; drop color A but do not cut; draw color B through lp on hook (one ch made—see *Fig 4*); continuing with color B, ch 1, 3 dc in ring; ch 2, 3 dc in ring; ch 2, join with a sl st in top of beg ch-3 of color A. Turn work. **Rnd 2 (right side):** Sk joining st, sl st in next ch st; sl st into ch-2 sp, ch 3; 2 dc in same sp, ch 1; work (3 dc, ch 2, 3 dc) all in next ch-2 sp for corner; ch 1, 3 dc in next corner ch-2 sp; ch 2, drop color B; with color A work 3 dc in same corner sp; ch 1, work (3 dc, ch 2, 3 dc) in next ch-2 sp, ch 1; over 2 sl sts of color B in beg corner sp work 3 dc; ch 2, join with a sl st in top of color B beg ch-3. Finish off, leaving approx 8″ lengths for joining.

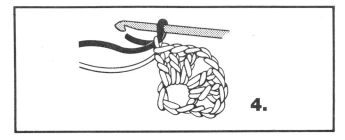

# USING THE CHART

Each square in the Chart represents one granny square and each square is identified by shading or a number. Use the Chart Key to find the color which applies to the shading or number which appears in the square.

The Chart Key also lists the number of squares of each color or combination of colors you will need to make for the afghan. Work from the Chart **and** the Chart Key to make your squares.

Make all of the squares one-by-one and join them when all have been completed **or** work row-by-row and join each row as it is completed **or** make squares which form parts of the picture (a car, a bird, a house, etc.), joining as you make them and adding one-color squares for the background later.

# JOINING SQUARES

Hold two squares with right sides tog, positioned (whenever possible) so sewing length is in upper right-hand corner. Thread yarn into tapestry needle. Carefully matching sts on front and back squares, sew with overcast st in **outer lps only** *(Fig 5)* across side, beg and ending with one corner st. When a sewing length is not available, sew with matching yarn. Be sure that all four-corner junctions are firmly joined. Weave in all yarn ends. Steam press lightly, if desired, before sewing finishing details to afghan.

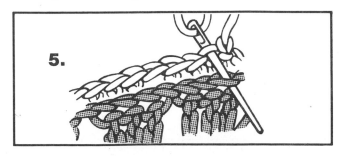

# DUTCH TULIPS

**SIZE:** Approx 54″ wide × 81″ long

**MATERIALS:** Dawn Sayelle* Worsted Size Yarn in 4-oz skeins, 6 Lemon, 7 Nile Green, 7 True Blue, 2 Flame; aluminum crochet hook size G (or size required for gauge).

**Materials Note:** Approx 40 squares can be made from one skein.

**GAUGE:** 1 square = 2¼″

## INSTRUCTIONS

First read General Instructions. Then work afghan using the Chart Key and Chart, making and joining squares per General Instructions.

*(Shown in color on the book jacket.)*

**DUTCH TULIPS CHART**

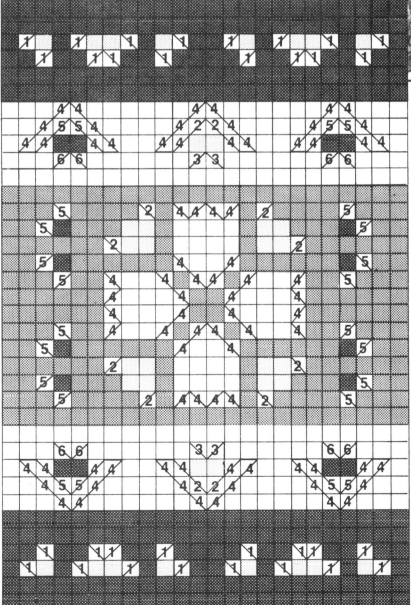

## DUTCH TULIPS CHART KEY
### ONE-COLOR SQUARES

| Key | Color | Number Needed |
|---|---|---|
| | Flame | 36 |
| | Nile Green | 216 |
| | True Blue | 256 |
| | Lemon | 196 |

### DIAGONAL TWO-COLOR SQUARES

| Key | Colors | Number Needed |
|---|---|---|
| 1 | Flame/True Blue | 32 |
| 2 | Flame/Nile Green | 12 |
| 3 | Flame/Lemon | 4 |
| 4 | Lemon/Nile Green | 80 |
| 5 | Nile Green/True Blue | 24 |
| 6 | Lemon/True Blue | 8 |

# MY HOME TOWN

**SIZE:** Approx 48″ wide × 67″ long

**MATERIALS:** Worsted weight yarn in 4-oz skeins, 4 dk green, 5 med green, 3 lt green, 2 blue, 2 white, 2 gray, 1 red, 1 brown, 1 black and 1 yellow; aluminum crochet hook size G (or size required for gauge).

**Materials Note:** Approx 40 squares can be made from one skein.

**GAUGE:** 1 square = 2¼″

## INSTRUCTIONS

First read General Instructions. Then work afghan using the Chart Key and Chart, making and joining squares per General Instructions. After all squares have been joined, work the following applique details.

### APPLIQUE DETAILS

As each roof outline is completed, sew to afghan using matching sewing thread (refer to photo and list below for placement). You will find that it's much easier to work in this manner, and it prevents the loss of small pieces which are easily mislaid.

**Roof Outlines:** With 2 strands of yarn held tog, make chains as listed below; weave in all yarn ends before sewing to afghan.

| Yarn Color | Length | Placement on Afghan |
|---|---|---|
| Black | 7″ | Church (upper right-hand corner) |
| Black | 3½″ | Church Tower |
| Black | 17″ | Red House (lower right-hand corner) |
| Black | 5½″ | Red Barn (adjacent to green house with yellow door) |
| Blue | 9½″ | White House with red door |
| Brown | 18″ | Yellow House with brown door (below church) |
| Brown | 12″ | Yellow House with green door (lower left-hand corner) |

## MY HOME TOWN CHART KEY

### ONE-COLOR SQUARES

| Key | Color | Number Needed |
|---|---|---|
| | White | 36 |
| | Light Green | 91 |
| | Medium Green | 151 |
| | Dark Green | 141 |
| 1 | Blue | 70 |
| 2 | Gray | 51 |
| 3 | Yellow | 30 |
| 4 | Red | 32 |
| 5 | Brown | 18 |
| 6 | Black | 23 |

### TWO-COLOR SQUARES

| Key | Colors | Number Needed |
|---|---|---|
| 7 | Gray (center)/White | 25 |
| 8 | Red (center)/White | 2 |
| 9 | White (center)/Brown | 2 |
| 10 | White (center)/Red | 2 |

### DIAGONAL TWO-COLOR SQUARES

| Key | Colors | Number Needed |
|---|---|---|
| 11 | Dark Green/Light Green | 7 |
| 12 | Dark Green/Medium Green | 4 |
| 13 | Medium Green/Light Green | 6 |
| 14 | Dark Green/Blue | 6 |
| 15 | Dark Green/Yellow | 4 |
| 16 | Dark Green/Brown | 3 |
| 17 | Dark Green/Black | 4 |
| 18 | Dark Green/Red | 5 |
| 19 | Medium Green/Yellow | 5 |
| 20 | Medium Green/Gray | 4 |
| 21 | Medium Green/White | 3 |
| 22 | Medium Green/Black | 2 |
| 23 | Medium Green/Red | 1 |
| 24 | Light Green/Blue | 2 |
| 25 | Light Green/Gray | 1 |
| 26 | Light Green/Brown | 3 |
| 27 | Light Green/Red | 3 |
| 28 | Black/White | 3 |
| 29 | Black/Blue | 3 |
| 30 | Black/Red | 2 |
| 31 | Black/Gray | 2 |
| 32 | Red/White | 8 |
| 33 | Red/Gray | 1 |
| 34 | Brown/Yellow | 2 |
| 35 | Brown/White | 1 |
| 36 | Gray/Yellow | 1 |
| 37 | Blue/White | 8 |

**MY HOME TOWN CHART**

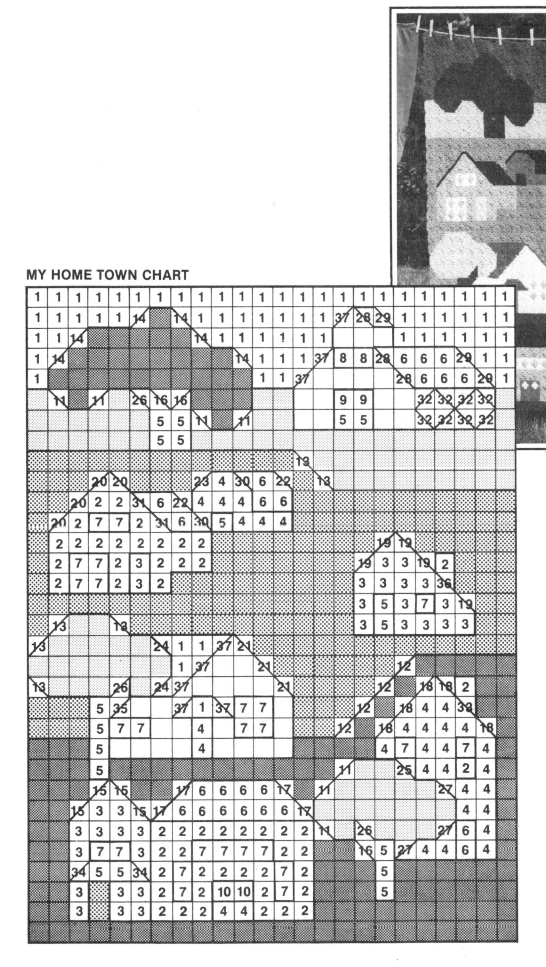

*(Shown in color on page 70.)*

# SUPPER TIME

**SIZE: Approx 45″ × 68″**

**MATERIALS: Dawn Sayelle\* Worsted Size Yarn in 4-oz skeins, 3 Bluebell, 7 Golf Green, 2 Flame, 3 White, 2 Coffee and 1 Black; aluminum crochet hook size G (or size required for gauge).**

**Materials Note: Approx 40 squares can be made from one skein.**

**GAUGE: 1 square = 2¼″**

## INSTRUCTIONS

First read General Instructions. Then work afghan using the Chart Key and Chart, making and joining squares per General Instructions.

**SUPPER TIME CHART**

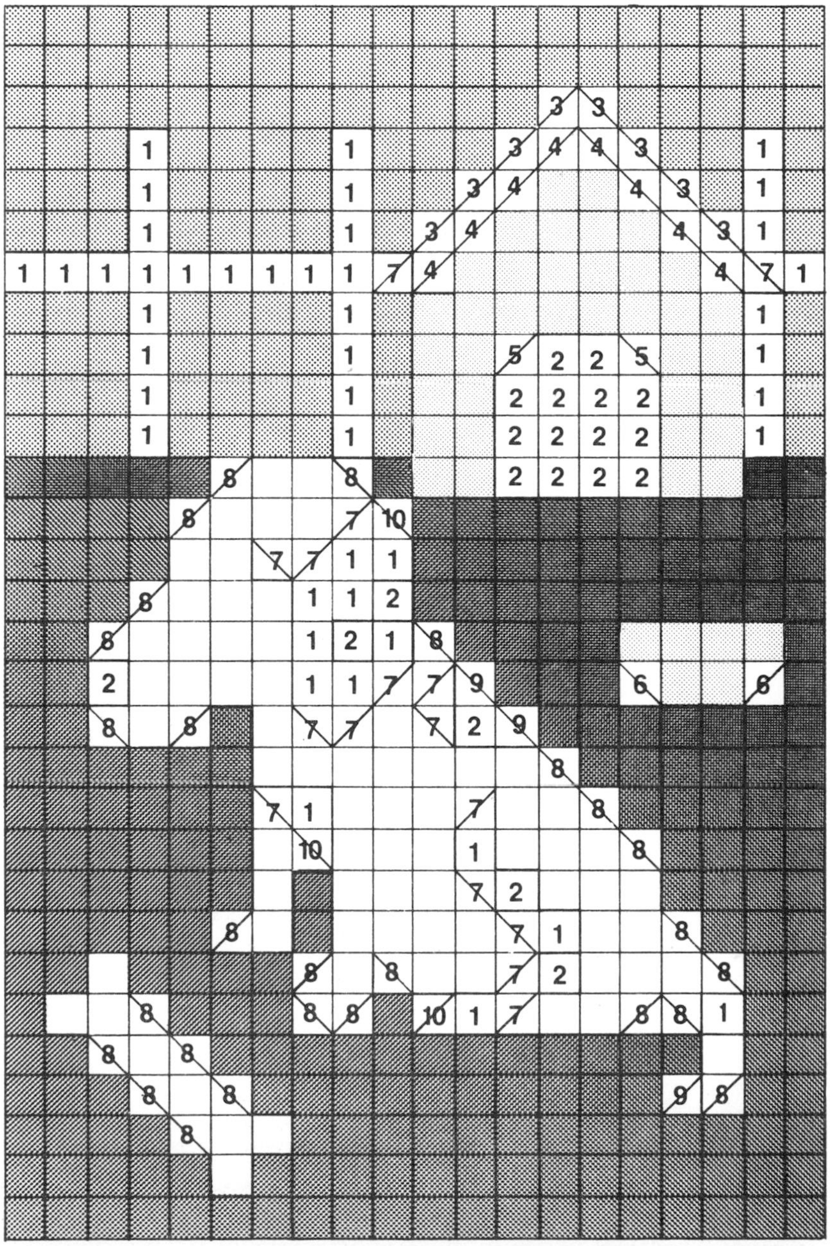

## SUPPER TIME CHART KEY

### ONE-COLOR SQUARES

| Key | Color | Number Needed |
|-----|-------|---------------|
| | Bluebell | 127 |
| | Golf Green | 227 |
| | Flame | 42 |
| | White | 71 |
| 1 | Coffee | 44 |
| 2 | Black | 20 |

### DIAGONAL TWO-COLOR SQUARES

| Key | Colors | Number Needed |
|-----|--------|---------------|
| 3 | Bluebell/White | 8 |
| 4 | Flame/White | 8 |
| 5 | Flame/Black | 2 |
| 6 | Golf Green/Flame | 2 |
| 7 | Coffee/White | 16 |
| 8 | Golf Green/White | 27 |
| 9 | Golf Green/Black | 3 |
| 10 | Golf Green/Coffee | 3 |

# WHEELS
## CHILD'S AFGHAN

**SIZE:** Approx 44″ × 66″ long

**MATERIALS:** Worsted weight yarn in 4-oz skeins, 7 blue, 3 bright red, 1 dark red, 2 yellow, 1 green, 1 off-white, 2 gray and 2 black; aluminum crochet hook size G (or size required for gauge).

**Materials Note:** Approx 40 squares can be made from one skein.

**GAUGE:** 1 square = 2¼″

## INSTRUCTIONS

First read General Instructions. Then work afghan using the Chart Key and Chart, making and joining squares per General Instructions. After all squares have been joined, work the following applique details.

### APPLIQUE DETAILS

As each detail is completed, sew to afghan using matching sewing thread (refer to photo for positions). You will find that it's much easier to work in this manner, and it prevents the loss of small pieces which are easily mislaid.

**Fire Engine Ladder: Rails (make 2):** With 2 strands of black held tog, ch 81; sc in 2nd ch from hook and in each rem ch across; finish off, weave in yarn ends.

**Rungs (make 8):** With 2 strands of black held tog, ch 8; sc in 2nd ch from hook and in each rem ch across; finish off, weave in yarn ends.

### WHEELS CHART KEY
**ONE-COLOR SQUARES**

| Key | Color | Number Needed |
|---|---|---|
| | White | 17 |
| | Gray | 50 |
| | Blue | 245 |
| | Bright Red | 75 |
| 1 | Yellow | 46 |
| 2 | Green | 25 |
| 3 | Dark Red | 33 |
| 4 | Black | 43 |

### DIAGONAL TWO-COLOR SQUARES

| Key | Colors | Number Needed |
|---|---|---|
| 5 | Blue/Dark Red | 5 |
| 6 | Blue/Black | 20 |
| 7 | Blue/Yellow | 5 |
| 8 | White/Dark Red | 2 |
| 9 | White/Bright Red | 1 |
| 10 | White/Yellow | 1 |
| 11 | Bright Red/Black | 10 |
| 12 | Dark Red/Black | 4 |
| 13 | Green/Black | 6 |
| 14 | Yellow/Black | 8 |
| 15 | Gray/Black | 4 |

### WHEELS CHART

*(Shown in color on page 71.)*

# CIRCUS CLOWN

**SIZE:** Approx 45" × 68"

**MATERIALS:** Worsted weight yarn in 4-oz skeins, 9 Baby Blue, 2 Lemon, 1 Orange, 1 Golf Green, 3 Flame, 1 White and 1 Black; aluminum crochet hook size G (or size required for gauge).

**Materials Note:** Approx 40 squares can be made from one skein.

**GAUGE:** 1 square = 2¼"

## INSTRUCTIONS

First Read General Instructions. Then work afghan using the Chart Key and Chart, making and joining squares per General Instructions. After all squares have been joined, work the following Applique Details.

*APPLIQUE DETAILS*

As each detail is completed, sew to afghan using matching sewing thread (refer to photo for position of details). You will find that it's much easier to work in this manner, and it prevents the loss of small pieces which are easily mislaid.

**Eyes (make 2):** With black, ch 3, join with a sl st to form a ring. **Row 1:** Ch 3, work 5 dc in ring; do **not** join, finish off. **Row 2:** Join blue with a sl st in top of beg ch-3 of prev row, ch 3, dc in same st; work 2 dc in each dc across = 12 dc (counting ch-3 as one dc). Finish off, weave in yarn ends.

**Nose:** With red, ch 4, join with a sl st to form a ring. **Rnd 1:** Ch 3, work 10 dc in ring, join with a sl st in top of beg ch-3. **Rnd 2:** Ch 3, 2 dc in next dc and in each dc around; join with a sl st in top of beg ch-3. Finish off, weave in yarn ends.

**Mouth:** With red, ch 22. **Row 1:** Dc in 4th ch from hook, work (dc in next ch, 2 dc in next ch) 8 times; dc in next ch, dc in last ch. **Row 2:** Ch 2, turn; dc in each dc across. Finish off, weave in all yarn ends.

**CIRCUS CLOWN CHART**

## CIRCUS CLOWN CHART KEY

### ONE-COLOR SQUARES

| Key | Color | Number Needed |
|---|---|---|
| ▓ | Baby Blue | 323 |
| ▨ | Flame | 99 |
| ░ | Lemon | 31 |
| □ | White | 28 |
| 1 | Orange | 3 |
| 2 | Golf Green | 5 |
| 13 | Black | 20 |

### DIAGONAL TWO-COLOR SQUARES

| Key | Colors | Number Needed |
|---|---|---|
| 3 | Flame/Lemon | 12 |
| 4 | Flame/Baby Blue | 31 |
| 5 | Orange/Baby Blue | 3 |
| 6 | Golf Green/Flame | 4 |
| 7 | Baby Blue/Lemon | 15 |
| 8 | Baby Blue/Black | 10 |
| 9 | Lemon/White | 9 |
| 10 | Lemon/Orange | 3 |
| 11 | Lemon/Black | 3 |
| 12 | Baby Blue/White | 1 |

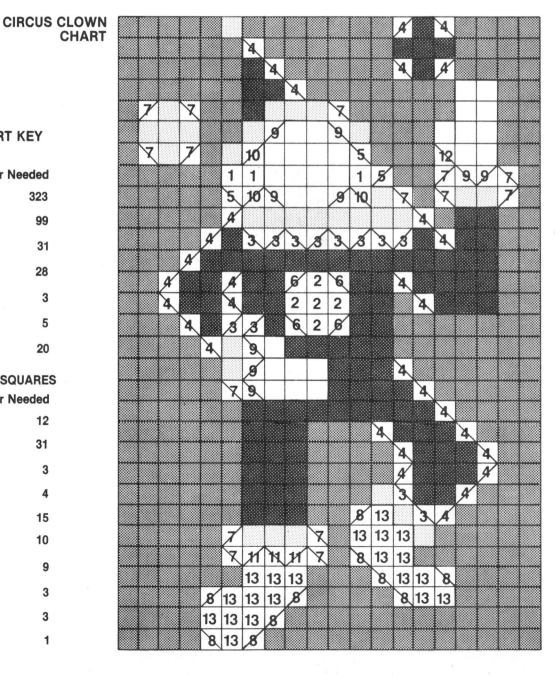

# PLAYFUL KITTENS

**SIZE:** Approx 45″ × 68″

**MATERIALS: Dawn Sayelle\* Worsted Size in 4-oz skeins, 9 Bluebell, 1 Golf Green, 1 Orange, 2 Amber, 1 Flame Red, 1 Lemon, 2 White, 1 Black, 1 Steel Gray and 1 Lt Gold; aluminum crochet hook size G (or size required for gauge).**

**Materials Note: Approx 40 squares can be made from one skein.**

**GAUGE: 1 square = 2¼″**

## INSTRUCTIONS

First read General Instructions. Then work afghan using the Chart Key and Chart, making and joining squares per General Instructions. After all squares have been joined, work the following applique details.

### APPLIQUE DETAILS

As each detail is completed, sew to afghan using matching sewing thread (refer to photo for position of details). You will find that it's much easier to work in this manner, and it prevents the loss of small pieces which are easily mislaid.

**Nose/Mouth (make 2):** With Black, make a chain to measure 10″. Finish off, weave in yarn ends. When sewing to afghan, sew right side of ch toward right side of afghan.

**Eyes (make 4):** With Golf Green, ch 4, join with a sl st to form a ring. Ch 2, work 6 dc in ring, join with a sl st in top of beg ch-2. Finish off, weave in yarn ends. With black, make four 2½″ chains; finish off, weave in yarn ends.

**Yarn Ends for Balls of Yarn (make 2):** With Flame, make a chain to measure 16″; finish off, weave in yarn ends. With Lemon, make a chain to measure 14″; finish off, weave in yarn ends. Sew in position, with wrong side of chain to right side of afghan.

## PLAYFUL KITTENS CHART KEY

### ONE-COLOR SQUARES

| Key | Color | Number Needed |
|---|---|---|
| | White | 41 |
| | Lt Gold | 41 |
| | Bluebell | 350 |
| | Amber | 50 |
| 1 | Black | 5 |
| 2 | Golf Green | 7 |
| 3 | Orange | 10 |
| 4 | Flame | 8 |
| 5 | Lemon | 6 |
| 6 | Steel Gray | 4 |

### DIAGONAL TWO-COLOR SQUARES

| Key | Colors | Number Needed |
|---|---|---|
| 7 | Lt Gold/Amber | 1 |
| 8 | Bluebell/Lt Gold | 4 |
| 9 | Bluebell/White | 14 |
| 10 | Bluebell/Black | 1 |
| 11 | Bluebell/Flame | 6 |
| 12 | Bluebell/Orange | 8 |
| 13 | Bluebell/Lemon | 4 |
| 14 | Bluebell/Golf Green | 5 |
| 15 | Bluebell/Steel Gray | 2 |
| 16 | Amber/White | 1 |
| 17 | Orange/Golf Green | 1 |
| 18 | Orange/White | 1 |
| 19 | Orange/Amber | 7 |
| 20 | Lemon/Golf Green | 1 |
| 21 | Lemon/Flame | 1 |
| 22 | Black/White | 5 |
| 23 | Steel Gray/White | 2 |
| 24 | Amber/Bluebell | 14 |

**PLAYFUL KITTENS CHART**

# SUMMER CAROUSEL

**SIZE: Approx 49″ × 72″**

**MATERIALS: Dawn Sayelle\* Worsted Size in 4-oz skeins, 9 White, 1 Antique Gold, 3 Lemon, 2 Flame, 2 Premier Green, 2 Blue and 1 Orange; aluminum crochet hook size G (or size required for gauge).**

**Materials Note: Approx 40 squares can be made from one skein.**

**GAUGE: 1 square = 2¼″**

## INSTRUCTIONS

First read General Instructions. Then work afghan using the Chart Key and Chart, making and joining squares per General Instructions. After all squares have been joined, work the following applique details.

### APPLIQUE DETAILS

As each detail is completed, sew to afghan using matching sewing thread (refer to photo for position of details). You will find that it's much easier to work in this manner, and it prevents the loss of small pieces which are easily mislaid.

**Eyes (make 2—1 red and 1 blue):** Ch 3, join with a sl st to form a ring. Ch 1, work 6 sc in ring; join with a sl st in beg ch-1. Finish off, weave in all yarn ends.

**Reins (make 2—1 red and 1 blue):** Make a chain to measure 12″ long; finish off, weave in yarn ends. When sewing to afghan, sew right side of ch toward right side of afghan.

**Tassels (make 6—1 red and 5 green):** Cut 10″ lengths of red and green yarn; following instructions for tassels in Chapter 8, using 10 strands for each. Tie tassels to afghan in positions shown in photo.

## SUMMER CAROUSEL CHART KEY
### ONE-COLOR SQUARES

| Key | Color | Number Needed |
|---|---|---|
| | Lemon | 58 |
| | White | 303 |
| | Orange | 17 |
| | Premier Green | 62 |
| 1 | Flame | 26 |
| 2 | Blue | 21 |
| 3 | Antique Gold | 21 |

### DIAGONAL TWO-COLOR SQUARES

| Key | Colors | Number Needed |
|---|---|---|
| 4 | Flame/White | 52 |
| 5 | Blue/White | 55 |
| 6 | Flame/Blue | 11 |
| 7 | Lemon/Orange | 20 |
| 8 | Lemon/Flame | 5 |
| 9 | Lemon/Premier Green | 20 |
| 10 | Lemon/White | 16 |
| 11 | Premier Green/White | 10 |
| 12 | Premier Green/Orange | 2 |
| 13 | Flame/Orange | 1 |
| 14 | Flame/Premier Green | 4 |

**SUMMER CAROUSEL CHART**

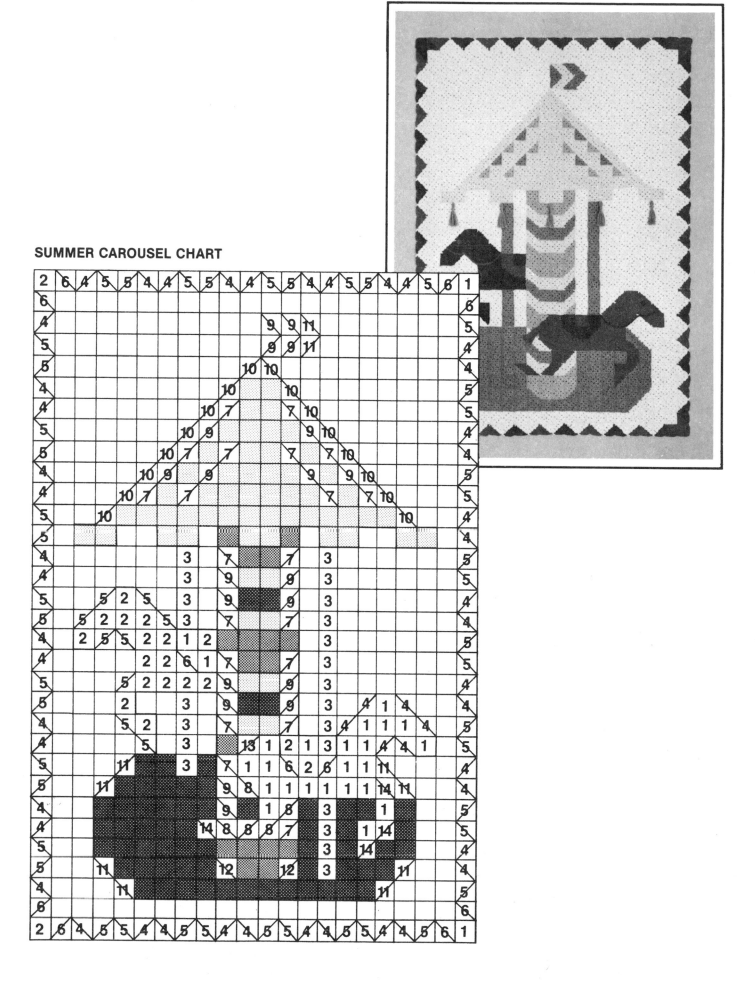

# THE BIRD WATCHER
## CHILD'S AFGHAN

**SIZE:** Approx 44″ wide × 66″ long

**MATERIALS:** Worsted weight yarn in 4-oz skeins, 8 turquoise, 3 dk green, 2 lt green, 2 beige, 1 brown and 1 orange; aluminum crochet hook size G (or size required for gauge).

**Materials Note:** Approx 40 squares can be made from one skein.

**GAUGE:** 1 square = 2¼ ″

## INSTRUCTIONS

First read General Instructions. Then work afghan using the Chart Key and Chart, making and joining squares per General Instructions. After all squares have been joined, work the following applique details.

### APPLIQUE DETAILS

As each detail is completed, sew to afghan using matching sewing thread (refer to photo for positions). You will find that it's much easier to work in this manner, and it prevents the loss of small pieces which are easily mislaid.

**Upper Bird's Beak:** With orange, ch 5; sc in 2nd ch from hook, hdc in next ch, dc in next ch, tr in last ch. Finish off, weave in yarn ends.

**Lower Bird's Beak:** With orange, ch 5. **Row 1:** Sc in 2nd ch from hook and in each ch to end = 4 sc. **Row 2:** Ch 1, turn; sk first sc, sc in next sc, decrease over last 2 sc [to decrease, * insert hook in next st, hook yarn and draw up a lp; rep from * once, YO and draw through all 3 lps now on hook—dec made]. **Row 3:** Ch 1, turn; sk first sc, sc in next sc. Finish off, weave in yarn ends.

**Mama Bird's Eye:** With beige, ch 4, join with a sl st to form a ring. Work 6 sc in ring, join with a sl st in first sc; finish off, weave in yarn ends.

**Mama Bird's Leg:** With 2 strands of brown held tog, make a 6½ ″ chain; finish off, weave in yarn ends.

**Worm for Mama Bird's Beak:** With 2 strands of beige held tog, make a 4½ ″ chain; finish off, weave in yarn ends.

**Cat's Nose/Mouth:** With brown, ch 5. **Row 1:** Sc in 2nd ch from hook and in each ch to end = 4 sc. **Row 2:** Ch 1, turn; sk first sc, sc in each of rem 3 sc. **Row 3:** Ch 1, turn; sc in first sc, dec over last 2 sc as before. **Row 4:** Ch 1, turn; sk first sc, sc in last sc, ch 20; finish off, weave in yarn ends.

**Cat's Eye:** With lt green, ch 3, join with a sl st to form a ring. **Rnd 1:** Work 6 sc in ring, join with a sl st in first sc. **Rnd 2:** Ch 1, sc in same sc as joining, work (2 sc in next sc, sc in next sc) twice; work 2 sc in last sc, join with a sl st in beg sc = 9 sc. Finish off lt green. **Rnd 3:** Join dk green with a sl st in any sc, work 2 sc in each of next 4 sc, sl st in next sc; finish off, weave in yarn ends.

## THE BIRD WATCHER CHART KEY
### ONE-COLOR SQUARES

| Key | Color | Number Needed |
|---|---|---|
| ☐ | Turquoise | 317 |
| ▒ | Light Green | 33 |
| ▓ | Dark Green | 73 |
| ▩ | Brown | 31 |
| 1 | Orange | 6 |
| 2 | Beige | 59 |

### DIAGONAL TWO-COLOR SQUARES

| Key | Colors | Number Needed |
|---|---|---|
| 3 | Light Green/Dark Green | 10 |
| 4 | Beige/Turquoise | 9 |
| 5 | Beige/Brown | 7 |
| 6 | Beige/Dark Green | 2 |
| 7 | Dark Brown/Turquoise | 5 |
| 8 | Turquoise/Dark Green | 15 |
| 9 | Turquoise/Light Green | 23 |
| 10 | Brown/Dark Green | 1 |
| 11 | Brown/Orange | 5 |
| 12 | Turquoise/Orange | 3 |
| 13 | Beige/Light Green | 1 |

## THE BIRD WATCHER'S CHART

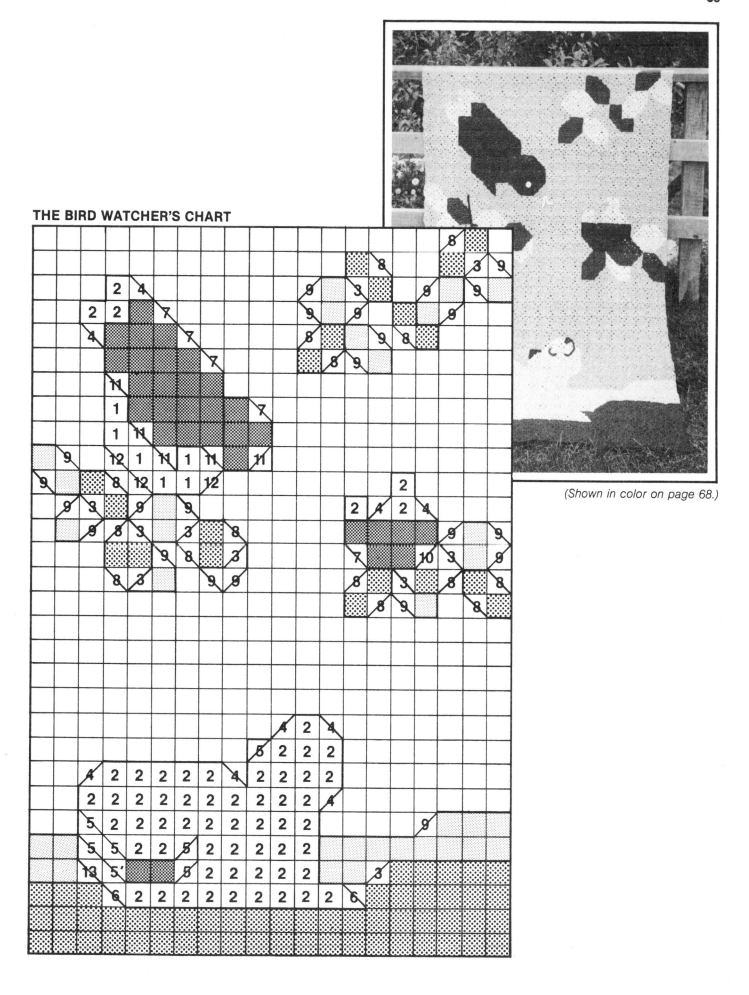

*(Shown in color on page 68.)*

# PUDDLE DUCKS
## CHILD'S AFGHAN

**SIZE: Approx 44″ wide × 66″ long**

**MATERIALS: Worsted weight yarn in 4-oz skeins, 4 white, 5 blue, 8 green, 1 yellow, 1 orange and a few yards black; aluminum crochet hook size G (or size required for gauge).**

**Materials Note: Approx 40 squares can be made from one skein.**

**GAUGE: 1 square = 2¼″**

## INSTRUCTIONS

First read General Instructions. Then work afghan using the Chart Key and Chart, making and joining squares per General Instructions. After all squares have been joined, work the following applique details.

### APPLIQUE DETAILS

As each detail is completed, sew to afghan using matching sewing thread (refer to photo for positions). You will find that it's much easier to work in this manner, and it prevents the loss of small pieces which are easily mislaid.

**Baby Duck's Beak (make 3):** With orange, ch 6; sc in 2nd ch from hook, sc in next ch, hdc in next ch, dc in next ch, tr in last ch; finish off, weave in yarn ends.

**Baby Duck's Long Leg and Foot (make 3):** With orange, ch 18; dc in 4th ch from hook, hdc in next ch, sc in next ch, sl st in each of rem 12 chs; finish off, weave in yarn ends.

**Baby Duck's Short Leg and Foot (make 3):** With orange, ch 10; dc in 4th ch from hook, hdc in next ch, sc in next ch, sl st in each of rem 4 chs; finish off, weave in yarn ends.

**Baby Duck's Eye (make 3):** With black, ch 3, join with a sl st to form a ring; work 3 sl sts into ring; finish off, weave in yarn ends.

**Mama Duck's Beak:** With orange, ch 9. **Row 1 (right side):** Sc in 2nd ch from hook and in each rem ch across = 8 sc. **Row 2:** Ch 1, turn; 2 sc in first sc, sc in each sc to last sc, 2 sc in last sc = 10 sc. **Row 3:** Ch 1, turn; sc in each sc across. **Row 4:** Rep Row 2 = 12 sc. **Rows 5 through 10:** Ch 1, turn; sc in each sc across. **Row 11:** Ch 1, turn; sc in each sc to last sc, 2 sc in last sc = 13 sc. **Row 12:** Ch 1, turn; sc in each sc across. **Rows 13 through 19:** Rep Rows 11 and 12 three times, then rep Row 11 once more. At end of Row 19, you should have 17 sc. **Row 20:** Ch 1, turn; sc in each of first 4 sc, do **not** work into rem 13 sc. **Row 21:** Ch 1, turn; sk first sc, sc in each rem sc across = 3 sc. **Row 22:** Ch 1, turn; sc in first sc, dec over next 2 sc [to dec, * insert hook in next st, hook yarn and draw up a lp; rep from * once, YO and draw through all 3 lps now on hook—dec made]. **Row 23:** Ch 1, turn; sk first sc, sc in last sc. Finish off, weave in yarn ends.

**Row 20A:** With right side facing you, join yarn with a sl st in first st at right-hand edge of Row 19 [where 13 sc were left unworked]. Ch 1, sc in same sc as joining; sc in each of next 9 sc, do **not** work in rem 3 sc = 10 sc. **Row 21A:** Ch 1, turn; sc in each sc to last sc, 2 sc in last

sc = 11 sc. **Row 22A:** Ch 1, turn; sc in each sc across. Finish off, weave in yarn ends.

**Mama Duck's Eye:** With black, ch 5, join with a sl st to form a ring. **Rnd 1:** Work 10 sc into ring, join with a sl st in first sc. **Rnd 2:** Ch 1, sc in same sc as joining; sc in each rem sc around, ch 5; finish off, weave in yarn ends.

**Mama Duck's Feet (make 2—one short and one long): Note:** Work all 68 rows for the long leg; finish off at end of Row 44 for short leg.

With orange, ch 5. **Row 1:** Sc in 2nd ch from hook and in each ch across = 4 sc. **Row 2:** Ch 1, turn; 2 sc in first sc, sc in each sc across to last sc, 2 sc in last sc = 6 sc. **Rows 3 through 8:** Rep Row 2 six times. At end of Row 8, you should have 18 sc. **Row 9:** Ch 1, turn; sc in each sc across. **Row 10:** Ch 1, turn; sc in each sc to last 2 sc, dec over last 2 sc = 17 sc. **Rows 11 through 32:** Rep Rows 9 and 10 eleven times. At end of Row 32, you should have 6 sc. **Row 33:** Ch 1, turn; sc in each sc across; ch 1, do **not** turn; working along top edge of foot, sc in end st of each of first 3 rows. **Row 34:** Ch 1, turn; sc in first sc, dc in each of next 2 sc = 3 sts. **Rows 35 through 38:** Ch 1, turn; sc in each st across. **Row 39:** Ch 1, turn; sc in each of first 2 sc, 2 sc in last sc = 4 sc. **Rows 40 through 44:** Ch 1, turn; sc in each sc across. **Note:** For short leg only, finish off now, weave in yarn ends. For long leg, continue as follows.

**Row 45:** Ch 1, turn; sc in each of first 3 sc, 2 sc in last sc = 5 sc. **Rows 46 through 50:** Ch 1, turn; sc in each sc across. **Row 51:** Ch 1, turn; sc in each of first 4 sc, 2 sc in last sc = 6 sc. **Rows 52 through 56:** Ch 1, turn; sc in each sc across. **Row 57:** Ch 1, turn; sc in each of first 5 sc, 2 sc in last sc = 7 sc. **Rows 58 through 62:** Ch 1, turn; sc in each sc across. **Row 63:** Ch 1, turn; sc in each of first 6 sc, 2 sc in last sc = 8 sc. **Rows 64 through 66:** Ch 1, turn; sc in each sc across. **Row 67:** Ch 1, turn; sk first sc, sc in each of next 5 sc, dec over last 2 sc = 6 sc. **Row 68:** Ch 1, turn; sk first sc, sc in each of next 3 sc, dec over last 2 sc = 4 sc. Finish off, weave in yarn ends.

## PUDDLE DUCKS CHART KEY
### ONE-COLOR SQUARES

| Key | Color | Number Needed |
| --- | --- | --- |
| ☐ | White | 111 |
| ▨ | Yellow | 15 |
| ▨ | Blue | 150 |
| ▨ | Green | 278 |

### DIAGONAL TWO-COLOR SQUARES

| Key | Colors | Number Needed |
| --- | --- | --- |
| 1 | Blue/White | 13 |
| 2 | Green/White | 16 |
| 3 | Blue/Green | 8 |
| 4 | Blue/Yellow | 1 |
| 5 | Green/Yellow | 8 |

**PUDDLE DUCKS CHART**

*(Shown in color on page 71.)*

# SUMMER GARDEN

**SIZE: Approx 48″ wide x 67″ long**

**MATERIALS: Worsted weight yarn in 4-oz skeins, 9 blue, 7 white, 2 dark green, 1 light green, 1 dark red, 1 red, 1 pink and 1 yellow; aluminum crochet hook size G (or size required for gauge).**

**Materials Note: Approx 40 squares can be made from 1 skein of yarn.**

**GAUGE: 1 square = 2¼″**

## INSTRUCTIONS

First read General Instructions. Then work afghan using the Chart Key and Chart, making and joining granny squares as in General Instructions. After all squares have been joined, work Applique Details.

*APPLIQUE DETAILS*

As each stem is completed, sew to afghan using matching sewing thread (refer to photo for positions). You will find that it's much easier to work in this manner, and it prevents the loss of small pieces which are easily mislaid.

**Flower Stems (make 11):** Make ch in color and length specified below, sl st in 2nd ch from hook and in each ch to end. Finish off; weave in yarn ends.

With dark green make 6 stems, one each in the following lengths: 12″, 56″, 28″, 19″, 3″ and 30″. With light green make 5 stems: 11″, 15½″, 23½″ and two 13″.

## SUMMER GARDEN CHART KEY

### ONE-COLOR SQUARES

| Key | Color | Number Needed |
|---|---|---|
| | White | 231 |
| | Blue | 314 |
| | Dark Green | 35 |
| | Red | 18 |
| 1 | Yellow | 12 |
| 2 | Pink | 4 |
| 3 | Light Green | 6 |

### DIAGONAL TWO-COLOR SQUARES

| Key | Colors | Number Needed |
|---|---|---|
| 4 | Red/White | 12 |
| 5 | Red/Blue | 18 |
| 6 | Red/Dark Red | 6 |
| 7 | Pink/White | 19 |
| 8 | Pink/Blue | 19 |
| 9 | Dark Red/White | 5 |
| 10 | Dark Red/Blue | 7 |
| 11 | Light Green/White | 2 |
| 12 | Light Green/Blue | 11 |
| 13 | Dark Green/White | 18 |
| 14 | Dark Green/Blue | 15 |
| 15 | Yellow/White | 6 |
| 16 | Yellow/Blue | 10 |

**SUMMER GARDEN CHART**

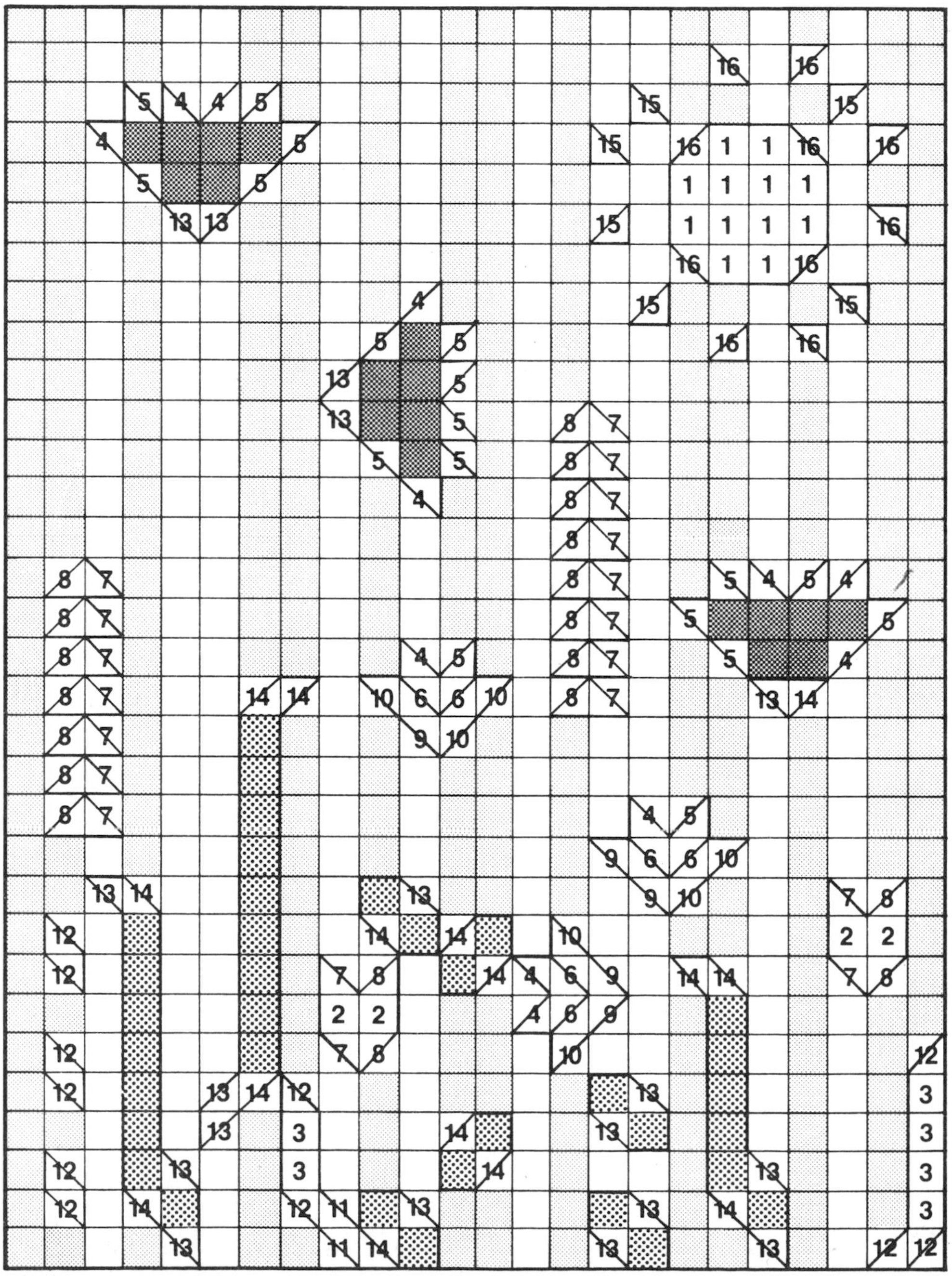

## Chapter 3

# Granny's Toy Shop

Toymaking is a labor of love, and it can be especially fun when toys are created of colorful, quick-to-make granny squares.

Our toy collection will appeal to all ages. The Sesame Street crowd will be fascinated by the large, stuffed letters of the alphabet; pre-teens will enjoy members of the dog family as decorative bed pillows; and the Jack and Jill dolls are sure to receive lots of hugs and kisses from their small owners.

## GENERAL INSTRUCTIONS

All of the animals are made of granny squares. Within each pattern in this chapter you will find:

a list of the number, color and kind of squares needed;

a chart showing placement of squares for assembling; and

instructions for any feature (ear, nose, tail, mouth, etc.) which will be made separately and then attached to the animal.

We have used five different kinds of squares:

a one-color **full** square;

a two-color **full** square with one color as the center

(Rnd 1) and the second color as the outside (Rnd 2);

a **diagonal** two-color full square which looks like two triangles joined;

a one-color **half** square which really looks like a triangle; and

a two-color **half** square.

Most of the animals use only two or three kinds of squares; instructions which follow are for each of the five different types, as well as methods of joining squares and stuffing.

When working features for animals, such as eyes or nose, the instruction "dec" means to decrease as follows: Insert hook in first st and pull up a lp, then insert hook in next st and pull up a lp; YO and draw through all 3 lps on hook—one dec has been made.

# GRANNY SQUARE INSTRUCTIONS

**Gauge: With rug yarn, 1 full square = 2½ "**
**With worsted weight yarn, 1 full square = 2"**
**With rug yarn, 1 half square = 2½ "**
**(see Note below)**
**With worsted weight yarn, 1 half square = 2"**
**(see Note below)**

**Note:** Measure on outside edge of square as shown in photos below.

## ONE-COLOR FULL SQUARE

With color specified in patt, ch 4, join with a sl st to form a ring.

**Rnd 1 (right side):** Ch 3, 2 dc in ring *(Fig 1)*; ch 1, * work 3 dc in ring, ch 1; rep from * twice, join with a sl st in top of beg ch-3 *(Fig 2)*.

**Rnd 2 (right side):** Sl st in each of next 2 dc and into ch-1 sp *(Fig 3)*; ch 3, work (2 dc, ch 1, 3 dc) all in same sp; *work (3 dc, ch 1, 3 dc) all in next ch-1 sp; rep from * twice, join with a sl st in top of beg ch-3. Finish off, leaving a 10″ yarn end for sewing later.

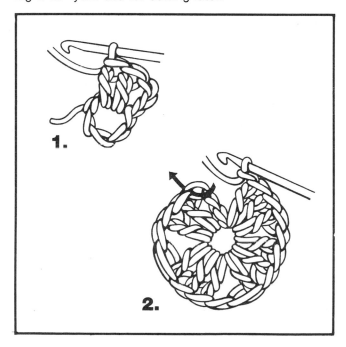

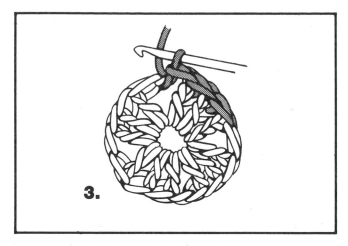

## ONE-COLOR HALF SQUARE

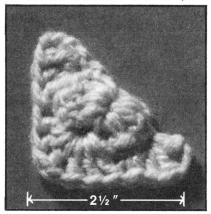

With color specified in patt, ch 4, join with a sl st to form a ring.

**Rnd 1 (wrong side):** Ch 3, work 3 dc in ring; ch 1, work 4 dc in ring.

**Rnd 2 (right side):** Ch 3, TURN; work 3 dc in first dc [at base of ch—Fig 4]; work (3 dc, ch 1, 3 dc) all in ch-1 sp; work 4 dc in top of Tch *(Fig 5)*. Finish off, leaving a 10″ yarn end for sewing later.

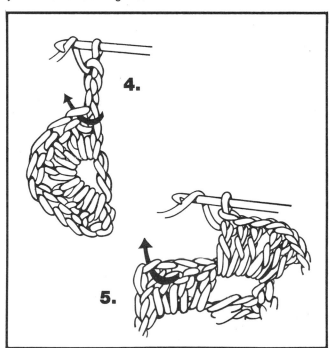

## TWO-COLOR HALF SQUARE

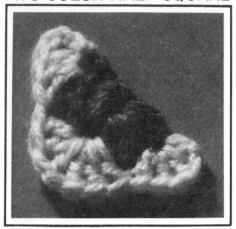

With center color (specified in patt), ch 4, join with a sl st to form a ring.

**Rnd 1 (wrong side):** Ch 3, work 3 dc in ring; ch 1, 4 dc in ring, finish off center color, TURN.

**Rnd 2 (right side):** With outer color (specified in patt), join with a sl st in first dc; ch 3, work 3 dc in first dc [at base of sl st—Fig 6]; work (3 dc, ch 1, 3 dc) all in ch-1 sp, 4 dc in top of ch-3. Finish off, leaving a 10″ yarn end for sewing.

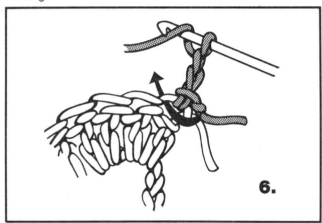

**6.**

## TWO-COLOR FULL SQUARE

With center color (specified in patt), ch 4, join with a sl st to form a ring.

**Rnd 1 (right side):** Ch 3, work 2 dc in ring, ch 1; * work 3 dc in ring, ch 1; rep from * twice, join with a sl st in top of beg ch-3. Finish off.

**Rnd 2 (right side):** With outer color (specified in patt), join with a sl st in any ch-1 sp; ch 3, work (2 dc, ch 1, 3 dc) all in same sp; * work (3 dc, ch 1, 3 dc) all in next ch-1 sp; rep from * twice, join with a sl st in top of beg ch. Finish off, leaving a 10″ yarn end for sewing.

## TWO-COLOR DIAGONAL SQUARE

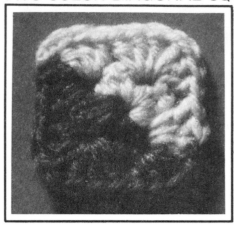

**Note:** Patterns list 2 colors for diagonal squares, such as: Black/White. Instructions below refer to "color A" and "color B." Either color listed in pattern (Black or White) can be "A" and the other color "B."

**Rnd 1 (wrong side):** With color A, ch 4, join with a sl st to form a ring. Ch 3, work 2 dc in ring; ch 1, 3 dc in ring; drop color A but do not cut off; draw color B through lp on hook [one ch made]; continuing with color B, work 3 dc in ring, ch 1; work 3 dc in ring, ch 1, join with a sl st in top of beg ch of color A.

**Rnd 2 (right side):** TURN; sl st into ch-1 sp, ch 3, 2 dc in same sp; work (3 dc, ch 1, 3 dc) in next ch-1 corner sp; 3 dc in next ch-1 corner sp, ch 1, drop color B; with color A work 3 dc in same corner sp; in next ch-1 corner sp, work (3 dc, ch 1, 3 dc); in beg corner sp [where beg sl st of color B was made], work 3 dc over sl st; ch 1, join with a sl st in top of beg ch of Color B. Finish off A and B, leaving 10″ yarn ends for sewing later.

# JOINING

Hold 2 squares with right sides tog and beg with yarn in upper right-hand corner; thread yarn into tapestry needle. Carefully matching sts on front and back squares, sew with overcast st in **outer lps only** (Fig 7) across side, joining corners at center sts. Finish off all yarn ends.

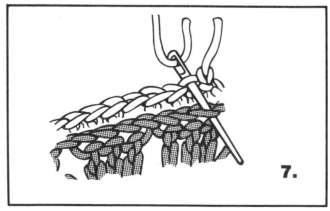

**7.**

# STUFFING

With wrong sides of front and back tog, join matching yarn with a sl st in outer corner sp of back; join front to back with sc, carefully matching sts and seams and working through **inner lps only.** As one section is joined (head, leg, etc.) begin stuffing. Stuff very firmly, pushing stuffing carefully into corners. Continue joining with sc around, stuffing as you go; at end, join with a sl st in first sc. Finish off.

# PIGGY

*designed by Eleanor Denner*

**SIZE: Approx 19″ wide (measured nose to tail) × 13″ high**

**MATERIALS: Aunt Lydia's Heavy Rug Yarn in 70-yd skeins: 8 skeins Med Pink, 1 skein Black; aluminum crochet hook size G (or size required for gauge); approx 2 lbs polyester filling for stuffing.**

## INSTRUCTIONS

First read General Instructions at beginning of this chapter; following Granny Square Instructions therein, make squares as listed below:

**ONE-COLOR FULL SQUARES: 75 Med Pink**
**ONE-COLOR HALF SQUARES: 12 Med Pink**

Arrange squares as shown in diagrams for front and back of body *(Fig 8);* join squares with joining method given in General Instructions. Squares which rem will be used for ears.

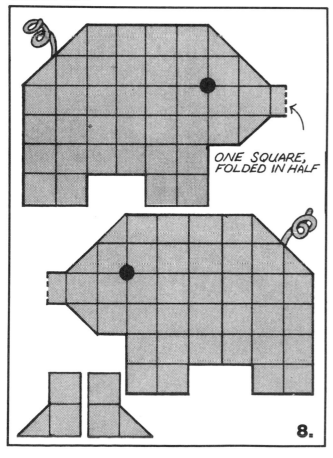

ONE SQUARE, FOLDED IN HALF

**8.**

**Eye (make 2):** With Black, ch 3; work 10 dc in 3rd ch from hook, join with a sl st in top of beg ch-3. Finish off, weave in yarn ends.

**Ear (make 2):** Join squares as shown in diagrams; sc around, working in outer lps only.

**Tail:** With Med Pink, ch 15; work 3 sc in 2nd ch from hook, 3 sc in each of next 10 chs, sl st in each of last 3 chs. Finish off.

*FINISHING*

With matching thread, sew eyes and ears as positioned in photo and diagrams. With stuffing method given in General Instructions, join front to back. Tie or sew tail to body.

# BABY ELEPHANT
*designed by Eleanor Denner*

**SIZE: Approx 13″ high by 15½″ wide**

**MATERIALS: Aunt Lydia's Heavy Rug Yarn in 70-yd skeins: 8 skeins Steel Gray and a few yards Black; aluminum crochet hook size G (or size required for gauge); approx 2 lbs polyester filling for stuffing.**

## INSTRUCTIONS

First read General Instructions at beginning of this chapter; following Granny Square Instructions therein, make squares as listed below with Steel Gray:

**73 ONE-COLOR FULL SQUARES**

**12 ONE-COLOR HALF SQUARES**

Arrange squares for front and back of body as shown in diagrams *(Fig 9);* join squares with joining method given in General Instructions.

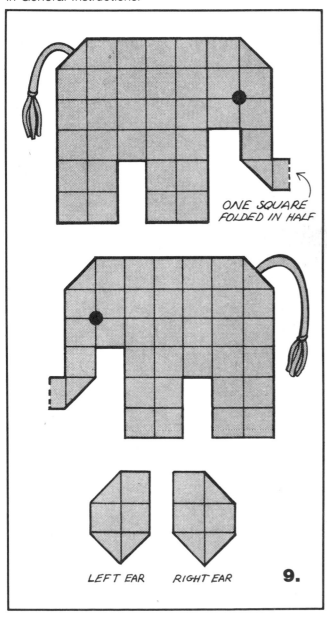

ONE SQUARE FOLDED IN HALF

LEFT EAR    RIGHT EAR    **9.**

**Tail:** With Steel Gray, ch 15, sl st in 2nd ch from hook and in each ch to end; finish off, weave in yarn ends. Cut 3 pieces of yarn each 6″ long and tie to end of tail.

**Ear (make 2):** Join squares as shown in diagrams; sew to body as positioned in photo.

**Eye (make 2):** With Black, ch 3; work 10 dc in 3rd ch from hook, join with a sl st in top of beg ch-3. Finish off, weave in yarn ends. With black sewing thread, sew eyes to body as positioned in photo.

*FINISHING*

With stuffing method given in General Instructions, join front to back. Tie or sew tail to body as positioned in diagrams.

# VINCENT VAN GATOR

*designed by Eleanor Denner*

**SIZE: Approx 7″ wide × 51″ long**

**MATERIALS: Aunt Lydia's Heavy Rug Yarn in 70-yd skeins: 13 Emerald Green, 4 Red, 1 White and few yds Black; aluminum crochet hook size G (or size required for gauge); approx 4 lbs polyester filling for stuffing.**

## INSTRUCTIONS

First read General Instructions at beginning of this chapter; following Granny Square Instructions therein, make squares as listed below:

**ONE-COLOR FULL SQUARES:**
**108 Emerald Green; 32 Red**
**ONE-COLOR HALF SQUARES:**
**20 Emerald Green; 4 Red**

Arrange squares for front and back as shown in diagrams *(Fig 10)*; 2 half squares which rem will be used later for eyes. Join squares with joining method given in General Instructions.

**Eye (make 2):** With Black, ch 2.

**Rnd 1:** Work 6 sc in 2nd ch from hook, join with a sl st in first sc. Finish off Black.

**Rnd 2:** Join white with a sl st in any sc, work 2 sc in same st and in each sc around = 12 sc. Do not join this or following rnds, but mark beg of each rnd.

**Rnds 3 and 4:** Sc in each sc around.

**Rnd 5:** Stuff, (dec over next 2 sc) 6 times. Finish off, leaving 10″ yarn end for sewing.

With Emerald Green, sc around each of rem half squares. Place over eyeball *(Fig 10)* and sew in position on head as shown in photo.

**Teeth (make 2—uppers and lowers):** With White, ch 2.

**Row 1:** Work 2 sc in 2nd ch from hook.

**Row 2:** Ch 1, turn; 2 sc in first sc.

Rep Row 2 until piece measures approx 34″ or is long enough to fit mouth. Finish off.

## FINISHING

With stuffing method given in General Instructions, join front to back. With matching thread, sew teeth as positioned in photo.

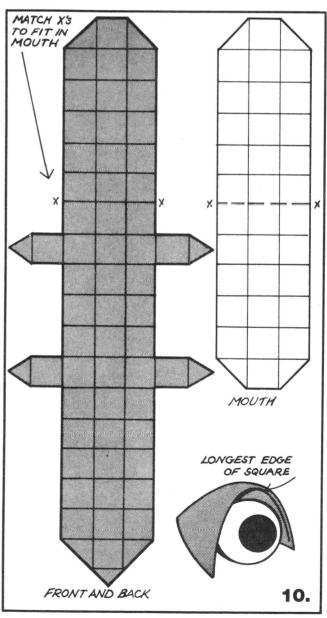

MATCH X's TO FIT IN MOUTH

MOUTH

LONGEST EDGE OF SQUARE

FRONT AND BACK

**10.**

# SHELLY TURTLE

*designed by Anis Duncan*

**SIZE: Approx 22″ wide × 25″ long**

**MATERIALS: Aunt Lydia's Heavy Rug Yarn in 70-yd skeins: 3 skeins Sunset, 4 skeins Yellow, 1 skein Red, 3 skeins Grass Green, 3 skeins Spring Green and a few yards each of Black and White; aluminum crochet hook size G (or size required for gauge); approx 4 lbs polyester filling for stuffing.**

## INSTRUCTIONS

First read General Instructions at beginning of this chapter; following Granny Square Instructions therein, make squares as listed below:

**ONE-COLOR FULL SQUARES**
**12 Grass Green**
**16 Spring Green**
**24 Yellow**
**16 Sunset**
**TWO-COLOR FULL SQUARES**
 **4 Red (center)/Sunset (outer)**
**12 Grass Green (center)/Yellow (outer)**
**DIAGONAL TWO-COLOR SQUARES**
**12 Spring Green/Red**
 **4 Sunset/Red**
**16 Sunset/Yellow**
**ONE-COLOR HALF SQUARES**
 **8 Spring Green**
 **8 Sunset**
**26 Grass Green**

Arrange squares as shown in diagrams *(Fig 11)*; join squares with joining method given in General Instructions. Rem half squares will be used later for eyes.

**Eye (make 2):** With Black, ch 2.

**Rnd 1:** Work 6 sc in 2nd ch from hook, join with a sl st in first sc. Finish off Black.

**Rnd 2:** Join white with a sl st in any sc, work 2 sc in same st and in each st around = 12 sc. Do not join this rnd or following rnds, but mark beg of each rnd.

**Rnds 3 and 4:** Sc in each sc around.

**Rnd 5:** Stuff, (dec over next 2 sc) 6 times. Finish off, leaving a 10″ yarn end for sewing.

With Grass Green, sc around each of rem half squares. Place over eyeball (Fig 10 same as alligator) and sew in position on head as shown in photo or diagrams.

*FINISHING*

With stuffing method given in General Instructions, join front to back—matching color of yarn with color of body. Feet and tail are stuffed and joined on all sides and then sewn to finished edge of shell.

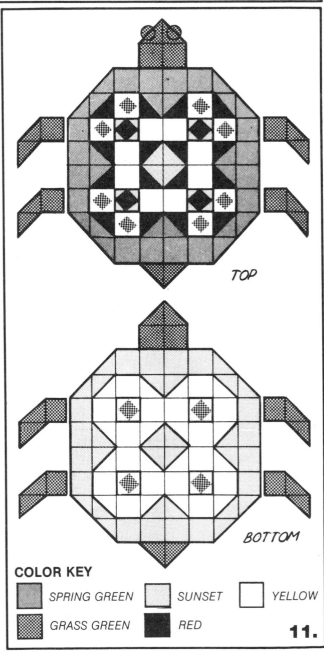

*TOP*

*BOTTOM*

**COLOR KEY**

| | | |
|---|---|---|
| SPRING GREEN | SUNSET | YELLOW |
| GRASS GREEN | RED | |

**11.**

# LEONARDO DA LION

*designed by Eleanor Denner*

**SIZE: Approx 21″ wide × 18″ high**

**MATERIALS:** Aunt Lydia's Heavy Rug Yarn in 70-yd skeins: 6 skeins Sunset, 1 skein Brown; few yards Black; aluminum crochet hook size G (or size required for gauge); approx 2 lbs polyester filling for stuffing.

## INSTRUCTIONS

**Important Note: The lion is made of 3-rnd squares.**

First read General Instructions at beginning of this chapter. Following Granny Square Instructions therein, make squares but at end of Rnd 2 do not finish off; continue by working from instructions for Rnd 3 which appear immediately following the list of squares needed:

**ONE-COLOR FULL SQUARES
(with 3rd rnd added*): 36 Sunset
ONE-COLOR HALF SQUARES
(with 3rd rnd added**): 6 Sunset**

***FULL SQUARE*
Rnd 3:** Sl st in each of next 2 dc and into ch-1 sp; ch 3, work (2 dc, ch 1, 3 dc) all in same sp; * work 3 dc in sp between corner groups for side; work (3 dc, ch 1, 3 dc) all in next ch-1 sp; rep from * twice, 3 dc in sp between corner groups; join with a sl st in top of ch-3. Finish off, leaving a 10″ yarn end for sewing.

****HALF SQUARE*
Rnd 3:** Ch 3, TURN, work 3 dc in first dc [at base of ch], 3 dc in sp between corner groups for side; work (3 dc, ch 1, 3 dc) all in next ch-1 sp; 3 dc in sp between corner groups, 4 dc in top of Tch. Finish off, leaving a 10″ yarn end for sewing.

Arrange squares for front and back as shown in diagrams *(Fig 12)*; join squares with joining method given in General Instructions.

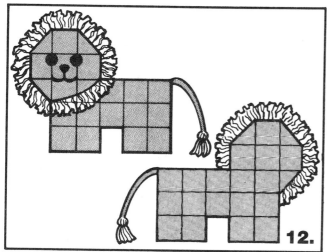

**12.**

**Eye (make 2):** With Black, ch 4, join with a sl st to form a ring.

**Rnd 1:** Ch 1, work 8 sc in ring, join with a sl st in beg ch-1. Finish off Black.

**Rnd 2:** Join Brown with a sl st in any sc, ch 2; hdc in same sp, 2 hdc in each sc around, join with a sl st in top of beg ch-2. Finish off, weave in yarn ends.

**Nose:** With Brown, ch 9.

**Row 1:** Sc in 2nd ch from hook and in each rem ch across = 8 sc.

**Row 2:** Ch 1, turn; dec over first 2 sc, sc in each of next 4 sc; dec over last 2 sc = 6 sc.

**Row 3:** Ch 1, turn; dec over first 2 sc, sc in each of next 2 sc; dec over last 2 sc = 4 sc.

**Row 4:** Ch 1, turn; dec over first 2 sc, dec over last 2 sc = 2 sc.

**Row 5:** Ch 1, turn; dec over rem 2 sc. Finish off, weave in yarn ends.

**Mouth:** With Brown, make a chain to measure 6″. Finish off, weave in yarn ends.

**Tail:** With Sunset, ch 6, join with a sl st to form a ring.

**Rnd 1:** Work 6 sc in ring, do not join this rnd or following rnds until specified.

**Rnd 2:** Sc in each sc around.

Stuffing as you work, rep Rnd 2 until tail measures 7″; then join with a sl st in beg sc of last rnd. Finish off, leaving a 10″ yarn end for sewing. [**Note:** It is easier to crochet from inside of work to outside to prevent hook from getting caught in work.]

**Tassel:** Cut 10 strands of Sunset yarn, each 10″ long and make tassel following Tassel Instructions in Chapter 8. Tie tassel to end of tail and weave in yarn ends.

**Fringe for Mane:** Cut 8″ strands of Sunset and Brown yarn. Using 3 Brown and 2 Sunset in each knot, tie a knot *(Fig 13)* in each sc around lion's head [working from back side] and in a circular line across squares to complete "head shape."

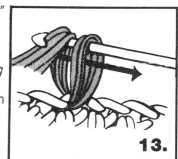

**13.**

## FINISHING

Position eyes, nose and ch mouth as shown in photo and diagrams; sew to head with sewing thread. With stuffing method given in General Instructions, join front to back. Sew tail to body.

# BONITA BURRO

*designed by Anis Duncan*

**SIZE:** 29″ wide (measures from nose to tail) × 28″ tall

**MATERIALS:** Aunt Lydia's Heavy Rug Yarn in 70-yd skeins: 1 Sunset, 1 Red, 1 Peacock, 2 Spring Green, 1 Beige, 11 Brown and a few yds Black; aluminum crochet hook size G (or size required for gauge); approx 4 lbs polyester filling for stuffing.

## INSTRUCTIONS

First read General Instructions at beginning of this chapter; following Granny Square instructions therein, make squares as listed below:

**ONE-COLOR FULL SQUARES: 84 Brown**

**ONE-COLOR HALF SQUARES: 24 Brown; 2 Red**

**DIAGONAL TWO-COLOR SQUARES: 8 Spring Green/Brown; 4 Spring Green/Sunset; 12 Spring Green/Peacock**

**TWO-COLOR FULL SQUARES: 12 Sunset (center)/Red (outer)**

Arrange squares for front and back of body as shown in diagrams *(Fig 14);* join squares with joining method given in General Instructions.

**Eye (make 2):** With Black, ch 3; work 12 dc in 3rd ch from hook, join with a sl st in top of beg ch-3. Finish off, weave in yarn ends. With black sewing thread sew eyes in place as indicated in diagrams.

**Nostrils (make 2):** With Black, ch 2; 6 sc in 2nd ch from hook, join with a sl st in top of beg ch. Finish off, weave in yarn ends. With black sewing thread sew in place as shown in diagrams.

**Tail:** With Beige, ch 6, join with a sl st to form a ring.

**Rnd 1:** Work 6 sc in ring, do not join this rnd or following rnds.

**Rnd 2:** Sc in each sc around.

Stuffing as you work, rep Rnd 2 until tail measures 6″ in length. [**Note:** It is easier to crochet from inside of work to outside; this prevents hook from getting caught in work.] Finish off, leaving 8″ end for sewing.

**Tassel:** Cut 20 strands of Beige yarn, each 12″ long and make tassel following Tassel Instructions in Chapter 8. Tie tassel to end of tail and weave in yarn ends.

## FINISHING

With stuffing method given in General Instructions, join front to back. Sew tail to body as positioned in diagrams.

**Fringe for Mane:** Cut strands of Beige yarn, each 6″ long. Using 2 strands in each knot, tie a knot *(Fig 15)* in each sc on burro's neck, working alternately from right and left sides of burro.

**15.**

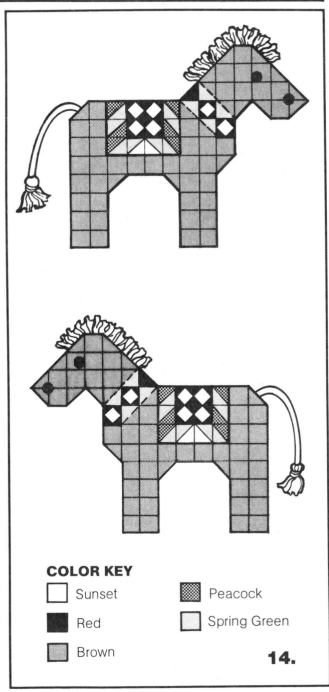

**COLOR KEY**

- ☐ Sunset
- ■ Red
- ▨ Brown
- ▨ Peacock
- ☐ Spring Green

**14.**

# GINNY GIRAFFE

*designed by Eleanor Denner*

**SIZE:** Approx 26″ wide (measured nose to tail) × 33″ high

**MATERIALS:** Aunt Lydia's Heavy Rug Yarn in 70-yd skeins: 9 Antique Gold, 4 Wood Brown and a few yds Green; aluminum crochet hook size G (or size required for gauge); approx 5 lbs polyester filling for stuffing.

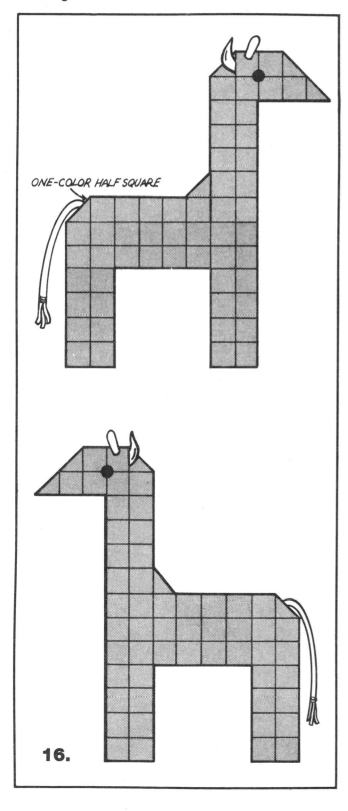

ONE-COLOR HALF SQUARE

**16.**

## INSTRUCTIONS

First read General Instructions at beginning of this chapter; following Granny Square Instructions therein, make squares as listed below:

**TWO-COLOR FULL SQUARES:**
106 Wood Brown (center)/Antique Gold (outer)

**TWO-COLOR HALF SQUARES:**
8 Wood Brown (center)/Antique Gold (outer)

**ONE-COLOR HALF SQUARES:**
4 Antique Gold

Arrange squares for front and back of body as shown in diagrams *(Fig 16)*; join squares with joining method given in General Instructions. Squares which rem will be used for ears.

**Ear:** With Antique Gold and right side of square facing, sc around each of rem 2 half squares. Finish off, weave in yarn ends.

**Horns (make 2):** With Wood Brown, ch 2.

**Rnd 1:** Work 6 sc in 2nd ch from hook, do not join but be sure to mark beg of each rnd.

**Rnd 2:** 2 sc in each sc around = 12 sc.

**Rnds 3 and 4:** Sc in each sc around = 12 sc.

**Rnd 5:** (Dec over 2 sc) 6 times = 6 sc.

**Rnds 6 through 8:** Work even on 6 sc. Join with a sl st; finish off, leaving a 10″ yarn end for sewing.

**Eye (make 2):** With Green, ch 4, join with a sl st to form a ring. Ch 2, work 8 hdc in ring, join with a sl st in top of beg ch. Finish off, weave in yarn ends.

**Tail:** With Antique Gold, ch 40; sl st in 2nd ch from hook and in each ch to end. Finish off, weave in yarn ends. Cut 3 pieces of yarn each 6″ long and tie to end of tail.

*FINISHING*

With matching thread, sew horns, eyes and ears as positioned in photo and diagrams. With stuffing method given in General Instructions, join front to back. Sew tail to body as positioned in photo.

# GRANNY'S CAT

*designed by Anis Duncan*

**SIZE: Approx 19½″ long × 9″ tall**

**MATERIALS: Aunt Lydia's Heavy Rug Yarn in 70-yd skeins: 4 skeins Sunset, 4 skeins Tangerine and few yds each of Dark Brown and Green; aluminum crochet hook size G (or size required for gauge); approx 2 lbs polyester filling for stuffing.**

## INSTRUCTIONS

First read General Instructions at beginning of this chapter; following Granny Square Instructions therein, make squares as listed below:

**ONE-COLOR FULL SQUARES:**
**25 Sunset; 16 Tangerine**
**DIAGONAL TWO-COLOR SQUARES:**
**13 Sunset/Tangerine**
**ONE-COLOR HALF SQUARES:**
**13 Sunset; 5 Tangerine**

Arrange squares for front and back as shown in diagrams *(Fig 17);* join squares using method given in General Instructions.

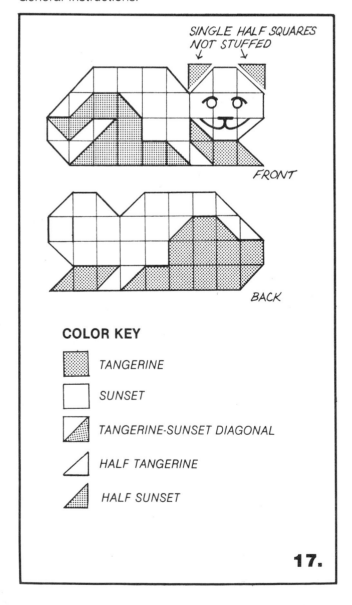

SINGLE HALF SQUARES NOT STUFFED

FRONT

BACK

**COLOR KEY**

TANGERINE

SUNSET

TANGERINE-SUNSET DIAGONAL

HALF TANGERINE

HALF SUNSET

**17.**

**Nose/Mouth:** With Dark Brown, make a chain to measure 10″; finish off, weave in yarn ends. With matching thread, sew as positioned in diagram.

**Eye (make 2):** With Green, ch 3, join with a sl st to form a ring. Ch 1, 6 sc in ring, join with a sl st in beg ch-1; finish off, weave in yarn ends. With matching thread, sew as positioned in diagram.

With Dark Brown, make two chains each 2½″ long; finish off, weave in yarn ends. With matching sewing thread, sew above eyes as positioned in diagram.

*FINISHING*

With stuffing method given in General Instructions, join front to back, working sc until you reach ears. Join each ear by placing it in position between front and back, then work sl st through correspsonding sts of all 3 pieces (front, ear, back). Continue in sc to other ear, then join it in same manner.

# DOODLE BUG

*designed by Barbara Luoma*

**SIZE: Approx 3½ " wide × 38½ " long**

**MATERIALS:** Worsted weight yarn, 4 oz light brown, several yards each of following colors: light gold, dark gold, light green, dark green, avocado green, light lavender, dark purple, light yellow, light orange, beige, rust, dark brown, bright red, light pink, white and black; aluminum crochet hook size G (or size required for gauge); polyester filling for stuffing.

**GAUGE: One square = 3½ "**

## INSTRUCTIONS

*BOTTOM SQUARE (make 10 light brown)*

**Note:** All rnds are worked on right side.

**Rnd 1:** Ch 4, work 2 dc in 4th ch from hook; * ch 3, 3 dc in same ch; rep from * twice more, ch 1, join with a hdc in top of beg ch-4.

**Rnd 2:** Ch 3, dc in sp under hdc, dc in same st as joining [where hdc was worked]; dc in **back lp only** of each dc to next ch-3 sp; * work (2 dc, ch 3, 2 dc) in ch-3 sp for corner, dc in **back lp only** of each dc to next ch-3 sp; rep from * twice more, work 2 dc in beg corner sp, ch 1, join with a hdc in top of beg ch-3 = 7 dc between each pair of corner sps.

**Rnd 3:** Rep Rnd 2; you should have 11 dc between each pair of corner sps. Finish off, weave in yarn ends.

*TOP SQUARE (make 10 in assorted colors)*

Make squares in colors of your choice or in the same colors we used which are listed below by square number. Instructions are the same as Bottom Square; however, at end of Rnd 3 do not finish off, work **Joining Rnd:** Hold one bottom square and one top square with wrong sides tog. Carefully match sts and work sc in each st around 3 sides; stuff lightly and then sc across last side. Finish off, leaving sewing length for joining.

| | COLORS USED IN RNDS 1 AND 2 | COLORS USED IN RND 3 AND JOINING RND |
|---|---|---|
| SQUARE 1 | Dk Brown | Dk Gold |
| SQUARE 2 | Bright Red | White |
| SQUARE 3 | Dk Purple | Lt Lavender |
| SQUARE 4 | Lt Green | Avocado Green |
| SQUARE 5 | Black | Bright Red |
| SQUARE 6 | Lt Pink | Dk Purple |
| SQUARE 7 | Lt Orange | Beige |
| SQUARE 8 | Lt Yellow | Lt Gold |
| SQUARE 9 | Dk Green | Lt Green |
| SQUARE 10 | Rust | White |

*HEAD (make 2—1 for Bottom and 1 for Top)*

**Rnd 1:** With lt brown, ch 4; work 9 dc in 4th ch from hook, join with a sl st in top of beg ch-4 = 10 dc.

**Rnd 2:** Ch 3, dc in same st; 2 dc in each rem dc around, join with a sl st in top of beg ch-3 = 20 dc.

**Rnd 3:** Ch 3, dc in same st, dc in next dc; * 2 dc in next dc, dc in next dc; rep from * around, join with a sl st in top of beg ch-3 = 30 dc.

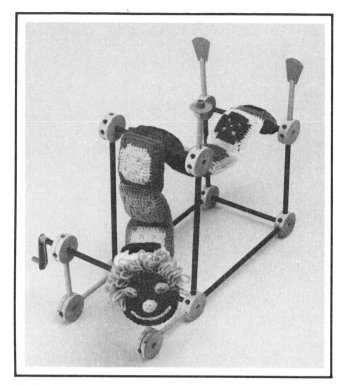

**Rnd 4:** Rep Rnd 3; you should have 45 dc. Bottom Piece Only: Finish off, weave in yarn ends. Top Piece: Do not finish off, continue with same yarn and join as follows: Hold both pieces with wrong sides tog; carefully match sts and work sc in each st around, stuffing lightly as you work. Finish off, leaving sewing length for joining.

*ASSEMBLY*

After all squares and head are stuffed and joined, hold squares side by side and whipstitch tog (see joining method 5 in Chapter 8), beg at tail with Square 1 and ending by joining Square 10 to head.

*FACIAL FEATURES*

**Eye (make 2):** With lt orange, ch 2, work 6 hdc in 2nd ch from hook, join with a sl st in beg hdc. Finish off, leaving approx 6" sewing length. Thread tapestry needle and sew to head as positioned in photo.

**Nose:** With lt pink, ch 2. **Rnd 1:** Work 6 sc in 2nd ch from hook; do not join until specified. **Rnd 2:** * Sc in next sc, 2 sc in next sc; rep from * twice = 9 sc. **Rnd 3:** Sc in each sc around, join with a sl st in beg sc. Finish off, leaving approx 6" sewing length. Thread tapestry needle and sew to head as positioned in photo.

**Mouth:** With lt pink and tapestry needle, embroider 8 chain sts for mouth as positioned in photo.

**Hair:** Work 3 rows of appliqued loop stitches, working from **left to right** at top of head as follows: With top side facing and lt green, beg in joining rnd at top of head and approx 6 sts to left of corner of Square 10. Join with a sl st around **post** of sc; hook yarn and draw up approx 1½ " lp through lp on hook, drop lp from hook. * Insert hook under **post** of next st [from right to left of st], hook yarn and draw up lp from under st; YO and draw up approx 1½ " lp through lp on hook, drop lp from hook; rep from * across to approx 6th st to right of corner of Square 10. Work in same manner on next 2 rnds below joining rnd.

# THE BARKER FAMILY

*designed by Eleanor Denner*

**SIZE: Approx height of Daddy Dog = 33″; Mama Dog = 26″; Baby Dog = 18″**

**MATERIALS: Aunt Lydia's Heavy Rug Yarn in 70-yd skeins, amounts listed below for each dog; aluminum crochet hook size G (or size required for gauge); polyester filling for stuffing, amounts for each dog listed below.**

**Materials Note:** Specific amounts given below are for each individual dog and includes one skein of Black for each; if you are making the set of all 3 dogs, one skein of Black will be sufficient for the set.

**DADDY DOG: 8 skeins Red, 7 skeins White, 1 skein Black; approx 4 lbs polyester filling for stuffing.**

**MAMA DOG: 8 skeins Red, 2 skeins White, 1 skein Black; approx 2 lbs polyester filling for stuffing.**

**BABY DOG: 3 skeins Red, 3 skeins White, 1 skein Black; approx one lb polyester filling for stuffing.**

**GAUGE: One 2-rnd square = 2½″**
**One 3-rnd square = 3½″**
**One 4-rnd square = 4½″**

**Gauge Note:** All squares are made from Granny Square Instructions with a different number of rnds for each dog: 2 rnds for Baby, 3 rnds for Mama, and 4 rnds for Daddy.

## BABY DOG
*TWO-RND SQUARES (make 26 White and 26 Red—One-Color Full Squares)*

Read General Instructions at beginning of this chapter; follow instructions therein for One-Color Full Squares and make 26 with White (Square A) and 26 with Red (Square B). Arrange squares for front and back as in Fig 18; join squares per instructions given in General Instructions.

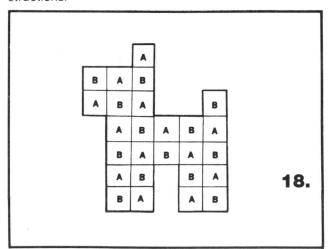

**18.**

**Eye (make 2):** With Black, ch 3, work 10 dc in 3rd ch from hook, join with a sl st in top of beg ch-3. Finish off, weave in yarn ends. With black sewing thread, sew eyes as positioned in photo. Now join front to back and stuff, using method given in General Instructions.

## MAMA DOG
*THREE-RND SQUARES (make 52—Two-Color Full Squares)*

Read General Instructions at beginning of this chapter; follow instructions therein for Two-Color Full Squares. Beg with White, work Rnd 1; work Rnd 2 with red but do not finish off at end of rnd. Continue with red for Rnd 3.

**Rnd 3:** Sl st in each of next 2 dc and into ch-1 sp, ch 3; work (2 dc, ch 1, 3 dc) all in same sp; * 3 dc between 3-dc groups along side, work (3 dc, ch 1, 3 dc) all in next ch-1 corner sp ; rep from * twice, 3 dc between 3-dc groups along last side, join with a sl st in top of beg ch-3. Finish off, leaving 10″ yarn end for sewing.

Arrange squares for front and back as in Fig 18; since Mama Dog squares are all identical, ignore the A and B marked in fig. Join squares per instructions in General Instructions.

**Eye (make 2):** With Black, ch 3, work 10 dc in 3rd ch from hook; join with a sl st in top of beg ch-3. Finish off, weave in yarn ends. With black sewing thread, sew eyes as positioned in photo. Now join front to back and stuff, using method given in General Instructions.

## PAPA DOG
*FOUR-RND SQUARES (make 26 Square A and 26 Square B)*

Read General instructions at beginning of this chapter; follow instructions therein for Two-Color Full Squares for first two rnds of each square, then work 3rd and 4th rnd from instructions below. For Square A, work Rnds 1 and 2 with Red; work Rnds 3 and 4 with White. For Square B, work Rnds 1 and 2 with White; work Rnds 3 and 4 with Red.

**Rnd 3:** Join new color with a sl st in any ch-1 corner sp, ch 3; work (2 dc, ch 1, 3 dc) all in same sp; * 3 dc between next two 3-dc groups for side; work (3 dc, ch 1, 3 dc) all in next ch-1 sp for corner; rep from * twice, 3 dc between next two 3-dc groups for last side, join with a sl st in top of beg ch-3.

**Rnd 4:** Sl st in each of next 2 dc and into ch-1 sp, ch 3; work (2 dc, ch 1, 3 dc) all in same sp; * 3 dc between 3-dc groups along side, work (3 dc, ch 1, 3 dc) all in next ch-1 sp for corner; rep from * twice, 3 dc between 3-dc groups along last side, join with a sl st in top of beg ch-3. Finish off, weave in yarn ends.

Arrange squares as positioned in Fig 18. Join squares for front and back per instructions given in General Instructions.

**Eye (make 2):** With Black, ch 3; work 12 dc in 3rd ch from hook, join with a sl st in top of beg ch-3. Finish off, weave in yarn ends. With black sewing thread, sew eyes as positioned in photo.

Now join front to back and stuff, using method given in General Instructions.

*(Shown in color on page 72.)*

# CH3-DC ROBOT

*designed by Eleanor Denner*

**SIZE: Approx 36″ tall without antenna**

**MATERIALS: Worsted weight yarn, 24 oz gray, ½ oz green, several yds red, and one yd white; aluminum crochet hook size G (or size required for gauge); approx 4 lbs polyester filling for stuffing; 3⅞″ diameter aluminum buttons.**

## INSTRUCTIONS

First read General Instructions at beginning of this chapter; following instructions therein for One-Color Full Square, make 239 gray squares and 3 green squares.

### ARRANGING SQUARES

Refer to diagrams in Fig 19 for arranging squares of each part of robot; see steps listed below for number of squares required in each part.

**STEP 1, HEAD: 42 gray squares**
**STEP 2, NECK: 6 gray squares**
**STEP 3, BODY: 123 gray and 3 green squares**
**STEP 4, ARM (make 2): 11 gray squares each**
**STEP 5, LEG (make 2): 23 gray squares each**

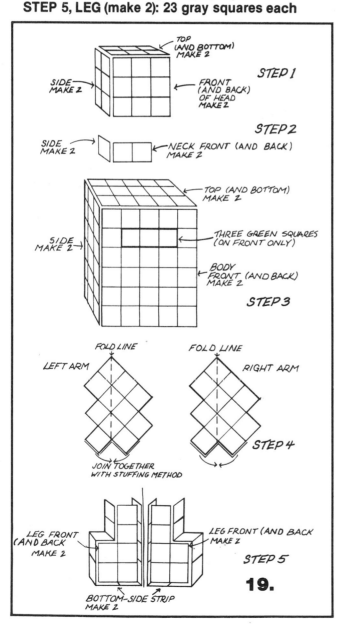

19.

### JOINING SQUARES

To form top, bottom, sides, etc. of each part, join squares using joining method given in General Instructions and referring to diagrams for placement. Do not join tops, bottoms and sides for Head or Body until appliqued features have been made and attached.

### APPLIQUÉD FEATURES FOR HEAD

**Eye (make 2):** With green, ch 2. **Rnd 1:** Work 6 sc in 2nd ch from hook; do not join until specified. **Rnd 2:** Work 2 sc in each sc around = 12 sc. **Rnd 3:** * Sc in next sc, 2 sc in next sc; rep from * 6 times, join with a sl st in beg sc. Finish off, leaving a 10″ yarn end for sewing. Thread tapestry needle, sew to front of Head as positioned in photo.

**Mouth:** With red, ch 23; sc in 2nd ch from hook and in each of next 2 chs, sk next 2 chs; sc in each of next 11 chs, sk next 2 chs; sc in each of last 4 chs; finish off, leaving a 10″ yarn end for sewing. Thread tapestry needle, sew to front of Head as positioned in photo.

**Antenna (make 2):** With gray, ch 2. **Rnd 1:** Work 6 sc in 2nd ch from hook, do not join until specified. **Rnd 2:** Sc in each sc around. Stuffing as you work, rep Rnd 2 until antenna measures 4″; join with a sl st in beg sc of last rnd. Finish off, leaving a 10″ yarn end for sewing. Thread tapestry needle, sew to top of Head as positioned in photo.

### APPLIQUÉD FEATURES FOR BODY

**Knob (make 4 red and 2 green):** Ch 2. **Rnd 1:** 6 sc in 2nd ch from hook, do not join until specified. **Rnd 2:** 2 sc in each sc around = 12 sc. **Rnds 3 and 4:** Sc in each sc around; at end of Rnd 4, join with a sl st in beg sc. Finish off, leaving a 10″ yarn end for sewing. Thread tapestry needle, sew 6 knobs and 3 buttons as positioned in photo.

### ASSEMBLING, JOINING AND STUFFING PARTS

Join tops, bottoms, fronts, backs, etc., for each part of robot using stuffing method given in General Instructions. Assemble and join parts tog in the following sequence: Join Neck to Head (Fig 20); join Head and Neck to Body (Fig 20); join each Arm to Body (Fig 21); and join each Leg to Body (Fig 22).

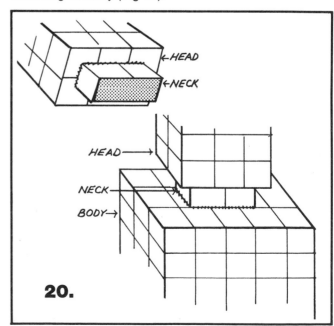

20.

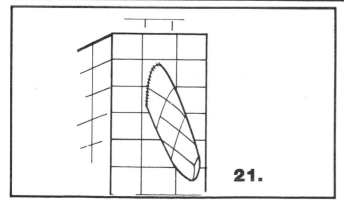

**21.**

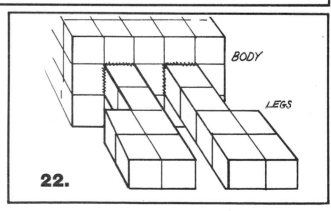

BODY

LEGS

**22.**

# ALPHABET

*designed by Eleanor Denner*

**SIZE: Each letter is approx 17″ high**

**MATERIALS: Aunt Lydia's Heavy Rug Yarn in 70-yd skeins: 30 skeins Black; 6 skeins Spring Green; 5 skeins each of Peacock, Red, Cerise; 4 skeins each of White, Yellow, Sunset, Grass Green, and Med Blue; 3 skeins each of Lt Blue, Med Pink, Burnt Orange, Tangerine, and Beige; 1 skein of Brown; aluminum crochet hook size G (or size required for gauge); approx 11 lbs polyester filling for stuffing.**

**Materials Note:** Yarn amounts given are needed to make the *entire* alphabet (26 letters) in color combinations shown in photo on book jacket. You may wish to make only a few letters, to spell out a name or initials, or an entire alphabet for toddlers learning their letters. You can make them with scraps of yarn in colors of your own choosing; but we suggest always using black or another dark color for the outer borders.

**GAUGE: One 3-rnd square = 3½″**

## INSTRUCTIONS

**Note: Letters are all made of 3-rnd squares.**

In our photo, we show each letter made up, clearly indicating position of squares (one-color Full squares and in some cases, one-color Half squares). Refer to photo to determine the number of squares required for front and back; in our set, backs and fronts of each letter are made with same color combination.

Read General Instructions at beginning of this chapter; following Granny Square Instructions therein, use any color except Black and work until Rnd 2 is completed. Then work third rnd (Border Rnd) as follows:

*FULL SQUARE*

**Border Rnd:** With right side of square facing, join Black with a sl st in any ch-1 corner sp. [**Note:** You may eliminate the need of many yarn ends to weave in, if you leave a 2″ end when joining Black and work each sc

over it.] Work 3 sc in same sp; * sc in each of next 6 dc to corner sp, 3 sc in ch-1 sp of corner; rep from * twice, sc in each of next 6 dc to first corner, join with a sl st in beg sc. Finish off, leaving a 10″ yarn end for sewing.

*HALF SQUARE*

**Border Rnd:** With right side of work facing, join Black with a sc in center ch-1 sp; 2 sc in same sp, sc in each of next 6 dc; 2 sc in top of last dc; working along sides of sts, 2 sc in side of dc and 2 sc in next ch-3; sc in ch where first groups were worked; 2 sc in side of next dc, 2 sc in side of next ch-3; 2 sc in top of same ch-3; sc in each of next 6 dc, join with a sl st in beg sc. Finish off, leaving a 10″ yarn end for sewing.

*ASSEMBLY*

Using joining method given in General Instructions, join squares in shape of letter in photo. Front view only of each letter is shown in photo; on a letter which does not have an identical front and back, you will need to sew square in reversed position for the back piece (see Fig 24 for the letter P, as an example).

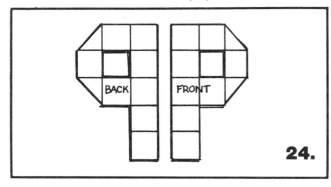

Join all squares for front, then all squares for back. Finish off all yarn ends before stuffing and joining tog.

Stuff front and back using method given in General Instructions. Note: For letter "R" only, the half and full square forming the lower right-hand part of the letter are joined and stuffed as a separate unit, then sewn to the rest of the letter.

*(Shown in color on the book jacket.)*

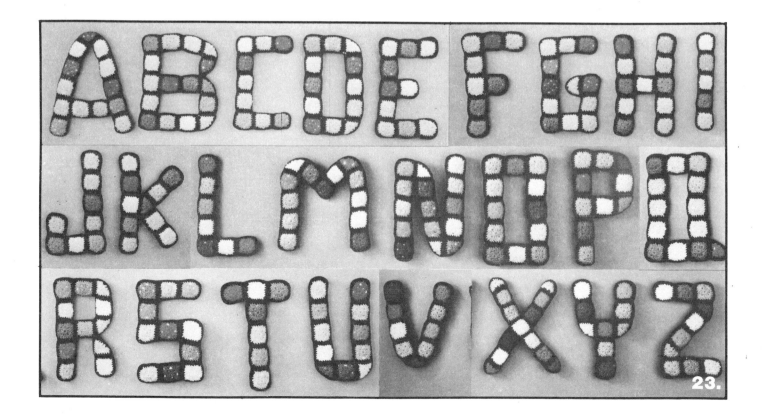

# GIANT DICE

*designed by Eleanor Denner*

**SIZE: Approx 4½ ″ cube**

**MATERIALS: Worsted weight yarn in 4-oz skeins: 2 skeins white and 1 skein red; aluminum crochet hook size G (or size required for gauge); one pound polyester filling.**

**GAUGE: One square = 4½ ″**

## INSTRUCTIONS

*SQUARE (make a total of 12 for pair)*

With white, ch 4, join with a sl st to form a ring.

**Rnd 1 (right side):** Ch 3, 2 dc in ring; ch 1, * work 3 dc in ring, ch 1; rep from * twice, join with a sl st in top of beg ch-3. Do not turn at end of this or following rnds; all rnds are worked on right side.

**Rnd 2:** Sl st in each of next 2 dc and into ch-1 sp, ch 3; work (2 dc, ch 1, 3 dc) all in same sp; * work (3 dc, ch 1, 3 dc) all in next ch-1 sp; rep from * twice, join with a sl st in top of beg ch-3.

**Rnd 3:** Sl st in each of next 2 dc and into ch-1 sp, ch 3; work (2 dc, ch 1, 3 dc) all in same sp for corner; * work 3 dc between next two 3-dc groups; in next ch-1 sp, work (3 dc, ch 1, 3 dc) for corner; rep from * twice, 3 dc between next two 3-dc groups, join with a sl st as before.

**Rnd 4:** Sl st in each of next 2 dc and into ch-1 sp, ch 3; work (2 dc, ch 1, 3 dc) all in same sp for corner: * work 3 dc between each pair of 3-dc groups along side; in next ch-1 corner sp, work (3 dc, ch 1, 3 dc); rep from * twice, work 3 dc between each pair of 3-dc groups along last side, join as before.

**Rnd 5:** Rep Rnd 4; finish off, weave in yarn ends.

*DOTS (make a total of 42 for pair)*

With red, ch 2, work 6 sc in 2nd ch from hook, join with a sl st in beg sc. Finish off, leaving 6″ yarn end for sewing. Thread tapestry needle and sew in positions shown on squares in Fig 25.

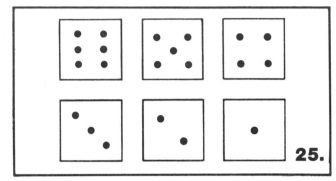

**25.**

*ASSEMBLING*

You will be first joining 4 squares in a row, then joining first square to last square; this will form a box-like shape with no top or bottom. Join a square at the top; stuff, then join last square at the bottom. The squares were joined with white with wrong sides tog; carefully match sts and work sc in each st across .

# JACK AND JILL DOLLS

*designed by Anis Duncan*

**SIZE:** Each approx 20″ tall

**MATERIALS:** Sport weight yarn, amounts for each doll listed individually below; aluminum crochet hook size G (or size required for gauge); miscellaneous items listed individually below.

**FOR JILL:** Sport weight yarn in 2-oz skeins: 2 skns each lt blue and white; 1 skn each lt pink, med pink and yellow; ¼″ wide white satin ribbon, 1 yd.

**FOR JACK:** Sport weight yarn in 2-oz skns: 2 skns red, 1 skn each lt blue, lt pink, med pink, white, black and yellow; three ⅝″ brass buttons; for insert in back pocket, 1 forked tree twig and rubber band.

**GAUGE:** One full square = 2″
In sc, 6 sts = 1″; 6 rnds = 1″

## INSTRUCTIONS

First read General Instructions at beginning of this chapter; following instructions therein, make squares as listed below:

**FOR JILL:**   **ONE-COLOR FULL SQUARES**
30 White
68 Blue
12 Lt Pink
**DIAGONAL TWO-COLOR FULL SQUARES**
22 Blue/White

**FOR JACK:**   **ONE-COLOR FULL SQUARES**
32 Blue
37 Red
12 Lt Pink
10 Black
**DIAGONAL TWO-COLOR FULL SQUARES**
2 Red/White
6 Red/Blue

Refer to diagrams in Fig 26 (page 64) for assembling front and back for body of doll; join squares using joining method given in General Instructions. Join front to back with stuffing method given in General Instructions.

## JILL

### FRONT OF HEAD *(make with pink)*

Ch 2. **Rnd 1:** Work 6 sc in 2nd ch from hook, do not join this rnd or following rnds unless specified. **Rnd 2:** 2 sc in each sc around = 12 sc (6 sts increased). **Rnd 3:** * 2 sc in next sc (inc made), sc in next sc; rep from * around = 18 sc (6 sts increased). **Rnd 4:** * 2 sc in next sc, sc in each of next 2 sc; rep from * around = 24 sc (6 sts increased). **Rnd 5:** * 2 sc in next sc, sc in each of next 3 sc; rep from * around = 30 sc (6 sts increased). **Rnds 6 through 16:** * 2 sc in next sc, work sc in same number of sc **plus one more** than prev rnd between incs; rep from * around = 6 sts increased each rnd. At end of Rnd 16, you should have 96 sc. **Rnds 17 through 19:** Sc in each sc around; at end of last rnd, join with a sl st in beg sc of rnd. Finish off, weave in yarn ends.

### BACK OF HEAD

With white, follow instructions for Front of Head. At end of Rnd 19 (last rnd), do not finish off white. **Joining Rnd:** Hold Front and Back with wrong sides tog and Front (pink) facing you. Remove lp from hook; insert hook into 2 lps of any sc in Front, hook dropped lp and pull through st. Ch 1, sc in each st around [inserting hook into 2 lps of pink and 2 lps of white to make each sc]. When approx half of joining has been completed, begin stuffing with polyester filling; continue to stuff as you work. At end of rnd, you should have 96 sc; sl st in beg sc of rnd. **Do not finish off;** continue with white for bonnet.

### BONNET

**Row 1:** With Front facing you, sc in each of first 4 sc; hdc in each of next 12 sc, dc in each of next 48 sc; hdc in each of next 12 sc, sc in each of next 4 sc; leave rem 16 sc unworked [for neck edge] = 80 sts. **Row 2:** Ch 1, turn; sc in each of first 4 sc, 2 hdc in each of next 12 hdc; 2 dc in each of next 48 dc, 2 hdc in each of next 12 hdc; sc in each of last 4 sc = 152 sts. **Row 3:** Ch 1, turn; sc in each of first 4 sc, dc in each st across to last 4 sc, sc in each of last 4 sc = 152 sts. **Row 4:** Ch 1, turn; sc in each of first 8 sts, work (dc, ch 1) in each st across to last 8 sts; sc in each of last 8 sts. **Row 5:** Ch 1, turn; sc in each of first 8 sts; * sc in next dc, ch 3, sl st in 3rd ch from hook [picot made]; rep from * across to last 8 sts, sc in each of last 8 sts. Finish off, weave in yarn ends.

### FRINGED HAIR

Cut strands of yellow yarn, each 3″ long. You will be using one strand for each knot of fringe and working single knot fringe (see instructions for single knot fringe in Chapter 8).

With pink side of head facing you, beg at the right-hand side of neck edge [where 16 sc were left unworked]. Beg in Rnd 19 of Head; * place 1 knot of fringe in **post** of each of first 4 sc, then place knots of fringe into sc in usual manner [inserting in 2 lps of each] around to last 4 sc at left-hand side of neck edge opening. **Note:** Within each row of fringe, knots can be worked in each sc OR some sc left unworked—depending on amount of thickness desired. In Rnds 17 and 16 of Head, beg and end by skipping 2 sc; in Rnds 15 and 14, beg and end by skipping 4 sc; in Rnds 13 and 12, beg and end by skipping 16 sc; in Rnd 11, sk first 30 sc, work fringe in next 20 sc only.

### FACIAL FEATURES

**Eye (make 2):** With blue, ch 3, join with a sl st to form a ring. Ch 1, work 9 sc in ring; join with a sl st in beg ch-1. Finish off, leaving approx 9″ sewing length.

**Cheek (make 2):** With med pink, ch 3, join with a sl st to form a ring. Ch 3, work 11 dc in ring; join with a sl st in top of beg ch-3. Finish off, leaving approx 9″ sewing length.

**Smile:** With med pink, ch 18, sc in 2nd ch from hook and in each rem ch across. Finish off, leaving approx 12″ sewing length.

### FINISHING

Sew features to face as positioned in photo; sew head to top of body. Cut ribbon in half; tack to bottom corners of bonnet ruffle, tie in a bow at chin.

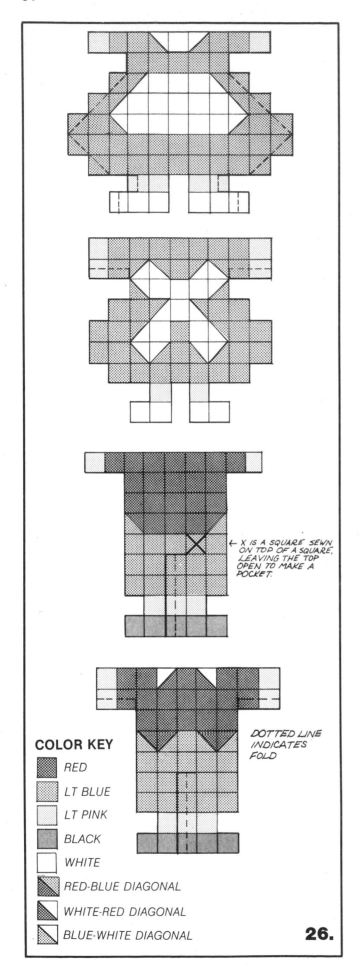

**COLOR KEY**

- ▨ RED
- ▨ LT BLUE
- ▨ LT PINK
- ▨ BLACK
- ☐ WHITE
- ◩ RED-BLUE DIAGONAL
- ◩ WHITE-RED DIAGONAL
- ◩ BLUE-WHITE DIAGONAL

← X IS A SQUARE SEWN ON TOP OF A SQUARE, LEAVING THE TOP OPEN TO MAKE A POCKET.

DOTTED LINE INDICATES FOLD

**26.**

## JACK

*TOP OF HEAD (make 2 with black)*
Ch 2. **Row 1:** Work 3 sc in 2nd ch from hook. **Row 2:** Ch 1, turn; 2 sc in each sc across = 6 sc [3 sc increased]. **Row 3:** Ch 1, turn; * 2 sc in next sc [inc made], sc in next sc; rep from * twice = 9 sc [3 sc increased]. **Row 4:** Ch 1, turn; * 2 sc in next sc, sc in each of next 2 sc; rep from * twice = 12 sc [3 sc increased]. **Row 5:** Ch 1, turn; * 2 sc in next sc, sc in next 3 sc; rep from * twice = 15 sc [3 sc increased]. **Rows 6 through 16:** Ch 1, turn; * 2 sc in next sc, sc in same number of sc **plus one more** between incs than in prev row; rep from * across = 3 sc increased each row. At end of Row 16, you should have 48 sc. **Rows 17 through 19:** Ch 1, turn; sc in each sc across. Finish off, weave in yarn ends. For 2nd piece made with black, do not finish off at end of Row 19; continue with same yarn for joining 2 black pieces tog.

**Joining:** With wrong sides tog, join by working sc into each st across in last row of both pieces; you should have 48 sc, join with a sl st in beg sc. Finish off, weave in yarn ends.

*BOTTOM OF HEAD (make 1 lt pink and 1 yellow)*
With lt pink [for face], follow instructions for Top of Head; finish off, weave in yarn ends. With yellow [for hair at back of head], follow instructions for Top of Head; do not finish off, continue with same yarn for joining. **Joining:** Rep instructions for joining Top of Head.

*FINISHING HEAD*
Join Top and Bottom with black yarn, carefully matching sts and joining seams. Work with wrong sides tog and Top [black piece] facing you, sc in end st of each row around. When half of joining has been completed, begin stuffing; continue to stuff as you work. You should have 74 sc around, join with a sl st in beg sc. **Do not finish off;** continue with black for brim of hat.

*HAT BRIM*
**Rnd 1:** Ch 3, * 2 dc in next sc, dc in each of next 2 sc; rep from * around to last sc, dc in last sc; join with a sl st in top of beg ch-3 = 98 dc. **Rnd 2:** Ch 3, dc in next dc; * 2 dc in next sc, dc in each of next 3 dc; rep from * around, join with a sl st in top of beg ch-3 = 122 dc. **Rnd 3:** Ch 1, work reverse sc in each st around [instructions for reverse sc appear in Chapter 8], join with a sl st in beg ch-1; finish off, weave in yarn ends.

*FACIAL FEATURES*
Follow instructions for Facial Features of Jill; sew features to face as positioned in photo. Sew head to top of body.

*FINISHING*
Sew buttons on front of body as positioned in photo. On back of body, sew 3 sides only of final square to body for pocket (as shown in Fig 26); make sling-shot with twig and rubber band and insert in pocket.

*(Shown in color on page 65.)*

JACK AND JILL DOLLS (see page 63)

CHRISTMAS AFGHAN (see page 83)

**TRADITIONAL GRANNY AFGHAN** (see page 20)

**GIANT FLOOR BALL** (see page 138)

*THE BIRDWATCHER AFGHAN* (see page 38)

*SNOWFIRE AFGHAN* (see page 10)

*MY HOMETOWN AFGHAN* (see page 26)

*WHEELS AFGHAN* (see page 30)

*PUDDLE DUCKS AFGHAN* (see page 40)

*SCATTER RUG* (see page 134)

*THE BARKER FAMILY* (see page 56)

**FOLDING FLOOR PILLOWS** (see page 132)

HOODED JACKET (see page 111)

BEACH COVER-UP (see page 119)

**BED JACKET** (see page 120)

*DAISY SUNDRESS* (see page 105)

**MARSHMALLOW LAYETTE**
(see page 94)

**TODDLER VEST** (see page 102)

**CHRISTMAS ORNAMENTS** (see page 85)

# Chapter 4

# Christmas at Granny's

Christmas decorations made with the granny square bring back warm memories of childhood days. Our collection ranges from a stocking to hang at the fireplace to a Christmas afghan; from a wall hanging to a door wreath.

These projects will become cherished family heirlooms, to be unwrapped proudly each holiday season.

# CHRISTMAS STOCKING

*designed by Mary Thomas*

**MATERIALS: Dawn Sayelle\* Knitting Worsted Size, for Version A: one 4-oz skein each Flame, Golf Green and White; for Version B: one 4-oz skein each Golf Green, Flame and Antique Gold; for both versions, aluminum crochet hook size I (or size required for gauge).**

**GAUGE: One Hexagon Motif = 3½ "**
       **(measured side to side)**
       **One Square Motif = 3 "**

## INSTRUCTIONS

Motifs and assembling are the same for both versions; use color in brackets when making Version B.

*HEXAGON MOTIF (make 16)*

With Flame [Golf Green], ch 4; join with a sl st to form a ring.

**Rnd 1 (right side):** Ch 2, hdc in ring, ch 1; * work 2 hdc in ring, ch 1; rep from * 4 times more, join with a sl st in top of beg ch-2. Finish off.

**Rnd 2:** With right side facing, join White [Antique Gold] with a sl st in any ch-1 sp, ch 2; work (hdc, ch 1, 2 hdc) in same sp as joining, * work (2 hdc, ch 1, 2 hdc) in next ch-1 sp; rep from * 4 times more, join with a sl st in top of beg ch-2. Finish off.

**Rnd 3:** With right side facing, join Golf Green [Flame] with a sl st in any ch-1 sp, ch 2; work (hdc, ch 1, 2 hdc) in same sp as joining (first corner made); work 2 hdc in sp between next two hdc groups (for side); * work (2 hdc, ch 1, 2 hdc) in next ch-1 sp (for corner); 2 hdc in sp between next two hdc groups (for side); rep from * 4 times more, join with a sl st in top of beg ch-2. Finish off.

**Rnd 4:** With right side facing, join Flame [Golf Green] with a sl st in any corner ch-1 sp, ch 1; work (sc, ch 1, 2 sc) in same sp as joining, work 2 sc in sp between each pair of hdc groups along side; * work (2 sc, ch 1, 2 sc) in next corner ch-1 sp; work 2 sc in sp between each pair of hdc groups along side; rep from * 4 times more, join with a sl st in beg ch-1. Finish off, weave in all yarn ends.

*SQUARE MOTIF (make one)*

Work same as Hexagon Motif **except** on each rnd, rep from * **twice** more instead of 4 times more.

*ASSEMBLING*

Join motifs as positioned in diagram *(Fig 1)*. To join, place 2 motifs with right sides tog. Thread Flame [Golf Green] into tapestry needle and sew motifs, working through outer lps only of each st *(Fig 2)*, carefully matching sts as you sew. When all motifs have been joined, fold in half as shown in Fig 1 and sew rem corresponding sides of motifs to form stocking.

*HANGER*

With Flame [Golf Green], ch 21, sl st loosely in 2nd ch from hook and in each rem ch across. Finish off; thread hanger through hdc groups at center back edge of stocking and sew ends tog to form a loop.

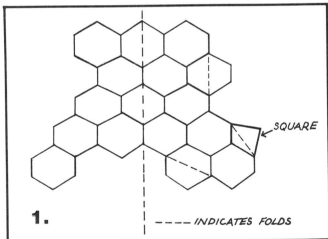

**1.** SQUARE — — — — INDICATES FOLDS

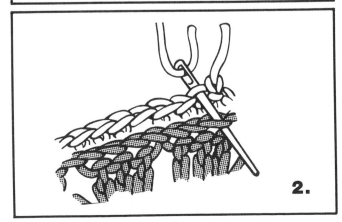

**2.**

# CHRISTMAS AFGHAN

*designed by Mary Thomas*

**SIZE: Approx 50″ x 66″**

**MATERIALS: Dawn Sayelle\* Knitting Worsted Size in 4-oz skeins: 11 White and 4 Flame; aluminum crochet hook size I (or size required for gauge).**

**GAUGE: One motif = 5½″ square**

## INSTRUCTIONS

*MOTIF (make 108)*

With Flame, ch 4, join with a sl st to form a ring.

**Rnd 1 (wrong side):** Ch 3, work 11 dc in ring, join with a sl st in top of beg ch-3 = 12 dc (counting ch 3 as one dc). Finish off Flame.

**Rnd 2 (right side):** TURN; join White with a sl st in any dc, ch 4; tr in same st as joining, tr in sp between last dc and next dc; * 2 tr in next dc, tr in sp between last dc and next dc; rep from * around, join with a sl st in top of beg ch-4 = 36 tr (counting ch 4). Finish off White.

**Rnd 3:** TURN; join Flame with a sl st in last tr of prev rnd, ch 1; sc in same st as joining and in next tr, work a **cluster** in next tr: (YO, insert hook in st; hook yarn and pull through st, YO and draw through 2 lps on hook) 3 times [4 lps now on hook]; YO and draw through all lps on hook, pushing cluster out to right side of work. * Sc in each of next 2 tr, work a cluster in next tr; rep from * around, join with a sl st in beg sc = 12 clusters. Finish off Flame.

**Rnd 4:** TURN; sk last cluster of prev rnd, join White with a sl st in next sc, ch 1; sc in same st as joining; * hdc in next st, dc in next st; work (dc, ch 1, tr, ch 1, dc) all in next st, dc in next st; hdc in next st, sc in each of next 4 sts; rep from * around, ending last rep by working sc in each of last 3 sts, join with a sl st in beg sc. Do not finish off.

**Rnd 5:** Ch 3, do NOT turn; dc in each of next 3 sts; * ch 2, sk ch-1 sp, work (dc, ch 1, tr, ch 1, dc) in next tr; ch 2,

sk ch-1 sp, dc in each of next 10 sts; rep from * around, ending last rep by working dc in each of last 6 sts, join with a sl st in top of beg ch-3. Finish off, weave in all yarn ends.

### ASSEMBLING

Afghan is 9 motifs wide by 12 motifs long. Motifs for the afghan in our photo were joined with White using Method 5 (see joining methods in Chapter 8).

*(Shown in color on page 66.)*

# CHRISTMAS WREATH

*designed by Mary Thomas*

**SIZE: Approx 13″ diameter**

**MATERIALS: Worsted weight yarn, 4 oz green and 1 oz red; aluminum crochet hook size G (or size required for gauge); polyester filling for stuffing.**

**GAUGE: In dc, 7 sts = 2″; 4 rows = 2″**

## INSTRUCTIONS

**Note: Ch 3 counts as one dc throughout patt.**

With green, ch 81 loosely; join with a sl st in first ch to make a ring, being careful not to twist chs.

**Rnd 1 (right side):** Ch 1, sc in same ch as joining and in each ch around, join with a sl st in beg sc = 81 sc.

**Rnd 2:** Ch 3, do not turn; work 3 dc in same sc as joining, sk 2 sc; * 4 dc in next sc, sk 2 sc; rep from * around, join with a sl st in top of beg ch-3 = 27 4-dc groups.

**Rnd 3:** TURN; sl st in sp between first and last 4-dc groups of prev rnd, ch 3, 3 dc in same sp; * 4 dc in next sp between dc groups; rep from * around, join with a sl st in top of beg ch-3.

**Rnd 4:** TURN; sl st in sp between first and last groups of prev rnd; work (dc, ch 1, 2 dc) in same sp; * work (2 dc, ch 1, 2 dc) in next sp between groups; rep from * around, join with a sl st in top of beg ch-3.

**Rnd 5:** TURN; sl st in sp between first and last groups of prev rnd, ch 3, dc in same sp; 2 dc in next ch-1 sp; * 2 dc in next sp between groups, 2 dc in next ch-1 sp; rep from * around, join with a sl st in top of beg ch-3 = 54 2-dc groups.

**Rnd 6:** TURN; sl st in sp between first and last groups of prev rnd, ch 3, dc in same sp; * work 2 dc in next sp between groups; rep from * around, join with a sl st in top of beg ch-3.

**Rnd 7:** TURN; sl st in sp between first and last groups of prev rnd, ch 3, 2 dc in same sp; * work 3 dc in next sp between groups; rep from * around, join with a sl st in top of beg ch-3.

**Rnd 8:** Rep Rnd 7.

**Rnd 9:** Ch 3, do NOT turn; dc in **back lp only** of next dc and each dc around, join with a sl st in top of beg ch-3 = 162 dc (counting ch 3). Now continue by working in **both** lps of each st.

**Rnd 10:** Ch 3, do NOT turn; dc in each of next 2 dc, decrease over next 2 dc as follows: Work dc in first st until 2 lps rem on hook; keeping the 2 lps on hook, YO and insert hook in next st; YO and draw through st [4 lps now on hook]; YO and draw through 2 lps [3 lps now on hook]; YO and draw through 3 lps [one lp rem on hook]—dec made. * Dc in each of next 3 dc, dec over next 2 dc as before; rep from * around, dc in each of next 2 dc, join with a sl st in top of beg ch-3 = 130 dc.

**Rnd 11:** Ch 3, do NOT turn; dc in each of next 2 dc, dec over next 2 dc; * dc in each of next 6 dc, dec over next 2 dc; rep from * around, dc in each of last 5 dc, join with a sl st in top of beg ch-3 = 114 dc.

**Rnd 12:** Ch 3, do NOT turn; dc in each of next 3 dc, dec; * dc in each of next 4 dc, dec; rep from * around, join with a sl st in top of beg ch-3 = 95 dc.

**Rnd 13:** Ch 3, do NOT turn; dc in next dc, dec; * dc in each of next 5 dc, dec; rep from * around, join with a sl st in top of beg ch-3 = 81 dc.

**Rnd 14:** Ch 3, do NOT turn; dc in next dc and in each dc around, join with a sl st in top of beg ch-3.

**Rnd 15:** Ch 1, do NOT turn; sc in same st as joining, sc in each dc around, join with a sl st in beg sc = 81 sc. Finish off, leaving approx 24″ sewing length.

### FINISHING

**Ribbon:** With red, make a ch approx 56″ long; work a hdc in 3rd ch from hook and in each rem ch across; finish off. Beg where rnds are joined and weave ribbon through 4-dc groups of first rnd; tie ends into a bow. Stuff wreath lightly; thread yarn end into tapestry needle and sew beg and last rnds tog with overcast st, carefully matching sts. Weave in all yarn ends.

# CHRISTMAS ORNAMENTS

Take an ordinary granny square, make it in a fine thread (bedspread-weight cotton, perle cotton, metallics); add starch, let dry—the result is a charming ornament for your Christmas tree, or to use as a package tie-on.

Three of our designs were created especially to be Christmas ornaments; the others are squares made from afghan and mat patterns in this book, using different fibers and color schemes.

## STARCHING

After crocheting each ornament, you'll need to starch it, using a thick solution of a commercial boilable starch (spray starches won't do the job) or a sugar-and-water starch that was traditionally used for old-fashioned doilies.

**Sugar Starch:** Mix ½ cup granulated sugar with ½ cup water in a small pan; heat to boiling (be careful not to burn the mixture), immediately remove from heat. Cool to room temperature.

Wet each ornament in clear water, then immerse in starch. Remove from starch (very wet—don't wring out the starch) and place on a padded surface covered with clean, white paper. Insert rust-proof pins at each corner of ornament, to hold tightly in shape. Evenly space a few pins along sides. Let ornaments dry thoroughly (this may take several days in muggy weather) before removing pins. Make loop hangers from white or translucent nylon thread.

## 1. SNOWFLAKE ORNAMENT
*designed by Kim Hubal*

**SIZE: Approx 2¼ " square**

**MATERIALS: Crochet cotton size #20, one ball of white; steel crochet hook size 11 (or size required for gauge).**

**GAUGE: One granny square = ¾ "**

*GRANNY SQUARE*
Ch 5, join with a sl st to form a ring.

**Rnd 1:** Ch 3, 2 dc in ring; * ch 1, 3 dc in ring; rep from * twice more, ch 1, join with a sl st in top of beg ch-3.

**Rnd 2:** Sl st in each of next 2 dc and into ch-1 sp, ch 3; work (2 dc, ch 2, 3 dc) in same sp; * ch 1, work (3 dc, ch 2, 3 dc) in next ch-1 sp; rep from * twice more, ch 1, join with a sl st in top of beg ch-3. Finish off, leaving approx 4" sewing length.

*INSTRUCTIONS*
Following Granny Square instructions above, make 4 squares. Hold 2 squares with right sides tog; thread end into tapestry needle. Sew with overcast sts, working into outer lps only of each st across, carefully matching sts; beg in one ch of corner sp and end in one ch of next corner sp. In same manner, join rem 2 squares then join first pair of squares to 2nd pair of squares being careful to securely join at intersection in center.

*EDGING*
**Rnd 1:** Join with a sl st in any ch-2 outer corner sp; * ch 6, sc in same sp; ch 6, sc in 3rd dc from ch-2 corner sp; work sc in each of next 3 dc, sc in next ch-2 sp; ch 6, sc in next ch-2 sp; sc in each of next 3 dc, sk next sp, sc in next dc; ch 6, sc in ch-2 outer corner sp; rep from * 3 times, ending last rep by joining with a sl st at base of beg ch-6.

**Rnd 2:** * Work 6 sc in ch-6 corner sp, sc in next sc; † work (hdc, 3 dc, tr, 3 dc, hdc) in next ch-6 sp †, sc in each of next 5 sc; rep from † to †, sc in each of next 5 sc; rep from † to †, sc in next sc; rep from * 3 times more, ending last rep by joining with a sl st at base of first ch-6 sp. Finish off, weave in all ends.

## 2. CHRISTMAS TREE ORNAMENT
*designed by Kim Hubal*

**SIZE: Approx 3½ " tall before tree top trim**

**MATERIALS: Bedspread-weight crochet cotton, one ball of white and one ball of red or green for edging; few yds silver or gold metallic crochet thread for tree top trim; steel crochet hook size 7 (or size required for gauge).**

**GAUGE: In dc, 8 sts = 1"**

*INSTRUCTIONS*

**Row 1 (right side):** With white, ch 5, work (3 dc, ch 1, 3 dc, ch 1, dc) in 5th ch from hook.

**Row 2:** TURN; sl st in first dc and into ch-1 sp; ch 4, work 3 dc in same sp; ch 1, work (3 dc, ch 1, 3 dc) in next ch-1 sp [for center]; ch 1, work (3 dc, ch 1, dc) in ch-5 sp.

**Row 3:** TURN; sl st in first dc and into ch-1 sp, ch 4; 3 dc in same sp, ch 1; 3 dc in next sp, ch 1; work (3 dc, ch 1, 3 dc) in center sp, ch 1; 3 dc in next sp, ch 1; work (3 dc, ch 1, dc) in Tch sp.

**Row 4:** TURN; sl st in first dc and into ch-1 sp, ch 4, 3 dc in same sp, ch 1; work (3 dc in next sp, ch 1) twice, work (3 dc, ch 1, 3 dc) in center sp, ch 1; work (3 dc in next sp, ch 1) twice, work (3 dc, ch 1, dc) in Tch sp.

**Row 5:** TURN; sl st in first dc and into ch-1 sp, ch 4; 3 dc in same sp, ch 1; work (3 dc in next sp, ch 1) 3 times, work (3 dc, ch 1, 3 dc) in center sp, ch 1; work (3 dc in next sp, ch 1) 3 times, work (3 dc, ch 1, dc) in Tch sp.

**Row 6:** TURN; sl st in each of the following sts: first dc, ch st, each of next 3 dc, next ch st, each of next 3 dc and into ch-1 sp; ch 4, 3 dc in same sp; work (ch 1, 3 dc in next sp) twice, ch 1; work (3 dc, ch 1, 3 dc) in center sp, work (ch 1, 3 dc in next sp) twice, ch 1; work (3 dc, ch 1, dc) in next sp.

**Row 7:** TURN; sl st in each of the following sts: first dc, ch st, each of next 3 dc, next ch st, each of next 3 dc and into next ch-1 sp; ch 4, 3 dc in same sp; ch 1, 3 dc in next sp; ch 1, work (3 dc, ch 1, 3 dc) in center sp; ch 1, 3 dc in next sp; ch 1, work (3 dc, ch 1, dc) in next sp.

**Row 8:** TURN; sl st in each of the following sts: first dc, ch st, each of next 3 dc, next ch st, each of next 3 dc and into next ch-1 sp; ch 4, 3 dc in same sp; ch 1, work (3 dc, ch 1, 3 dc) in center sp; ch 1, (3 dc, ch 1, dc) in next sp.

**Row 9:** TURN; sl st in each of the following sts: first dc, ch st, each of next 3 dc, ch st and next dc; work (3 dc, ch 2, 3 dc) in center sp, sk next 2 dc, sl st in each of the following sts: next dc, ch st, each of next 3 dc and into next sp; finish off, leaving approx 3" end for weaving in.

*EDGING*
With wrong side facing, join red or green with a sl st in first ch of beg ch-5 sp of Rnd 1; ch 1.

**Rnd 1:** Sc in same sp, work 12 sc evenly spaced to ch-1 sp at lower corner of tree, work 3 sc in corner sp; * work even in sc to next outer edge ch-1 sp, 3 sc in outer sp [for branch tip shaping]; rep from * twice, work even in sc to ch-2 sp at top of tree; 5 sc in sp at top of tree, rep from first * to 2nd * 4 times, work 12 sc evenly spaced to beg sc, join with a sl st in beg sc.

**Rnd 2:** Ch 1, TURN; sc in each sc to 3-sc group at first corner, sc in first sc, 3 sc in center sc; sc in each sc to within 2 sc of 3-sc group at next branch tip, dec over 2 sc. [To dec: pull up a lp in each of next 2 sc; YO and draw through all 3 lps now on hook.] * Sc in first sc of 3-sc group, 3 sc in center sc; sc in each sc to within 2 sc of 3-sc group of next branch tip, dec over 2 sc; rep from * once more, sc in each sc to 5-sc group at top of tree; sc in each of first 2 sc, 5 sc in center sc of 5-sc group; ** sc in each sc to next 3-sc group, sc in first sc, 3 sc in center sc, sc in next sc; dec over 2 sc; rep from ** twice more, sc in each sc to 3-sc group at corner, sc in first sc, 3 sc in next sc, sc in each rem sc, join with a sl st in beg sc. Finish off, weave in ends.

*TREE TOP TRIM (A OR B)*
**Tree Top A**
Join silver or gold with a sl st in center sp at top of tree; ch 3, work (2 dc, ch 3, 3 dc) in same sp; ch 1, turn; work sc in each of first 3 dc, work (2 sc, ch 2, 2 sc) in ch-3 sp; sc in each of next 2 dc, sc in top of ch-3; finish off, weave in ends.

**Tree Top B**
With silver or gold,, * ch 3, sl st in 2nd ch from hook; hdc in rem ch, rep from * 4 times more, join with a sl st in first ch of beg ch, then sl st in center sp at top of tree. Finish off, weave in ends.

## 3. GRANNY'S WREATH ORNAMENT
*designed by Kim Hubal*
**SIZE: 3½″ measured from side to side**

**MATERIALS: Bedspread-weight crochet cotton, one ball each of white, red and medium green; steel crochet hook size 7 (or size required for gauge).**

**GAUGE: In dc, 8 sts = 1″**

*INSTRUCTIONS*
**Note:** All rnds are worked on right side.
With white, ch 6, join with a sl st to form a ring.

**Rnd 1:** Ch 3 (counts as first dc of rnd), dc in ring; ch 1, work (2 dc in ring, ch 1) 5 times, join with a sl st in top of beg ch-3; you should have six 2-dc groups.

**Rnd 2:** Sl st in next dc and into ch-1 sp; work (ch 3, dc, ch 1, 2 dc) all in same sp [first corner made]; * ch 1 [for side], work (2 dc, ch 1, 2 dc) all in next ch-1 sp [for corner]; rep from * 4 times, ch 1, join with a sl st in top of beg ch-3 = 6 corners and 6 sides made. Finish off white.

**Note:** In next rnd, you will work alternately with red and green; always carry color not in use loosely across back of work, working over it when possible.

**Rnd 3:** Join green with a sl st in any ch-1 corner sp; ch 3 (counts as first dc of rnd), work (dc, ch 1, dc) in same sp; * work another dc in **same** sp but only until 2 lps rem on hook; drop green, pick up red and complete dc with red; continuing with red, ch 1, dc in next ch-1 side sp; in **same** sp, work another dc until 2 lps rem on hook; drop red, pick up green; continuing with green, complete dc, ch 1; work (2 dc, ch 1, dc) all in next ch-1 corner sp; rep from * 5 times, ending last rep by working ch 1 with green, join with a sl st in top of beg ch-3. Finish off red only.

**Rnd 4:** Continuing with green, sl st in next dc and into next ch-1 corner sp; work (ch 3, dc, ch 1, 2 dc) all in same sp, * ch 1, work (2 dc in next ch-1 side sp, ch 1) twice; in next corner sp, work (2 dc, ch 1, 2 dc); rep from * 4 times, ch 1, work (2 dc in next side sp, ch 1) twice, join with a sl st in top of beg ch-3. Finish off green.

**Rnd 5:** Join white with a sl st in any ch-1 corner sp; ch 3, work (dc, ch 1, 2 dc) in same sp; * ch 1, † work 2 dc in next side sp, ch 1 †; rep from † to † to next corner sp, work (2 dc, ch 1, 2 dc) in corner sp; rep from * 4 times, rep from † to † across last side, join with a sl st in top of beg ch-3.

**Rnd 6:** Sl st in next dc and into ch-1 corner sp; ch 3, work (dc, ch 1, 2 dc) in same sp; beg at * and follow instructions of Rnd 5.

**Rnd 7:** Sl st in next dc and into ch-1 corner sp; ch 6 [for hanger], sc in same sp; sc in each dc around, skipping ch-1 side sps and working 3 sc in each corner sp; join with a sl st in base of beg ch-6. Finish off, weave in all ends.

## 4. SNOWFIRE ORNAMENT
**SIZE: 3¼″ square**

**MATERIALS: Bedspread-weight crochet cotton, one ball each of white and red; steel crochet hook size 7 (or size required for gauge).**

**GAUGE: In dc, 8 sts = 1″**

*INSTRUCTIONS*
Make one square following Square Instructions for Snowfire Afghan in Chapter 1 on page 10.

## 5. STARBURST ORNAMENT
**SIZE: 2¼″ square**

**MATERIALS: Bedspread-weight crochet cotton, one ball each of white and green; steel crochet hook size 7 (or size required for gauge).**

**GAUGE: In dc, 8 sts = 1″**

*INSTRUCTIONS*
Make one motif following Basic Motif Instructions for Starburst Afghan in Chapter 1 on page 16 using white for Rnds 1 and 2 and green for Rnds 3 and 4.

## 6. RING OF HOLLY BERRIES ORNAMENT

**SIZE: 2¼" square**

**MATERIALS: Bedspread-weight crochet cotton, one ball each of white and red; steel crochet hook size 7 (or size required for gauge).**

**GAUGE: In dc, 8 sts = 1"**

*INSTRUCTIONS*
Make one motif following Motif Instructions for Christmas Afghan in Chapter 4 on page 83.

## 7. SNOWFLAKE ORNAMENT

**SIZE: 2" square**

**MATERIALS: Bedspread-weight crochet cotton, one ball of white; steel crochet hook size 7 (or size required for gauge).**

**GAUGE: In dc, 8 sts = 1"**

*INSTRUCTIONS*
Following Square Instructions for Aztec-Tile Mat in Chapter 7 on page 134, work Rnds 1 through 4; finish off.

*(Shown in color on page 80.)*

# SANTA PILLOW

*designed by Anis Duncan*

**SIZE: Approx 15″ square**

**MATERIALS: Aunt Lydia's Heavy Rug Yarn in 70-yd skeins: 4 skeins Red; 2 skeins White; 1 skein each Green and Lt Pink and a few yds each of Blue and Dk Pink; aluminum crochet hook size G (or size required for gauge); approx one lb polyester filling for stuffing.**

**GAUGE: One square = 2½ ″**

## ONE-COLOR SQUARE

With color specified in patt, ch 4, join with a sl st to form a ring.

**Rnd 1 (right side):** Ch 3, 2 dc in ring *(Fig 1);* ch 1, * work 3 dc in ring, ch 1; rep from * twice, join with a sl st in top of beg ch-3 *(Fig 2).*

**Rnd 2 (right side):** Sl st in each of next 2 dc and into ch-1 sp *(Fig 3);* ch 3, work (2 dc, ch 1, 3 dc) all in same sp; * work (3 dc, ch 1, 3 dc) all in next ch-1 sp; rep from * twice, join with a sl st in top of beg ch-3. Finish off, leaving a 10″ yarn end for sewing later.

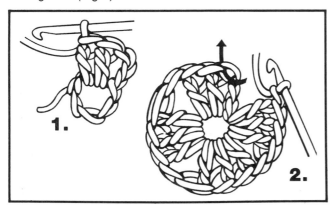

## DIAGONAL TWO-COLOR SQUARE

**Rnd 1 (wrong side):** With color A, ch 4, join with a sl st to form a ring. Ch 3, work 2 dc in ring; ch 1, 3 dc in ring; drop color A but do not cut off; draw color B through lp on hook [one ch made]; continuing with color B, work 3 dc in ring, ch 1; work 3 dc in ring, ch 1, join with a sl st in top of beg ch of color A.

**Rnd 2 (right side):** TURN; sl st into ch-1 sp, ch 3, 2 dc in same sp; work (3 dc, ch 1, 3 dc) in next ch-1 corner sp; 3 dc in next ch-1 corner sp, ch 1, drop color B; with color A work 3 dc in same corner sp; in next ch-1 corner sp,

work (3 dc, ch 1, 3 dc); in next corner sp [where beg sl st of color B was made], work 3 dc over the sl st; ch 1, join with a sl st in top of color B beg ch. Finish off A and B, leaving 10″ yarn ends for sewing later.

## INSTRUCTIONS

Following One-Color Square and Diagonal Two-Color Square instructions above, make squares listed below:

### ONE-COLOR SQUARES

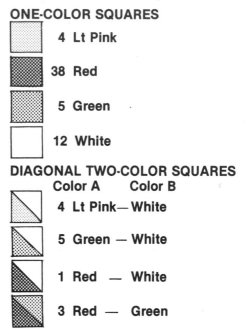

| | |
|---|---|
| | **4 Lt Pink** |
| | **38 Red** |
| | **5 Green** |
| | **12 White** |

### DIAGONAL TWO-COLOR SQUARES

| | Color A | Color B |
|---|---|---|
| | **4 Lt Pink — White** | |
| | **5 Green — White** | |
| | **1 Red — White** | |
| | **3 Red — Green** | |

*BACK*
Assemble 36 red one-color squares, 6 squares wide and 6 squares long. Join 2 squares with right sides tog and yarn end in upper right-hand corner. Thread yarn into tapestry needle; carefully matching sts on both squares, sew with overcast st in outer lps only (see joining Method 5 in Chapter 8) of each st across, beg in center ch of one corner and ending in center ch of next corner. Join four more squares in same manner for first row of squares. When squares have been joined for all six rows, join rows in same manner being careful that each 4-corner intersection is firmly secured. Finish off, weave in all yarn ends.

*FRONT*
Assemble rem squares as shown in Fig 4. Join in same manner as back, then work facial features per instructions which follow. Note: As each facial feature is made, use matching thread and sew to front of pillow as positioned in photo.

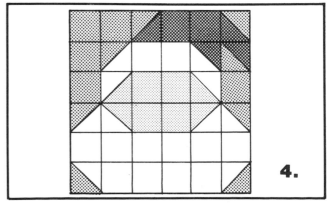

**Nose:** With red, ch 3, join with a sl st to form a ring. Ch 3, work 11 dc in ring, join with a sl st in top of beg ch-3. Finish off, weave in yarn ends. Before sewing to front of pillow, stuff with small amount of polyester filling.

**Left Eye:** With blue, ch 3, join with a sl st to form a ring.
**Row 1 (wrong side):** Ch 1, work 5 sc in ring.
**Row 2:** Ch 1, turn; sc in first sc, 2 sc in next sc; 2 hdc in each of next 2 sc, 2 dc in last sc, 2 dc in beg ch-1 of Row 1. Finish off, weave in yarn ends.

**Right Eye:** With blue, ch 3, join with a sl st to form a ring.
**Row 1 (wrong side):** Ch 1, work 5 sc in ring.
**Row 2:** Ch 3, turn; dc in first sc, 2 dc in next sc; 2 hdc in each of next 2 sc, 2 sc in next sc; 2 sc in ch-1. Finish off, weave in yarn ends.

**Left Cheek:** With dk pink, ch 3, join with a sl st to form a ring.
**Row 1 (right side):** Ch 3, work 5 dc in ring.
**Row 2:** Ch 3, turn; dc in first dc, 2 dc in each of rem 4 dc, 2 dc in top of ch-3 of prev row.
**Row 3:** TURN; sl st in next dc, ch 1; hdc in next dc, 2 dc

in each of next 8 dc, 2 dc in top of ch-3. Finish off, weave in yarn ends.

**Right Cheek:** With dk pink, ch 3, join with a sl st to form a ring.
**Row 1 (right side):** Ch 3, work 5 dc in ring.
**Row 2:** Ch 3, turn; dc in first dc, 2 dc in each of rem 4 dc, 2 dc in top of ch-3 of prev row.
**Row 3:** Ch 3, turn; dc in next dc, 2 dc in each of next 8 dc; hdc in next dc, sc in top of ch-3. Finish off, weave in yarn ends.

*FINISHING*
Hold front and back of pillow with wrong sides tog; join red with a sl st in ch st of any outer corner sp; ch 1, sc in same st. Carefully matching sts and seams and working through inner lps only, sc in corresponding sts of both pieces around; beg stuffing when more than half of pillow has been joined and continue to stuff as you go. At end, join with a sl st in beg sc; finish off, weave in yarn ends.

**Pompon:** Following instructions in Chapter 8, make a 2″ white pompon and sew to pillow as positioned in photo.

# TREE SKIRT

*designed by Mary Thomas*

**SIZE: Approx 44″ diameter**

**MATERIALS: Worsted weight yarn, 24 oz green and 6 oz red; aluminum crochet hook size J (or size required for gauge).**

**GAUGE: In dc, 3 sts = 1″**

## INSTRUCTIONS

*2-RND MOTIF (make 16)*

With red, ch 8, join with a sl st to form a ring.

**Rnd 1 (right side):** Ch 3, 2 dc in ring, ch 2; * 3 dc in ring, ch 2; rep from * 6 times more, join with a sl st in top of beg ch-3. Finish off red.

**Rnd 2:** With right side facing, join green with a sl st in any ch-2 sp; ch 3, work (2 dc, ch 3, 3 dc) in same sp for beg corner; work (3 dc, ch 3, 3 dc) all in next ch-2 sp for corner, 3 dc in next ch-2 sp for side; work (3 dc, ch 3, 3 dc) all in next ch-2 sp for corner; work 3 dc in each of next two ch-2 sps for side; work (3 dc, ch 3, 3 dc) all in next ch-2 sp for last corner; 3 dc in last ch-2 sp for side, join with a sl st in top of beg ch-3. Finish off, weave in yarn ends. You should have two 3-dc groups along "inner" edge, four 3-dc groups along "outer" edge, and three 3-dc groups along each side edge of motif.

*4-RND MOTIF (make 16)*

Work same as 2-Rnd Motif but do not finish off green at end of Rnd 2.

**Rnd 3:** Ch 1, turn; sl st in sp between beg and end 3-dc groups of prev rnd, ch 3; 2 dc in same sp, 3 dc in next sp between pair of 3-dc groups; * work (3 dc, ch 3, 3 dc) all in next corner sp, work 3 dc in each sp between pairs of 3-dc groups along side; rep from * twice, work (3 dc, ch 3, 3 dc) all in last corner sp, join with a sl st in top of beg ch-3.

**Rnd 4:** Ch 1, turn; sl st in sp between beg and end 3-dc groups of prev rnd, ch 3, 2 dc in same sp; * work (3 dc, ch 3, 3 dc) all in next corner sp, work 3 dc in each sp between pairs of 3-dc groups along side, rep from * twice, work (3 dc, ch 3, 3 dc) all in last corner sp, 3 dc in each of last 2 sps between pairs of 3-dc groups, join with a sl st in top of beg ch-3. Finish off, weave in yarn ends.

You should have four 3-dc groups along inner edge, six 3-dc groups along outer edge, and five 3-dc groups along each side edge of motif.

*6-RND MOTIF (make 16)*

Work same as 4-Rnd Motif but do not finish off green at end of Rnd 4.

**Rnd 5:** Ch 1, turn; sl st in sp between beg and end 3-dc groups of prev rnd, ch 3; 2 dc in same sp, 3 dc in each of next 2 sps between pairs of 3-dc groups; * work (3 dc, ch 3, 3 dc) all in next corner sp, work 3 dc in each sp between pairs of 3-dc groups along side; rep from * twice, work (3 dc, ch 3, 3 dc) all in last corner sp, 3 dc in last sp between pair of 3-dc groups, join with a sl st in top of beg ch-3.

**Rnd 6:** Ch 1, turn; sl st in sp between beg and end 3-dc groups of prev rnd, ch 3; 2 dc in same sp, 3 dc in next sp between pair of 3-dc groups; * work (3 dc, ch 3, 3 dc) all in next corner sp, work 3 dc in each sp between pairs of 3-dc groups along side; rep from * twice, work (3 dc, ch 3, 3 dc) all in last corner sp, 3 dc in each of last 3 sps between pairs of 3-dc groups, join with a sl st in top of beg ch-3. Finish off. You should have six 3-dc groups along inner edge, eight 3-dc groups along outer edge, and seven 3-dc groups along each side edge of motif.

*ASSEMBLING*

To join motifs, use method 5 (see joining methods in Chapter 8); beg and ending in corner ch adjacent to 3-dc groups leaving center ch free [center ch is used when joining at 4 corners on strips]. For each strip: first join outer edge of 2-Rnd Motif to inner edge of 4-Rnd Motif [4 3-dc groups along each edge], carefully matching sts; then join outer edge of 4-Rnd Motif to inner edge of 6-Rnd Motif [6 3-dc groups along each edge], carefully matching sts. When all 16 strips have been made, join tog in same manner, carefully matching sts along side edges of each strip. Do not join first and last strips tog; this will be referred to as "opening" in Edging instructions.

*INNER EDGING*

Hold skirt with wrong side facing you and inner edge across top; beg with opening at your right and join green with a sl st in upper right-hand corner sp.

**Row 1:** Ch 3, dc in same sp, 3 dc in next sp between corner groups; * 2 dc in each of next 2 corner sps [sp on each side of joining], 3 dc in next sp between corner groups; rep from * across, ending 2 dc in upper left-hand corner sp at opening.

**Row 2:** Ch 3, turn; 2 dc in first sp [sp between last 2-dc and 3-dc groups of prev row]; * 3 dc in next sp between 3-dc and 2-dc groups, dc in next sp between pair of 2-dc groups, 3 dc in next sp between 2-dc and 3-dc groups; rep from * across, ending 2 dc in last sp between 3-dc and 2-dc groups, dc in top of ch-3.

**Row 3:** Ch 3, turn; 3 dc in first sp between 2-dc and 3-dc groups, * dc in dc between 3-dc groups, 3 dc in next sp between pair of 3-dc groups; rep from * across, ending last rep by working 3 dc in last sp between 3-dc and 2-dc groups, dc in top of Tch.

**Row 4:** Ch 3, turn; dc in first sp between last dc and 3-dc group of prev row; * 2 dc in next sp between 3-dc group and dc, 2 dc in next sp between dc and 3-dc group; rep from * across, ending dc in sp under Tch, dc in top of Ich.

**Row 5:** Ch 3, turn; dc in next dc and in each dc across, ending dc in top of Tch.

**Row 6:** Ch 1, turn; sc in last dc of prev row and in each dc across, ending sc in top of Tch. Finish off, weave in all yarn ends.

*OUTER EDGING*

Hold skirt with right side facing you and outer edge across top. Beg with opening at your right and join red with a sl st in upper right-hand corner sp; ch 3, 2 dc in same sp; work 3 dc in each sp between 3-dc groups and in each corner sp [on each side of joining] across, ending 3 dc in upper left-hand corner sp at opening. Finish off, weave in all yarn ends.

# NOEL WALL HANGING

*designed by Anis Duncan*

**SIZE: Approx 18″ wide x 7½″ long**

**MATERIALS: Bedspread-weight crochet cotton, one ball green; metallic crochet thread, two balls silver; steel crochet hook size 1 (or size required for gauge); ¼″ diameter dowel rod, 19″ long.**

**GAUGE: One square = 1½″**

## ONE-COLOR GRANNY SQUARE
### (make 14 green and 28 silver)

Ch 4, join with a sl st to form a ring.

**Rnd 1 (wrong side):** Ch 3, 2 dc in ring, ch 2; * work 3 dc in ring, ch 2; rep from * twice, join with a sl st in top of beg ch-3: Turn work.

**Rnd 2 (right side):** Sk joining st, sl st in next ch st; sl st into ch-2 sp, ch 3; work 2 dc in same sp, ch 1; * work (3 dc, ch 2, 3 dc) all in next ch-2 sp for corner, ch 1; rep from * twice; work 3 dc in beg corner, ch 2, join with a sl st in top of beg ch-3. Finish off, leaving approx 6″ sewing length.

## DIAGONAL TWO-COLOR
## GRANNY SQUARE (make 18)

With green, ch 4, join with a sl st to form a ring.

**Rnd 1 (wrong side):** Ch 3, 2 dc in ring; ch 2, 3 dc in ring, drop green but do not cut; draw silver through lp on hook [one ch st made]; continuing with silver, ch 1, 3 dc in ring; ch 2, 3 dc in ring; ch 2, join with a sl st in top of beg ch-3. Turn work, continue with silver.

**Rnd 2 (right side):** Sk joining st, sl st in next ch st; sl st into ch-2 sp, ch 3; work 2 dc in same sp, ch 1; work (3 dc, ch 2, 3 dc) all in next ch-2 sp for corner; ch 1, 3 dc in next ch-2 corner sp; ch 2, drop silver; with green, work 3 dc in same corner sp; ch 1, work (3 dc, ch 2, 3 dc) in next ch-2 sp; ch 1, work 3 dc in beg corner sp [over 2 sl sts of silver]; ch 2, join with a sl st in top of beg ch-3. Finish off green and silver, leaving 6″ sewing lengths.

## INSTRUCTIONS

First make specified number of squares following Granny Square instructions. Hanging is 12 squares wide and 5 squares long; arrange squares as positioned in Fig 1.

**Joining:** Hold 2 squares with right sides tog; thread matching thread into tapestry needle. Carefully sew with overcast st in **outer lps only** *(Fig. 2)* across side, beg and ending with one corner st. Be sure that all four-corner intersections are firmly joined. Weave in all ends.

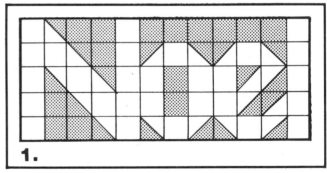

1.

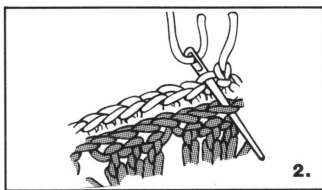

2.

**Top Edging:** Hold hanging with right side facing you; join green with a sl st in upper right-hand corner sp, ch 1, sc in same sp; * ch 8, sc in next ch-1 sp between corner groups; (ch 8, sc in next ch-2 corner sp of square) twice; rep from * across top edge, ending last rep by working sc in upper left-hand corner sp. Finish off, weave in ends. Insert dowel rod.

# Chapter 5

# Granny's Little Ones

Granny fashions are delightful gifts for children—from babies to toddlers. Our collection includes a three-piece layette in soft, fluffy marshmallow stitch, a warm snuggly bunting, and a variety of appealing garments for pre-schoolers.

# MARSHMALLOW FLUFF BABY LAYETTE

## to fit newborn to three months

designed by Barbara Retzke

This charming baby layette is soft and fluffy, thanks to the interesting Marshmallow Stitch. Although not difficult to do, we suggest you work a sample swatch of the stitch before starting your garment. To make the swatch, first ch 16; then following Foundation Row instructions given below, work 6 MS ending in last ch, work dc in last ch.

**Next Row:** Ch 3 and turn; then follow Patt Row instructions, beg in sp between dc and MS and work 6 MS across ending in last sp [between MS and ch 3], work dc in last sp. Work several more rows in this manner until you are familiar with the technique.

## MARSHMALLOW STITCH

(abbreviated MS)

**Foundation Row:** First MS is worked as follows: YO, insert hook in 4th ch from hook and pull up a lp to measure ½"; sk one ch, insert hook in next ch and pull up a ½" lp [4 lps now on hook—Fig 1]; YO and draw through all 4 lps on hook, ch 1 [first MS made].

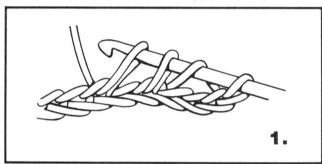

**1.**

Next and each following MS is worked as follows: YO, insert hook in **same** ch [where MS was completed] and pull up a ½" lp; sk one ch, insert hook in next ch and pull up a ½" lp; YO and draw through all 4 lps on hook, ch 1 [MS made].

**Patt Row:** First MS is worked as follows: YO, insert hook in sp between first 2 sts and pull up a ½" lp; insert hook in next sp [between sts] and pull up a ½" lp; YO and draw through all 4 lps on hook, ch 1 [first MS made].

Next and each following MS is worked as follows: YO, insert hook in **same** sp [where MS was completed] and pull up a ½" lp; insert hook in next sp [between sts] and pull up a ½" lp; YO and draw through all 4 lps on hook, ch 1 [MS made].

The Cluster Stitch also is used in the layette patterns. To practice it, continue across your sample swatch, working in the sps.

## CLUSTER STITCH

(abbreviated CL)

YO, insert hook in next st or sp (as specified in patt) and pull up a ½" lp; YO, insert hook in **same** st or sp and pull up a ½" lp [5 lps now on hook]; YO and draw through first 4 lps only, then YO and draw through rem 2 lps [CL made].

## JACKET and BONNET

**JACKET MEASUREMENTS:**

| | |
|---|---|
| chest | 19" |
| length from neck to bottom edge | 9" |
| sleeve length | 5" |

**MATERIALS:** Sport weight yarn, 12 oz white and 1 oz pink (or blue); aluminum crochet hook sizes E and F (or sizes required for gauge); ⅜" wide white satin ribbon, 1 yd each for jacket and bonnet.

**GAUGE:** With smaller size hook, 1 motif = 2¾" square
With larger size hook in Marshmallow St, 3 sts = 1"; 2 rows = ¾"

## INSTRUCTIONS

JACKET

**Body:** Beg at neckline with larger size hook and white, ch 62 loosely.

**Foundation Row (wrong side):** Following Foundation Row instructions in Marshmallow Stitch, work 6 MS; work (CL, ch 2, CL) all in **same** ch where last MS was completed, ch 1; beg in **same** ch [where two CL were worked] and work 4 MS, work (CL, ch 2, CL) in same ch as last MS, ch 1; beg in same ch and work 9 MS, work (CL, ch 2, CL) all in same ch, ch 1; beg in same ch and work 4 MS, work (CL, ch 2, CL) all in same ch, ch 1; beg in same ch and work 6 MS ending in last ch, dc in last ch.

**Note:** On all following rows, MS is worked following Patt Row instructions of Marshmallow Stitch.

**Row 1:** Ch 3, turn; beg in first sp [between dc and MS] and work 7 MS ending in ch-2 sp between CL; work CL set of (CL, ch 2, CL) in same sp, ch 1; beg in same sp and work 6 MS ending in next ch-2 sp, work CL set in same sp, ch 1; beg in same sp and work 11 MS ending in next ch-2 sp, work CL set in same sp, ch 1; beg in same sp and work 6 MS ending in next ch-2 sp, work CL set in same sp, ch 1; beg in same sp and work 7 MS ending in last sp, dc in last sp.

**Row 2:** Ch 3, turn; work (8 MS, CL set in ch-2 sp, ch 1) twice; 13 MS, work (CL set, ch 1, 8 MS) twice, dc in last sp.

**Row 3:** Ch 3, turn; work 9 MS, CL set, ch 1; 10 MS, CL set, ch 1; 15 MS, CL set, ch 1; 10 MS, CL set, ch 1; 9 MS, dc in last sp.

**Row 4:** Ch 3, turn; work 10 MS, CL set, ch 1; 12 MS, CL set, ch 1; 17 MS, CL set, ch 1; 12 MS, CL set, ch 1; 10 MS, dc in last sp.

**Row 5:** Ch 3, turn; work 11 MS, CL set, ch 1; 14 MS, CL set, ch 1; 19 MS, CL set, ch 1; 14 MS, CL set, ch 1; 11 MS, dc in last sp.

**Row 6:** Ch 3, turn; work 12 MS, CL set, ch 1; 16 MS, CL set, ch 1; 21 MS, CL set, ch 1; 16 MS, CL set, ch 1; 12 MS, dc in last sp.

**Row 7:** Ch 3, turn; work 13 MS, CL set, ch 1; 18 MS, CL set, ch 1; 23 MS, CL set, ch 1; 18 MS, CL set, ch 1; 13 MS, dc in last sp.

**Row 8 (divide for armholes):** Ch 3, turn; work 14 MS ending in ch-2 sp of first CL set; work next MS in same sp and in next ch-2 sp of 2nd CL set skipping 18 MS [for armhole]; work 25 MS ending in ch-2 sp of 3rd CL set, work next MS in same sp and in next ch-2 sp of 4th CL

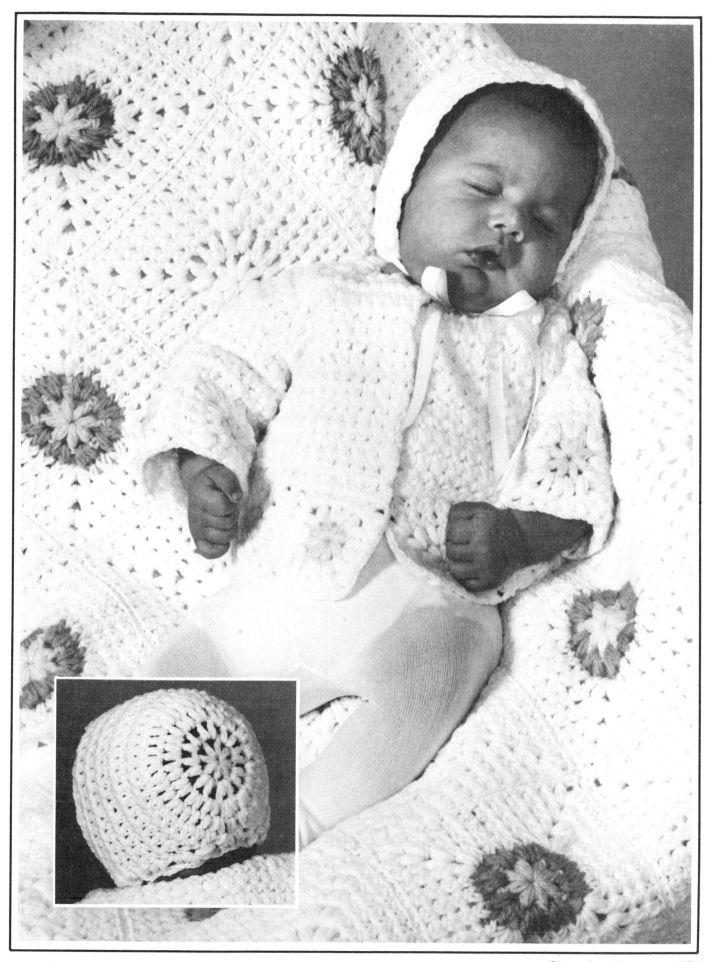

(Shown in color on page 78.)

set skipping 18 MS [for armhole]; work 14 MS, dc in last sp = 55 MS.

**Row 9:** Ch 3, turn; work 55 MS across (omitting sts of each armhole), dc in last sp.

**Rows 10 through 14:** Rep Row 9 five times or until jacket measures approx 3″ less than desired length. Finish off, weave in yarn ends.

**Right Sleeve:** Hold jacket with right side facing and last row of Body held at your right; with larger size hook, join white with a sl st in ch-2 sp of 2nd CL set at armhole.

**Rnd 1 (wrong side):** Ch 3, turn; beg in same sp and work 21 MS around armhole ending in beg sp, join with a sl st in top of beg ch-3.

**Rnd 2:** Ch 3, turn; beg in sp between ch 3 and last MS of prev rnd and work 21 MS ending in beg sp, join with a sl st in top of beg ch-3.

**Rnds 3 through 5:** Rep Rnd 2 three times or until sleeve measures approx 3″ less than desired length. Finish off, weave in yarn ends.

**Left Sleeve:** Hold jacket with right side facing and last row of Body held at your left; work in same manner as Right Sleeve.

**Floral Motifs (make 14):** With pink (or blue) and smaller size hook, ch 5, join with a sl st to form a ring.

**Note:** On Rnds 1 and 2 *only* work each CL with ¼″ lps instead of ½″ lps.

**Rnd 1 (right side):** Pull up lp on hook to measure ¼″, work in ring (CL, ch 2) 8 times, join with a sl st in top of beg CL (*Fig 2*). Finish off.

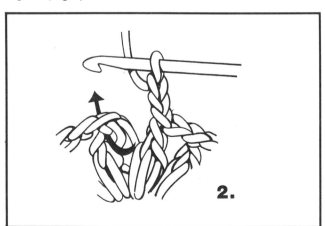

**2.**

**Rnd 2:** With right side facing, join white with a sl st in any ch-2 sp and pull up lp on hook to measure ¼″; work (CL, ch 3, CL) in same sp for beg corner, ch 1; * work (CL, ch 1, CL) in next sp, ch 1; work (CL, ch 3, CL) in next sp for corner, ch 1; rep from * twice, work (CL, ch 1, CL) in last sp, ch 1, join with a sl st in top of beg CL.

**Rnd 3:** Do not turn; sl st into beg ch-3 sp and pull up lp on hook to measure ½″. **Note:** Remember to work each following CL with ½″ lps. Work (CL, ch 3, CL) in same sp, ch 1; beg in same sp and work 4 MS ending in next corner sp, * work (CL, ch 3, CL) in corner sp, ch 1; beg in same sp and work 4 MS ending in next corner sp; rep from * twice, ending last rep in beg corner sp, join with a sl st in top of beg CL. Finish off, leaving approx 8″ sewing length.

**Bottom Edging:** Hold 2 motifs with right sides tog; thread yarn end into tapestry needle. Carefully matching st by st, sew with overcast st in **outer lps only,** beg with center ch st of one corner and end with center ch st of next corner. [For more details on joining, see joining method 5 in Chapter 8.] Add 6 more motifs in same manner to form a row of 8 motifs.

Then work one row of edging across long edge of joined motifs as follows. Hold joined motifs with right side facing and long edge across top; use larger size hook and join white with a sl st in upper right-hand corner sp. Ch 3, beg in same sp and work 55 MS across working in each corner sp and in sps between MS of each motif, ending in upper left-hand corner sp, dc in corner sp. You should have 6 MS across each motif and 1 MS at each joining. Finish off, leaving approx 30″ sewing length; thread into tapestry needle. Sew edging row on joined motifs to bottom row on jacket; holding pieces with right sides tog and carefully matching sts, sew with overcast st through **both lps** of corresponding sts across.

**Sleeve Edging (make 2):** Join 3 motifs as before to form a row; then join ends of row to form a circle. Then work one rnd of edging around one edge of joined motifs as follows. With right side facing, use larger size hook and join white with a sl st in ch-3 corner sp of any motif. Ch 3, working into **each** sp around, beg in same sp as joining and work 21 MS ending in beg sp, join with a sl st in top of beg ch-3. Finish off, leaving approx 14″ sewing length. Sew motifs to sleeve in same manner as Bottom Edging.

**Neck Edging:** With right side facing, beg at upper right-hand corner of jacket neck edge; use larger size hook and join white with a sl st in first skipped ch st of foundation ch. Pull up lp on hook to measure ½″ and work CL in same st; work CL in each skipped ch st across = 29 CL. Finish off, weave in yarn ends. Weave ribbon through sps between CL and trim ends neatly.

*BONNET*

With larger size hook and pink (or blue), ch 5, join with a sl st to form a ring.

**Rnd 1:** Pull up lp on hook to measure ½″, work in ring (CL, ch 2) 8 times, join with a sl st in top of beg CL (*Fig 2*) = 8 CL. Finish off.

**Rnd 2:** With white, sl st into next sp, pull up lp on hook to measure ½″ as before; work (CL, ch 2, CL) in same sp, ch 2; * work (CL, ch 2, CL) in next sp, ch 2; rep from * around, join with a sl st in top of beg CL = 16 CL.

**Rnd 3:** Sl st into next sp and pull up lp on hook; work (CL, ch 1, CL) in same sp, ch 1; * work (CL, ch 1, CL) in next sp, ch 1; rep from * around, join with a sl st in top of beg CL = 32 CL.

**Rnd 4:** Sl st into next sp and pull up lp on hook; work CL in same sp, ch 1; work (CL, ch 1) in each of next 2 sps, work (CL, ch 1, CL) in next sp, ch 1; * work (CL, ch 1) in each of next 3 sps, work (CL, ch 1, CL) in next sp, ch 1; rep from * around, join with a sl st in top of beg CL = 40 CL. You will now begin working in rows to shape crown.

**Row 1:** Sl st into next sp and pull up lp on hook; work CL in same sp, ch 1; beg in **next** sp and work 37 MS ending in 2nd sp from end, work CL in last sp.

**Row 2:** Turn; pull up lp on hook and work CL in first sp, ch 1; beg in **next** sp and work 35 MS ending in 2nd sp from end, work CL in last sp.

**Row 3:** Turn; pull up lp on hook and work CL in first sp, ch 1; beg in **next** sp and work 33 MS ending in 2nd sp from end, work CL in last sp.

**Row 4:** Turn; pull up lp on hook and work CL in first sp, ch 1; beg in **same** sp and work 33 MS ending in **last** sp, work CL in last sp.

**Rows 5 through 10:** Rep Row 4 six times.

**Edging Rnd:** Turn; sc in first sp, * pull up lp on hook to measure ½", YO, insert hook in same sp and pull up ½" lp; YO, insert hook in next sp and pull up a ½" lp [5 lps now on hook]; YO and complete st as CL, sc in same sp and in next sp; rep from * across last row of crown. Across neck edge, work (ch 1, CL) in each of first 9 sps, work (ch 1, CL) twice in next sp at center, work (ch 1, CL) in each of rem 9 sps, ch 1; 2 sc in beg sp, join with a sl st in beg sc.

Finish off, weave in yarn ends. Weave ribbon through sps between CL at neck edge and trim ends neatly.

## AFGHAN

**SIZE: Approx 40" square**

**MATERIALS: Sport weight yarn, 16 oz white, ½ oz each pink and blue, 1 oz green; aluminum crochet hooks sizes E and F (or size required for gauge).**

**GAUGE: With larger size hook, one 6-rnd motif = 5¼" square**

*6-RND MOTIF INSTRUCTIONS*

**Note:** Before working motif, see instructions for Marshmallow and Cluster Stitches on page 94; every rnd of motif is worked on right side.

With larger size hook, ch 5, join with a sl st to form a ring.

**Rnd 1:** Pull up lp on hook to measure ½", work in ring (CL, ch 2) 8 times, join with a sl st in top of beg CL *(Fig 2)*.

**Rnd 2:** Sl st in any sp and pull up lp on hook to measure ½"; beg in same sp and work (CL, ch 2) twice in each sp around, join with a sl st in top of beg CL = 16 CL.

**Rnd 3:** Sl st in next sp and pull up lp on hook to measure ½"; work (CL, ch 2, CL) in same sp for beg corner, ch 1; beg in same sp and work 4 MS, * work (CL, ch 2, CL) in same sp [where last MS was completed] for corner ch 1; beg in same sp and work 4 MS; rep from * twice, ending last rep in beg corner sp, join as before.

**Rnd 4:** Sl st in beg corner sp and pull up lp on hook to measure ½"; work (CL, ch 2, CL) in same sp, ch 1; beg in same sp and work 6 MS ending in next corner sp, * work (CL, ch 2, CL) in same sp, ch 1; beg in same sp and work 6 MS ending in next corner sp; rep from * twice, ending last rep in beg corner sp, join.

**Rnd 5:** Work in same manner as Rnd 4, having 8 MS between corner sps.

**Rnd 6:** Work in same manner as Rnd 4, having 10 MS between corner sps.

Finish off, leaving approx 12" yarn end for sewing.

*AFGHAN INSTRUCTIONS*

Follow 6-Rnd Motif Instructions above and make:
   25 motifs using white for each rnd
   12 motifs using pink for Rnd 1, green for Rnd 2 and white for Rnds 3 through 6
   12 motifs using blue for Rnd 1, green for Rnd 2 and white for Rnds 3 through 6

See Fig 3 for arranging motifs; join motifs using joining method 5 in Chapter 8.

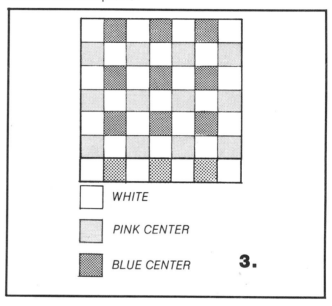

WHITE

PINK CENTER

BLUE CENTER

**3.**

**Edging:** With right side facing and smaller size hook, join white with a sl st in any outer corner sp of afghan.

**Rnd 1:** Pull up lp on hook to measure ½"; beg in same sp and work (CL, ch 2, CL) for corner, ch 2; counting each joining as a sp, * sk next sp, work (CL, ch 1, CL) in next sp, ch 2; rep from * across edge to next corner sp of afghan. Work rem corners and sides in same manner, join with a sl st in top of beg CL.

**Rnd 2:** Sl st into corner sp and pull up lp on hook to measure ½"; work (CL, ch 2, CL) in same sp, ch 2; * work (CL, ch 1, CL) in next sp, ch 2; rep from * across to next corner sp. Work rem corners and sides in same manner, join with a sl st in top of beg CL. Finish off, weave in all yarn ends.

# BUNTING

*designed by Mary Thomas*

**SIZE: Newborn to 3 months**

**MATERIALS: Sport weight yarn, 6 oz white and 4 oz yellow; aluminum crochet hook size F (or size required for gauge); 16″ zipper for front closure.**

**GAUGE: One square = 3″**

## INSTRUCTIONS

*SQUARE (make 64)*

With yellow, ch 4, join with a sl st to form a ring.

**Rnd 1 (right side):** Ch 3, work 15 dc in ring, join with a sl st in top of beg ch-3 = 16 dc (counting ch 3). Finish off yellow.

**Rnd 2:** With right side facing and working in each **sp** between dc around, join white with a sl st in any sp; ch 3, dc in same sp; 2 dc in each of rem 15 sps, join with a sl st in top of beg ch-3 = 32 dc (counting ch 3). Finish off white.

**Rnd 3:** With right side facing and working in **back lp only** of each dc around, join yellow in any dc; ch 2, hdc in same dc as joining and in next dc; * 2 hdc in next dc, hdc in next dc; rep from * around, join with a sl st in top of beg ch-2 = 48 hdc (counting ch 2). Finish off yellow.

**Rnd 4:** With right side facing and working in **both lps** of each hdc around, join white with a sl st in any hdc; ch 5, work (2 dc, tr) in same hdc as joining; * sk 2 hdc, hdc in each of next 2 hdc; sc in each of next 3 hdc, hdc in each of next 2 hdc; sk 2 hdc, work (tr, 2 dc, ch 2, 2 dc, tr) all in next hdc; rep from * 3 times, ending last rep by working (tr, dc) in same hdc as joining [where (2 dc, tr) were worked at beg of rnd], join with a sl st in 3rd ch of beg ch-5. Finish off, leaving 12″ sewing length.

### FINISHING

**Assembling:** Position squares for bunting, hood and bottom sections as shown in Fig 1. Use white and joining method 5 in Chapter 8 and join squares leaving 16″ opening at center front for zipper. When all squares have been joined, place right side down on padded ironing board and lightly steam. Allow pieces to remain on board until completely dry. Fold bunting in half with right sides tog matching corresponding edges; beg at bottom side edge in center sts of first squares and join side edges tog using same joining method. Join other side of bunting in same manner. Insert bottom section and join edges tog as before. Join bottom edge of hood to neck edge of bunting leaving one square on each side of center front free; then extend seam just made (approx ¾″ on each side) by joining matching corner sts of motif on hood to motif left free at center front.

**Edging:** With right side facing, join white with a sl st in corner sp at left center neck edge, ch 1. Working across edges on each side of front opening, work sc in same sp, sc in each st and corner sp of squares and sc in sp at each joining, ending by working sc in corner sp at right center neck edge. Working across edges of neck and hood, work (sl st, ch 3, dc) in same sp, dc in each st and corner sp of squares, ending 2 dc in corner sp at left center neck edge. Working from left to right in reverse sc (see Chapter 8) back across edges of neck and hood,

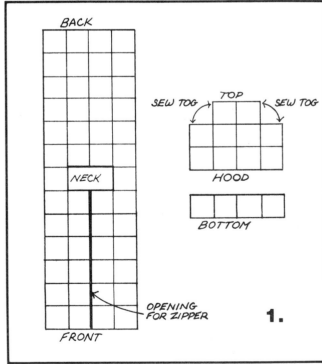

**1.**

work one st in each dc, ending sl st in top of ch 3 at right center neck edge. Finish off, weave in all yarn ends. Sew zipper in place at center front.

**Tie:** With one strand each of yellow and white held tog, make a chain to measure 36″. Weave tie through dc around edge of hood. Following Pompon Instructions in Chapter 8, make two 1″ diameter pompons using equal amounts of yellow and white; attach one pompon to each end of tie.

# GINGHAM BABY AFGHAN

*designed by Jean Leinhauser*

**SIZE:** Approx 35″ square before edging

**MATERIALS:** Worsted weight yarn, 12 oz lt blue, 10 oz white, 6 oz med blue; aluminum crochet hook size G (or size required for gauge).

**GAUGE:** One granny square measures 2¼″

## GRANNY SQUARE INSTRUCTIONS

Ch 4, join with a sl st to form a ring.

**Rnd 1:** Ch 3 (counts as first dc), 2 dc in ring; * ch 2, 3 dc in ring; rep from * twice, ch 2, join with a sl st in top of beg ch-3.

**Rnd 2:** Sl st in each of next 2 dc, sl st into ch-2 corner sp; ch 3, work (2 dc, ch 2, 3 dc) in same sp; * work (3 dc, ch 2, 3 dc) in next corner sp; rep from * twice, join with a sl st in top of beg ch-3. Finish off, weave in yarn ends.

## AFGHAN INSTRUCTIONS

Following Granny Square Instructions above, make 113 squares with lt blue, 56 squares with med blue and 56 squares with white. Afghan has 15 rows with 15 squares in each row. Every odd-numbered row contains 8 lt blue squares and 7 med blue squares (alternate lt blue and med blue squares, beg and ending with lt blue). Every even-numbered row contains 8 white squares and 7 lt blue squares (alternate white and lt blue squares, beg and ending with white).

**Joining:** Hold 2 squares with right sides tog; thread yarn into tapestry needle. Work across 8 sts of each motif; carefully matching sts, beg in ch st at corner and sew with overcast st in **outer lps only,** ending in first ch st of next corner. Join **all** squares in this manner whether joining squares for a row or joining rows of squares. Do not join at four-corner junctions—this will leave small openings as shown in photo.

**Edging:** With right side facing, join white with a sl st in any corner sp of afghan, ch 1.

**Rnd 1:** * Work 3 sc in corner sp of afghan, sc in each of next 6 dc across square; work (sc in next corner sp of same square, sc in corner sp of **next** square, sc in each of next 6 dc) 14 times; rep from * 3 times, join with a sl st in first sc of rnd.

**Rnd 2:** Sl st in next sc, ch 5; dc in same st, sk next sc; * work (dc, ch 2, dc) all in next sc, sk next sc; rep from * around, join with a sl st in 3rd ch of beg ch-5.

**Rnd 3:** Sl st in first sp; ch 3, work (dc, ch 3, 2 dc) all in same sp; work (2 dc, ch 3, 2 dc) in each ch-2 sp around, join with a sl st in top of beg ch-3. Finish off, weave in yarn ends.

# BABY BONNET
*designed by Nancy Dent*

**SIZE: Fits ages 3 to 9 months, weight approx 11 to 18 lbs.**

**MATERIALS: Sport weight yarn, 2 oz each white and yellow; aluminum crochet hook size D (or size required for gauge).**

**GAUGE: 1 granny square = 3¼″**

## INSTRUCTIONS
*GRANNY SQUARE (make 8)*

With yellow, ch 5, join with a sl st to form a ring.

**Rnd 1:** Ch 3 [counts as first dc], work 15 more dc in ring; join with a sl st while changing colors as follows: With yellow lp on hook, insert hook in top of beg ch-3; drop yellow, pick up white and complete the sl st by drawing white through lps on hook. Finish off yellow. **Note:** Join new color in this manner throughout patt.

**Rnd 2:** Sl st into sp between ch-3 and next dc; ch 3, work (dc, ch 1, 2 dc) in same sp [for beg shell]; ch 1, sk one dc; * in sp between **next** 2 dc, work a shell of (2 dc, ch 1, 2 dc); ch 1, sk one dc; rep from * 6 times more, join with a sl st changing to yellow as before. You should have 8 shells.

**Rnd 3:** Sl st in next dc, sl st into next ch-1 sp; make a beg cluster in same sp as follows: Ch 3, † YO, insert hook in sp and draw up a ½″ lp, YO and draw through 2 lps on hook †; rep from † to † once more, then YO and draw through 3 lps now on hook—beg cluster made. Ch 2, * make a cluster in next ch-1 sp [by repeating from † to † 3 times, then YO and draw through 4 lps on hook]. Ch 2, rep from * 14 times more; join with a sl st in top of beg cluster, changing to white.

**Rnd 4:** Ch 2, * work (2 sc in next ch-2 sp, ch 1) 3 times; work a shell of (3 dc, ch 2, 3 dc) all in next ch-2 sp, ch 1; rep from * 3 times more, join with a sl st in top of beg ch-2. Finish off, weave in yarn ends.

### FINISHING

**Assembling:** Sew squares tog (4 squares long and 2 squares wide), carefully matching sts and being sure that all right sides face up. Use overcast st and tapestry needle threaded with white. Fold joined squares in half; with fold at top, sew sides of squares tog to the right **or** left of fold for back seam.

**Trim:** With right side facing, join white with a sl st in ch-2 sp at left front corner. Ch 1, work 3 sc in same sp; across neck edge, work sc in each **st** across [be sure to sk all ch-1 sps and seams between squares] to right front corner; work 3 sc in ch-2 sp at corner; continue to work sc in each rem **st** around as before, join with a sl st in beg sc. Now continue to work one row across neck edge, work sc in each st across to right front corner. Finish off, weave in yarn ends.

**Ties (make 2):** With 2 strands of white held tog, make a ch to measure 12″ long for each tie.

**Pompons (make 3):** With equal amounts of white and yellow yarn, make 1″ diameter pompons (see Pompon Instructions in Chapter 8). Sew one pompon to top of hood; attach one pompon to one end of each tie and fasten other end of ties to right and left corners of bonnet.

# TRADITIONAL GRANNY AFGHAN
## FOR BABY
*designed by Jean Leinhauser*

**SIZE: Approx 24″ x 36″**

**MATERIALS: Worsted weight yarn, 8 oz white, 4 oz baby blue and a few yds each of other assorted colors [see Note below]; aluminum crochet hook size H (or size required for gauge).**

**Materials Note:** The white yarn specified in materials is used only for Rnds 4 and 6 of each square; work the other rnds of each square with your leftovers, in any colors of your choice. Even a yard of yarn is enough to work the first rnd of a square. Do not work two rnds with the same color—change colors at the end of every rnd. Light and bright colors will create the prettiest afghan. The baby blue yarn specified is used *only* for the edging. Do not use this yarn for rnds in the squares, or you will not have enough for the edging.

**GAUGE: One granny square = 6″**

## INSTRUCTIONS
*GRANNY SQUARE (make 24)*

With first color, ch 4, join with a sl st to form a ring.

**Rnd 1:** Ch 3, 2 dc in ring; * ch 3, work 3 dc in ring; rep from * twice, ch 3, join with a sl st in top of beg ch-3. Finish off.

**Rnd 2:** Join new color with a sl st in any ch-3 sp, ch 3; work (2 dc, ch 3, 3 dc) in same sp [for corner], * work (3 dc, ch 3, 3 dc) all in next ch-3 sp [for corner]; rep from * twice, join with a sl st in top of beg ch-3. Finish off.

**Rnd 3:** Join new color with a sl st in any ch-3 corner sp, ch 3; work (2 dc, ch 3, 3 dc) in same sp, * work 3 dc between next two 3-dc groups [for side], work (3 dc, ch 3, 3 dc) in next corner sp; rep from * twice, work 3 dc between next two 3-dc groups [for last side], join with a sl st in top of beg ch-3. Finish off.

**Rnd 4:** Join white with a sl st in any corner sp, ch 3; work (2 dc, ch 3, 3 dc) in same sp, * work 3 dc between each pair of 3-dc groups along side; in next corner sp, work (3 dc, ch 3, 3 dc); rep from * twice; work 3 dc between each pair of 3-dc groups along last side, join with a sl st in top of beg ch-3. Finish off.

**Rnd 5:** Join new color with a sl st in any corner sp, ch 3; work (2 dc, ch 3, 3 dc) in same sp, * work 3 dc between each pair of 3-dc groups along side; in next corner sp, work (3 dc, ch 3, 3 dc); rep from * twice; work 3 dc between each pair of 3-dc groups along last side, join with a sl st in top of beg ch-3. Finish off.

**Rnd 6:** Make a slip knot on hook with blue; join with a sc in any corner sp, work 2 sc in same sp; * sc in each dc across to next corner sp, work 3 sc in corner sp; rep from * twice; sc in each dc to beg corner, join with a sl st in first sc. Finish off, weave in all yarn ends.

**Joining:** Hold 2 squares with right sides tog; thread tapestry needle with white. Carefully matching sts, beg in center sc at corner and sew with overcast st in **outer lps only,** ending in center sc at next corner. Join squares in 4 rows of 6 squares each, then join rows in same manner.

**Edging:** Make a slip knot on hook with blue; with right side facing, join with a sc in center sc of 3-sc group at any corner of afghan.

**Rnd 1:** Work 2 more sc in same sc as joining, * sc in each sc across to center sc of 3-sc group at next corner of afghan, work 3 sc in center sc; rep from * twice; sc in each sc along last side to beg sc, join with a sl st in beg sc.

**Rnd 2:** TURN; with wrong side facing, * ch 3, sl st in next sc; rep from * around, ending by working a sl st in last sc, join with a sl st in base of beg ch-3. Finish off, weave in yarn ends.

# VEST FOR TODDLERS

*designed by Eleanor Denner*

**Designed to fit toddler sizes 2 to 4**

**MATERIALS: Pompadour Baby Yarn in 1-oz skeins: 2 skeins each green and white, 1 skein each pink, blue and yellow; steel crochet hook size 00 (or size required for gauge); eight ½" white buttons for side tabs.**

**GAUGE: One square = 2¼"**

## INSTRUCTIONS

*SQUARE (make 32 total—8 each of yellow, pink, blue and green)*

**Note:** Ch 3 counts as one dc throughout patt.

Ch 4, join with a sl st to form a ring.

**Rnd 1 (right side):** Ch 3, work 15 dc in ring, join with a sl st in top of beg ch-3.

**Rnd 2:** Ch 3, work 4 dc in same st as joining for beg corner; * ch 1, sk one dc, dc in next dc; ch 1, sk one dc, 5 dc in next dc for corner; rep from * twice; ch 1, sk one dc, dc in next dc; ch 1, sk last dc, join with a sl st in top of beg ch-3.

**Rnd 3:** Sl st in each of next 2 dc, ch 3; work 4 dc in same st where last sl st was made, * work (ch 1, dc in next ch-1 sp) twice, ch 1; 5 dc in center dc of 5-dc corner group; rep from * twice; work (ch 1, dc in next ch-1 sp) twice, ch 1, join with a sl st in top of beg ch-3. Finish off, weave in yarn ends.

**Rnd 4:** With right side facing, join white with a sl st in center st of any 5-dc corner group, ch 1, 3 sc in same st; * sc in each dc and in each ch-1 sp across to center st of next corner, work 3 sc in center st at corner; rep from * twice; sc in each dc and in each ch-1 sp across last side, join with a sl st in beg sc. You should have 3 sc at each corner and 9 sc between corners. Finish off, leaving approx 12" sewing length for joining.

### ASSEMBLING AND JOINING

Refer to Fig 1 for arranging squares of front and back. Join squares by holding 2 squares with right sides tog; thread yarn end into tapestry needle and sew with overcast st working into **outer lps only** (see joining method 5 in Chapter 8). Be sure that each 4-corner intersection is secure when joining strips of squares.

### BACK YOKE AND SHOULDER STRAPS

**Back Yoke:** Hold back with right side facing you; counting from upper right-hand corner, sk 3-sc group and next 2 sc; join green with a sl st in next sc.

**Row 1:** Ch 3, dc in each of next 8 sc of first square; * on next square, beg in center sc of corner group and work 13 dc across ending in center sc of next corner group of same square; rep from * once; on last square, beg in center sc of corner group and work dc in each of next 9 sc. You should have 44 dc (counting ch 3).

**Row 2:** Ch 3, turn; dec over next 2 dc [to dec: work dc in first st until there are 2 lps on hook; keeping the 2 lps on hook, YO, insert hook in next st; YO and draw through st (4 lps now on hook); YO and draw through 2 lps, YO and draw through rem 3 lps on hook—dec made]. Work dc in

each st across to within 3 sts of end, dec as before over next 2 dc, dc in top of ch-3 = 42 dc.

**Row 3:** Ch 3, turn; dec over next 2 dc, dc in each st across to within 3 sts of end, dec over next 2 dc, dc in top of Tch = 40 dc.

**Row 4:** Rep Row 3; you should have 38 dc. Do not finish off.

**Left Shoulder Strap: Row 1:** Ch 3, turn; dc in next dc and in each of next 7 dc = 9 dc (counting ch 3). **Row 2:** Ch 3, turn; dc in each of next 7 dc, dc in top of Tch. Rep Row 2 until strap measures approx 7½" or desired length. Finish off, leaving approx 12" sewing length.

**Right Shoulder Strap:** Hold back with wrong side facing and counting from left shoulder strap, sk center 20 dc of back, join green with a sl st in next dc. **Row 1:** Ch 3, do **not** turn; dc in each of next 8 sts. **Row 2:** Ch 3, turn; dc in each of next 7 dc, dc in top of ch-3. Rep Row 2 until measurement is same as other strap. Finish off, leaving approx 12" sewing length.

### FINISHING

Join left shoulder strap to front as follows. Thread yarn end into tapestry needle; hold right side facing you, sk 3-sc group at upper right-hand corner and next 5 sc; then align 9 sts of strap with next 6 sts on first square, center sc and next 2 sc of 2nd square. Use overcast method and sew through **both** lps of each st across. Sew other strap to front in same manner.

**Edging:** With right side facing, join white with a sl st in center sc of 3-sc group at any outer corner; ch 1, 3 sc in same st as joining, sc in each st of squares and each row of straps around entire edge of garment, ending at beg corner; join with a sl st in first sc made. Then work one rnd in reverse sc around entire edge [see instructions for reverse sc in Chapter 8].

**Tab (make 4):** With white, ch 19 for foundation chain.

**Rnd 1:** Dc in 4th ch from hook, dc in each of next 14 chs, 5 dc in last ch; now continue by working in unworked lps of foundation ch as follows: dc in each of next 14 chs, 3 dc in last ch, join with a sl st in top of ch-3 left unworked at beg of rnd. **Rnd 2:** Ch 1, sc in first dc and in each dc around, join with a sl st in beg sc. **Rnd 3:** Work reverse sc as before in each sc around. Finish off, weave in yarn ends. Sew one button on each end of each tab. Attach 2 tabs at each side by inserting buttons in ch-1 sps of squares.

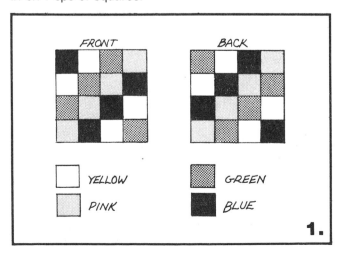

FRONT    BACK

☐ YELLOW    ▨ GREEN

▨ PINK    ■ BLUE

**1.**

(Shown in color on page 79.)

# DAISY SUNDRESS

*designed by Jean Leinhauser*

**Designed to fit toddler sizes 3 and 4**

**MATERIALS: Sport weight yarn, 1 oz white and 6 oz bright golden yellow; aluminum crochet hook size F (or size required for gauge); three ⁵⁄₁₆″ diameter white pearl buttons.**

**GAUGE: One daisy square = 2½″**

## INSTRUCTIONS

*DAISY SQUARE (make 10)*

With yellow, ch 4, join with a sl st to form a ring.

**Rnd 1 (right side):** Ch 4, work beg petal in ring as follows: keeping last lp of each st on hook, work 2 tr [3 lps now on hook], YO and draw through all 3 lps [beg petal made]; ch 3, * work petal in ring as follows: keeping last lp of each st on hook, work 3 tr [4 lps now on hook], YO and draw through all 4 lps [petal made], ch 3; rep from * 6 times more, join with a sl st in top of beg petal = 8 petals. Finish off yellow.

**Rnd 2:** With right side facing, join white with a sl st in any ch-3 sp; ch 3, work (2 dc, ch 2, 3 dc) all in same sp for beg corner; * 3 dc in next ch-3 sp, work (3 dc, ch 2, 3 dc) all in next ch-3 sp for corner; rep from * twice more, 3 dc in last ch-3 sp, join with a sl st in top of beg ch-3; finish off and weave in yarn ends.

*ASSEMBLING*

Refer to Fig 1 for arranging squares of yoke. Use white and joining method 5 in Chapter 8 and join daisy squares leaving squares at center back unjoined. When joining is completed, place yoke right side down on padded ironing board and lightly steam, taking care not to let iron touch the squares. Leave on board until completely dry.

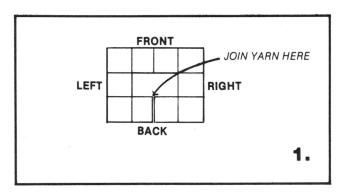

1.

*YOKE EDGING*

With right side of yoke facing you, make a slip knot on hook with white and join with a sc in corner sp at left back center neck edge (see *Fig 1*), sc in same sp. Work sc in each dc and in each corner sp of squares around neck edge and at each inner corner (where 3 squares are joined) also work one sc in corner sp of center square, ending 2 sc in corner sp at right back center neck edge [you should have 11 sc across each square, one sc at each inner corner and 2 sc at each corner at center back]. Now continue working around rem edges of yoke by working sc in each dc and in each corner sp of squares, sc in sp at each joining and 2 sc in each outer corner sp, ending at bottom corner sp of left back center edge; working across back center edge, 2 sc in corner sp, * sc in next dc, ch 1, sk one dc (for buttonhole), sc in next dc; rep from * twice, ending in corner sp at left back center neck edge. Join with a sl st in beg sc; finish off.

*SKIRT*

Hold yoke with right side facing and back lower edge across top. Join yellow with a sl st in 2nd sc at upper right-hand corner of square to the left of center opening.

**Foundation Row:** Working across 2 squares of right back, * work (ch 5, dc) in same st as joining [beg shell made]; † sk next sc, work (dc, ch 2, dc) all in next sc [shell made] †; rep from † to † across, ending in 2nd sc at next corner; * break yarn. Sk 3 squares for armhole and join yellow with a sl st in 2nd sc at next corner. Working across 4 squares of front, rep from * to * once; break yarn. Sk 3 squares for armhole and join yellow with a sl st in 2nd sc at next corner. Working across 2 squares of left back, rep from * to * once; do not break yarn, sl st in 3rd ch of ch-5 of beg shell on right back.

**Joining Rnd:** Sl st into sp of beg shell and work beg shell of (ch 3, dc, ch 2, 2 dc) in same sp; work shell of (2 dc, ch 2, 2 dc) in ch-2 sp of each shell and in sp of each beg shell across right back, front and left back edges, join with a sl st in top of beg ch-3.

**Patt Rnd:** Sl st in top of next dc and into ch-2 sp of beg shell, work beg shell of (ch 3, dc, ch 2, 2 dc) in same sp; work shell of (2 dc, ch 2, 2 dc) in ch-2 sp of each shell around, join with a sl st in top of beg ch-3.

Rep Patt Rnd until skirt measures, from bottom edge of yoke, approx 11½″ for size 3 dress or 12½″ for size 4 dress (or desired length). Finish off, weave in all yarn ends. Sew on buttons.

(Shown in color on page 77.)

# TODDLER ROBE

*designed by Jean Leinhauser*

**SIZES: Toddler 2 and 3**

**Size Note:** Instructions are the same for both sizes; size difference is achieved by changing hook sizes. Refer to **Materials** and **Gauge** for recommended hook size and specified gauge.

**MATERIALS:** Sport weight yarn, 4 oz baby pastels ombre; 2 oz pastel pink; aluminum crochet hook size F for size 2 garment or size G for size 3 garment (or size required for gauge); four ⅜" diameter white buttons.

| GAUGE: | For Size 2 | For Size 3 |
|---|---|---|
| One granny square = | 2½ " | 2¾ " |
| In dc, | 9 sts = 2" | 8 sts = 2" |

## INSTRUCTIONS

*GRANNY SQUARE (make 36)*

With pink, ch 4, join with a sl st to form a ring.

**Rnd 1 (right side):** Ch 3, 2 dc in ring; * ch 2, 3 dc in ring; rep from * twice more, ch 2, join with a sl st in top of beg ch-3.

**Rnd 2:** Sl st in each of next 2 dc and into ch-2 sp; ch 3, work (2 dc, ch 2, 3 dc) all in same sp for beg corner; * in next ch-2 sp, work (3 dc, ch 2, 3 dc) for corner; rep from * twice, join with a sl st in top of beg ch-3. Finish off pink.

**Rnd 3:** With right side facing, join ombre with a sl st in any ch-2 corner sp; ch 3, work (2 dc, ch 3, 3 dc) all in same sp; * 3 dc in sp between next two 3-dc groups; in corner ch-2 sp, work (3 dc, ch 2, 3 dc); rep from * twice, 3 dc in sp between last two 3-dc groups, join with a sl st in top of beg ch-3. Finish off, weave in all yarn ends.

*ASSEMBLING*

Arrange squares as shown in Fig 1; with tapestry needle threaded with ombre yarn, sew squares with right sides tog using overcast st (see joining method 5 in Chapter 8). Leave squares unjoined at center front as indicated, for front opening. Place joined squares right side down on padded ironing board, and lightly steam. Allow garment to remain on board until completely dry. Fold in half lengthwise; with same sewing method, join side yoke and sleeve seams leaving last 2 squares at each sleeve cuff edge unjoined.

*NECKLINE*

With right side facing, join pink with a sl st in ch-2 corner sp at right front center neck edge.

**Row 1:** Ch 1, beg in same sp and work sc in each corner sp and in each dc of squares around neck edge and at each inner corner (where 3 squares are joined) also work one sc in corner sp of center square, ending in ch-2 corner sp at left front center neck edge. You should have 11 sc across each square and one sc at each inner corner for a total of 70 sc.

**Row 2:** Ch 3, turn; dc in each of next 10 sc, sk next sc at corner; dc in each of next 11 sc, sk next sc at corner; dc in each of next 22 sc, sk next sc at corner; dc in each of next 11 sc, sk next sc at corner; dc in each of last 11 sc = 66 dc (counting ch 3).

**Row 3:** Ch 3, turn; dc in each of next 9 dc, sk 2 dc at corner; dc in each of next 9 dc, sk 2 dc at corner; dc in each of next 20 dc, sk 2 dc at corner; dc in each of next 9 dc, sk 2 dc at corner; dc in each of last 9 dc, dc in top of Tch = 58 dc.

**Row 4:** Ch 3, turn; dc in each of next 8 dc, sk 2 dc at corner; dc in each of next 7 dc, sk 2 dc at corner; dc in each of next 18 dc, sk 2 dc at corner; dc in each of next 7 dc, sk 2 dc at corner; dc in each of last 8 dc, dc in top of Tch = 50 dc. Finish off, weave in yarn ends.

*SKIRT*

Hold garment with right side facing and bottom edge of yoke across top; join ombre with a sl st in upper right-hand corner sp.

**Row 1:** Ch 3 (counts as first dc of row), beg in next dc and work dc in each dc and in each corner sp across squares and work dc in sp at each joining, ending in upper left-hand corner sp = 95 dc.

**Row 2 (beading row):** Ch 5 (counts as first tr and first ch-1 sp of row), sk next dc; * tr in next dc, ch 1, sk one dc; rep from * across, ending tr in top of ch-3.

**Row 3:** Ch 3, turn; * dc in ch-1 sp, dc in next dc; rep from * across, ending last rep by working dc in 3rd ch of ch-5 = 95 dc.

**Row 4:** Ch 3, turn; dc in next dc and in each dc across, dc in top of Tch.

**Rows 5 through 7:** Rep Row 4 three times.

**Row 8 (inc row):** Ch 3, turn; dc in each of next 23 dc, 2 dc in each of next 2 dc; dc in each of next 43 dc, 2 dc in each of next 2 dc; dc in each rem dc across, dc in top of Tch = 99 dc.

**Rows 9 and 10:** Rep Row 4 twice.

**Row 11 (inc row):** Ch 3, turn; dc in each of next 24 dc, 2 dc in each of next 2 dc; dc in each of next 45 dc, 2 dc in each of next 2 dc; dc in each rem dc across, dc in top of Tch = 103 dc.

**Row 12:** Rep Row 4.

**Row 13 (inc row):** Ch 3, turn; dc in each of next 25 dc, 2 dc in each of next 2 dc; dc in each of next 47 dc, 2 dc in each of next 2 dc; dc in each rem dc across, dc in top of Tch = 107 dc.

**Row 14:** Rep Row 4.

**Row 15 (inc row):** Ch 3, turn; dc in each of next 26 dc, 2 dc in each of next 2 dc; dc in each of next 49 dc, 2 dc in each of next 2 dc; dc in each rem dc across, dc in top of Tch = 111 dc. Now rep Row 4 until piece measures 18" from Row 1 of Skirt, or desired length. **Note:** You may wish to make garment an inch or so longer than currently needed and hem the excess length; garment can then be lengthened as the child grows. Finish off, weave in all yarn ends.

*FRONT AND NECK EDGING*

With right side facing, join pink with a sl st in st at lower corner of right front center edge.

**Row 1:** Ch 1, beg in same st and work sc evenly spaced (keeping work flat) along right front center edge to Beading Row; work 4 sc in tr sp, sc in top and side of next dc; work sc in each corner sp and in each dc across next 2 squares of yoke, work 6 sc evenly spaced to corner at

right neck edge; around neck edge, work 3 sc in first dc (corner made), sc in each dc, 3 sc in top of Tch (corner made); then work sc along left front center edge to correspond with right front center edge, ending in st at lower corner of left front center edge.

**Row 2:** Ch 1, turn; sc in each sc to 3-sc corner group at left neck edge, sc in first sc, 3 sc in center sc; sc in next sc and each sc around neck edge to 3-sc corner group at right neck edge, sc in first sc, 3 sc in center sc, sc in next sc; * ch 1, sk one sc (for buttonhole), sc in each of next 6 sc; rep from * 3 times, sc in each rem sc.

**Row 3:** Ch 1, turn; sc in each sc and in each ch-1 buttonhole sp. Finish off, weave in yarn ends.

*SLEEVE EDGING (make 2)*
With right side facing, join pink with a sl st at underarm seam (where 2 squares were left unjoined). Ch 1, work sc in each corner sp and in each dc of squares around working 2 sc in each outer corner sp of sleeve, join with a sl st in beg sc. Finish off, weave in yarn ends.

*BELT*
With pink, make a chain to measure 45″; hdc in 2nd ch from hook and in each rem ch across; finish off. Make two 1½″ tassels with ombre following Tassel Instructions in Chapter 8. Weave belt through Beading Row, then attach one tassel to each end of belt. Sew on buttons.

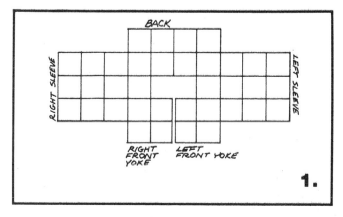

# HANKY TOP FOR TODDLERS
*designed by Eleanor Denner*

| SIZES: | Small | Medium | Large |
|---|---|---|---|
| Fits Toddlers | 2 yrs | 3 yrs | 4 yrs |

**Size Note:** Instructions are written for sizes as follows: Small(Medium-Large).

**MATERIALS: Sport weight yarn, 4(6-8) oz white; aluminum crochet hook size F (or size required for gauge).**

**GAUGE: First 7 rnds of Granny Square = 6″**

## GRANNY SQUARE

**Note:** Each rnd is worked with right side facing you.

With white, ch 4, join with a sl st to form a ring.

**Rnd 1:** Ch 3, 2 dc in ring; * ch 2, 3 dc in ring; rep from * twice more, ch 2, join with a sl st in top of beg ch-3.

**Rnd 2:** Sl st in each of next 2 dc and into ch-2 sp; ch 3, work (2 dc, ch 2, 3 dc) in same sp [for beg corner]; * ch 1, work (3 dc, ch 2, 3 dc) in next ch-2 sp [for corner]; rep from * twice more, ch 1, join with a sl st in top of beg ch-3.

**Rnd 3:** Sl st in each of next 2 dc and into ch-2 corner sp; ch 3, work (2 dc, ch 2, 3 dc) in same sp [for beg corner]; * ch 1, work 3 dc in next ch-1 sp [for side]; ch 1, work (3 dc, ch 2, 3 dc) in next ch-2 corner sp; rep from * twice more, ch 1, 3 dc in next ch-1 sp [for last side]; ch 1, join with a sl st in top of beg ch-3.

**Rnd 4:** Sl st in each of next 2 dc and into ch-2 corner sp; ch 3, work (2 dc, ch 2, 3 dc) in same sp [for beg corner]; * ch 1, work (3 dc in next sp, ch 1) twice [for side]; work (3 dc, ch 2, 3 dc) in next ch-2 corner sp [for corner]; rep from * twice more, ch 1, work (3 dc in next ch-1 sp, ch 1) twice [for last side], join with a sl st in top of beg ch-3.

**Rnd 5 and all following Rnds:** Sl st in each of next 2 dc and into ch-2 corner sp; ch 3, work (2 dc, ch 2, 3 dc) in same sp [for beg corner]; * ch 1, work (3 dc, ch 1) in each sp to next corner; work (3 dc, ch 2, 3 dc) in corner sp; rep from * twice more, ch 1; work (3 dc, ch 1) in each sp across last side, join with a sl st in top of beg ch-3.

## INSTRUCTIONS

Follow Granny Square instructions above; working 11(13-15) rnds for each square, make 4 squares: one for Front, one for Back, one for Right Sleeve and one for Left Sleeve.

See diagram in Fig 1. Right Sleeve and Left Sleeve are joined to Front by working across from points A to B as follows: Hold Right Sleeve and Front with right sides tog; join yarn with a sl st in corner sp (A) of both squares, sc in same sp of both pieces, * ch 3, sc in next ch-1 sp [inserting hook into corresponding sp of both pieces]; rep from * 6(7-8) times more; finish off, weave in yarn ends. You have just formed Right Front raglan seam; work in same manner for Left Front raglan seam [A to B]. Work raglan seams on Back in same manner [a to b].

Join Front to Back by folding work in half with right sides tog (*Fig 2*); join yarn with a sl st in corner sp at C of Front and c of Back; work one sc in same sp, sl st in same sp;

finish off, weave in yarn ends. Front is left open between B and C; Back is left open between b and c.

For each sleeve underarm seam, hold sleeve folded in half with right sides tog; beg at end of sleeve [x in *Fig 2*]; join yarn with a sl st in corner sp, sc in same sp of both corners; * ch 3, sc in next ch-1 sp [insert hook into corresponding sp of both pieces]; rep from * 3(5-6) times more, ending in same sp used for last sc made when sleeves were attached to Front and Back.

**Drawstring:** Make a chain to measure 36(40-44)″; sl st in 2nd ch from hook and in each rem ch across; finish off, weave in ends. Weave drawstring through sps around neck opening; beg and ending in ch-2 corner sp at point A at top of Front.

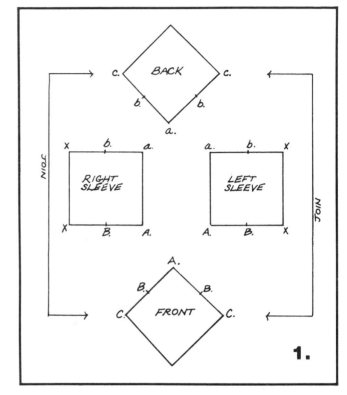

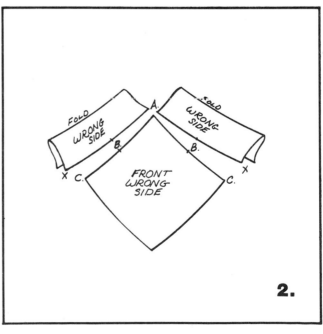

# Chapter 6

# The Fashionable Granny

Granny projects can be practical, useful, decorative—and even fashionable!

Our collection of granny fashions features both garments made entirely of granny motifs (the tabard, the beach cover-up), and designs with the granny squares serving as accent (the hooded jacket, the bed jacket).

For those of you who have previously used granny squares only for afghans, here's a chance to experiment with a delightful new use for the versatile square.

# HOODED JACKET

*designed by Doris England*

An unusual method of seaming adds an attractive finishing detail to this lovely garment, complementing the pattern stitch in the body of the jacket and the granny squares in the trim. The seaming detail is achieved by first working an edging in sc around all garment pieces before sewing seams with backstitching on right side of garment.

| SIZES: | Small | Medium | Large |
|---|---|---|---|
| Body Bust: | 32" | 36" | 40" |
| **Garment Measurements:** | | | |
| bust | 38" | 42" | 46" |
| length from bottom edge | | | |
| to shoulder | 26" | 27" | 27" |
| sleeve length | 18" | 18" | 18" |

**Size Note:** Instructions are written for sizes as follows: Small(Medium-Large).

**MATERIALS: Worsted weight yarn, 32(36-40) oz light gray heather, 4(6-8) oz charcoal gray, 2 oz white; aluminum crochet hook size H for all sizes plus hook size I for medium and large sizes only (or hook sizes required for gauge); five 1¼" square charcoal gray buttons; one black dress snap fastener size 2 for neck closure.**

**GAUGE:** With size H hook, in patt,
      7 sts = 2"; 7 rows = 2"
     **With size H hook,**
      one 5-rnd granny square = 4½"
     **With size I hook,**
      one 5-rnd granny square = 4¾"

**Gauge Note:** To test gauge in pattern stitch and determine correct hook size, use smaller size hook and ch 22. Following Pattern Stitch instructions below, first work Foundation Row = 21 sts; then work Rows 1 and 2, ten times. You should have a total of 21 rows with 21 sts in each row and your swatch should measure 6" square.

## PATTERN STITCH
*(WORKED ON UNEVEN NUMBER OF STS)*

**Foundation Row (right side):** Sc in 2nd ch from hook, * dc in next ch, sc in next ch; rep from * across.

**Patt Row 1:** Ch 1, turn; sc in first sc, sc in next dc; * dc in next sc, sc in next dc; rep from * across to last st, sc in last sc.

**Patt Row 2:** Ch 1, turn; sc in first sc, dc in next sc; * sc in next dc, dc in next sc; rep from * across to last st, sc in last sc. Rep Patt Rows 1 and 2 for pattern stitch.

## INSTRUCTIONS

**Note:** Use smaller size hook throughout patt unless otherwise specified.

### JACKET

**Back:** Beg at lower edge with lt gray heather, ch 68(74-82). Following Pattern Stitch instructions, beg on right side with Foundation Row and work in patt on 67(73-81) sts until back measures approx 26(27-27)", ending by working Patt Row 1. Do not finish off; you will now shape neck of right front.

**Right Front: Row 1 (right side):** Ch 1, turn; sc in first sc and mark this st with a small safety pin or a piece of con-

*(Shown in color on page 74.)*

trasting yarn to be used later for working sleeve; work (dc in next sc, sc in next dc) 11(12-13) times = 23(25-27) sts [center 21(23-27) sts are left unworked for neck opening; rem 23(25-27) sts will be worked later for left front]. **Rows 2 through 11:** Work Patt Rows 1 and 2, five times; ending last row at neck edge. **Row 12:** Ch 15(17-19), turn; sc in 2nd ch from hook, sc in next ch; work (dc in next ch, sc in next ch) 6(7-8) times; then work (dc in next sc, sc in next dc) 11(12-13) times, ending sc in last sc = 37(41-45) sts.

Neck shaping is now completed; beg with Patt Row 2 and continue by working even in patt until right front measures same as back, ending by working Patt Row 2. Finish off.

**Left Front:** With right side facing, hold jacket with back neck edge across top and neck shaping just worked to your right. Sk center 21(23-27) sts for neck opening; join lt gray heather with a sl st in next st [dc]. **Row 1 (right side):** Ch 1, sc in same st as joining, work (dc in next sc, sc in next dc) 10(11-12) times; dc in next sc, sc in last sc and mark this st to be used later for working sleeve = 23(25-27) sts. **Rows 2 through 12:** Work Patt Rows 1 and 2, five times; then work Patt Row 1 once more. You should now be at neck edge. **Row 13:** Ch 9(9-11), turn; sc in 2nd ch from hook, dc in next ch; work (sc in next ch, dc in next ch) 3(3-4) times, sc in next sc; then work (dc in next sc, sc in next dc) 10(11-12) times, ending dc in next sc, sc in last sc = 31(33-37) sts.

Neck shaping is now completed; beg with Patt Row 1 and continue by working even in patt until left front measures same as back, ending by working Patt Row 2. Finish off.

**Right Sleeve:** Hold jacket with wrong side facing and marked armhole edge of right front across top. Counting from marker to your right, join lt gray heather with a sl st in 29th(31st-33rd) row. **Row 1 (wrong side):** Ch 1, sc in same sp as joining and in each row to marker; sc in marked row and in each of next 29(31-33) rows = 59(63-67) sc. **Row 2:** Ch 1, turn; sc in first sc, * dc in next sc, sc in next sc; rep from * across = 59(63-67) sts. Now beg with Patt Row 1 and work even in patt until sleeve measures approx 6″, ending by working Patt Row 1. Then work shaping as follows. **Shaping: Row 1 (dec row):** Ch 1, turn; dec over first 2 sc [to dec: draw up a lp in each of 2 sc (3 lps now on hook), YO and draw through all 3 lps—dec made]; * sc in next dc, dc in next sc; rep from * across to last 3 sts, sc in next dc, work dec over last 2 sc as before = 57(61-65) sts. **Row 2:** Ch 1, turn; sc in first st, * dc in next sc, sc in next dc; rep from * across to last 2 sts, dc in next sc, sc in last st. **Rows 3 and 4:** Work Patt Rows 1 and 2. **Row 5 (dec row):** Ch 1, turn; dec over first 2 sts [sc, dc], * dc in next sc, sc in next dc; rep from * across to last 3 sts, dc in next sc, dec over last 2 sts [dc, sc] = 55(59-63) sts. **Row 6:** Ch 1, turn; sc in first st, * sc in next dc, dc in next sc; rep from * across to last 2 sts, sc in next dc, sc in last st. **Row 7:** Work Patt Row 2. **Row 8:** Work Patt Row 1. Rep last 8 rows twice = 47(51-55) sts. Now beg with Patt Row 2 and work even in patt until sleeve measures approx 18″ or desired length, ending by working Patt Row 1. Finish off.

**Left Sleeve:** Hold jacket with wrong side facing and marked armhole edge of left front across top; then work same as Right Sleeve. At end of last row, do not finish off; ch 1, turn and work edging on right side of garment.

**Edging:** Across last row of sleeve, † work 3 sc in first st (for corner), sc in each st to last st, 3 sc in last st (for corner).† Across long edge of sleeve and side edge of back, work sc in **next** row and in each row to inside corner at underarm; dec over next 2 rows, sc in each row to last row at bottom edge [sk last row]. Rep from † to † across lower edge of back. Across side edge of back and long edge of right sleeve, work sc in **next** row and in each row to inside corner at underarm; dec over next 2 rows, sc in each row to last row at wrist edge of sleeve [sk last row]. Work across last row of right sleeve, long edge of sleeve and side edge of right front as before; then rep from † to † across bottom edge of right front. Across center edge of right front, work sc in **next** row and in each row to last row at neck edge [sk last row]. Across neck edge, work 3 sc in first st (for corner), sc in each of next 5(5-7) sts; sc in next st and mark this st to be used later in joining hood, sc in each of next 6(8-8) sts; dec over next st and next row at first inside corner, sc in each of next 9 rows along right neck shaping; dec over next row and next st at 2nd inside corner, sc in each of next 19(21-25) sts along back neck edge; dec over next st and next row at 3rd inside corner, sc in each of next 10 rows along left neck shaping; dec over next row and next st at last inside corner, sc in each of next 6(6-8) sts, 3 sc in last st at left center neck edge (for corner). Work center edge of left front to correspond to center edge of right front; then work bottom edge of left front, side edge of left front and long edge of left sleeve as before. Join with a sl st in beg sc; finish off.

**Side and Sleeve Seams:** Thread lt gray heather into tapestry needle and with wrong sides tog, carefully match sts and sew seams with backstitching through **both** lps of corresponding sts (Fig 1) along side and sleeve edges. Be careful not to pull sts tightly as this will cause seam to pucker.

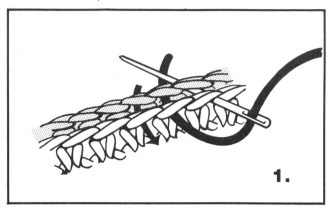

**1.**

**Granny Square Right Front Trim:** Following Granny Square instructions below, make 5 squares, using size H hook (or size required for 4½″ square) for size small garment; or size I hook (or size required for 4¾″ square) for sizes medium and large garments.

*GRANNY SQUARE*
With white, ch 3, join with a sl st to form a ring.

**Rnd 1:** Ch 4, 2 tr in ring, ch 1; * 3 tr in ring, ch 1; rep from * twice, join with a sl st in top of beg ch-4. Finish off.

**Rnd 2:** With right side facing, join lt gray heather with a sl st in any ch-1 sp; ch 3, work (2 dc, ch 1, 3 dc) all in same sp for beg corner; * work (3 dc, ch 1, 3 dc) all in next ch-1 sp for corner; rep from * twice, join with a sl st in top of beg ch-3.

**Rnd 3:** Sl st in each of next 2 dc and into ch-1 corner sp; ch 3, work (2 dc, ch 1, 3 dc) all in same sp, 3 dc between next two 3-dc groups for side; * work (3 dc, ch 1, 3 dc) all in next ch-1 corner sp, 3 dc between next two 3-dc groups for side; rep from * twice, join with a sl st in top of beg ch-3. Finish off.

**Rnd 4:** With right side facing, join charcoal gray with a sl st in any ch-1 corner sp; ch 3, work (2 dc, ch 1, 3 dc) all in same sp, 3 dc between each pair of 3-dc groups along side; * work (3 dc, ch 1, 3 dc) all in next ch-1 corner sp, 3 dc between each pair of 3-dc groups along side; rep from * twice, join with a sl st in top of beg ch-3.

**Rnd 5:** Ch 1, sc in same st as joining; sc in each of next 2 dc, * 3 sc in ch-1 corner sp, sc in each of next 12 dc; rep from * 3 times, ending last rep by working sc in each of last 9 dc, join with a sl st in beg sc. Finish off, weave in all yarn ends.

**Assembling:** Join 2 squares by holding squares with wrong sides tog. Carefully matching sts, with charcoal gray, beg in center st at one corner and sew with backstitching through **both** lps of corresponding sts across, ending in center st at next corner. Join rem squares in same manner to form a row of 5 squares. Before sewing joined squares to right front, lightly steam joinings and then work one rnd of edging as follows. Hold joined squares with right side facing and short edge across top. With same size hook used to make squares, join charcoal gray with a sl st in center st at upper right-hand corner. * Across short edge, work sc in each of next 14 sts to center st at next corner, 3 sc in next st. Across long edge, work sc in each of 14 sts along edge of each square and 2 sc at each joining, ending at center st at next corner, 3 sc in next st; rep from * once, join with a sl st in beg sc; finish off. With same sewing method used in side and sleeve seams and light gray heather, join long edge of joined motifs to center edge of right front.

### HOOD

**Note:** Remember to use smaller size hook unless otherwise specified.

Beg at top with lt gray heather, ch 92. **Row 1:** Work Patt Foundation Row = 91 sts. **Rows 2 through 9:** Work Patt Rows 1 and 2, four times. At end of last row, finish off; TURN for back shaping.

**Back Shaping: Row 1:** Sk first 36 sts, join lt gray heather with a sl st in next st [sc]; ch 1, sc in same st, sc in next dc; work (dc in next sc, sc in next dc) 8 times, sc in next sc = 19 sts [rem 36 sts are left unworked]. Beg with Patt Row 2 and work 4(12-24) rows even in patt, ending by working Patt Row 1. Now work Rows 1 through 8 of Shaping on Right Sleeve 3(2-1) time(s) = 7(11-15) sts.

**For small and medium sizes only:** Work Rows 1 through 7 of Shaping on Right Sleeve once = 3(7) sts; do not finish off, ch 1, TURN and work edging.

**For large size only:** Work Rows 1 through 3 of Shaping on Right Sleeve once = 13 sts; do not finish off, ch 1, TURN and work edging.

**Edging:** Across row just completed, work 3 sc in first st (for corner), sc in each of next 1(5-11) sts, 3 sc in last st (for corner). Across next 2 edges (on each side of inside corner), work sc in each of **next** 34 rows along side of back shaping, dec over last row and next st at inside corner; sc in each of next 34 sts, 3 sc in last st (for corner). Across next edge, work sc in each of next 8 rows. Across long front edge, work 3 sc in first st (for corner), sc in each st to last st, 3 sc in last st (for corner). Work across rem edges in same manner, join with a sl st in beg sc. Finish off.

**Granny Square Trim:** Following Granny Square instructions in Granny Square Right Front Trim, use size H hook (or size required for 4½ " square) for all sizes and make 6 squares. With charcoal gray, join squares in a row in same manner as right front trim. Lightly steam joinings; with lt gray heather, sew long front edge of hood to long edge of joined squares in same manner as side and sleeve seams, matching sts of hood [91 sts] to sts of joined squares [14 sts across each square and one st at each joining = 91 sts].

**Seams:** With same method used for sewing side and sleeve seams and lt gray heather, sew back seams of hood (see Fig 2). Then sew hood and neck seam aligning one center corner st of hood with center corner st at left center neck edge of jacket and other center corner st of hood with marked st on right neck edge of jacket, and omitting one st on each side of 4 seams on hood.

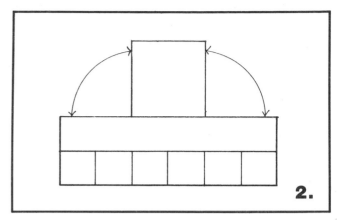

**2.**

### POCKET

Following Granny Square instructions in Granny Square Right Front Trim, use size H hook for all sizes and work Rnds 1 through 4 only; at end of last rnd, do not finish off.

**Rnd 5:** Continuing with charcoal gray, sl st in each of next 2 dc and into ch-1 corner sp; ch 3, work (2 dc, ch 1, 3 dc) all in same sp, 3 dc between each pair of 3-dc groups along side; * work (3 dc, ch 1, 3 dc) all in next ch-1 corner sp, 3 dc between each pair of 3-dc groups along side; rep from * twice, join with a sl st in top of beg ch-3.

**Rnd 6:** Rep Rnd 5; finish off.

**Rnd 7:** With right side facing, join charcoal gray with a sl st in any ch-1 corner sp; ch 1, 2 sc in same sp, sc in each st to next ch-1 corner sp; * work 3 sc in corner sp, sc in each st to next ch-1 corner sp; rep from * twice, ending sc in beg corner sp, join with a sl st in beg sc. Do not finish off; you will now begin edging.

**Edging:** Ch 1, working from **left** to **right** in reverse sc (see Chapter 8), work one st in each st around 3 sides, ending in first st at 3rd corner. Finish off. With charcoal gray, sew side edges of pocket to right front, aligning edge of pocket without reverse sc with bottom edge of right front; and side edge of pocket with side seam of jacket [bottom edges of pocket and right front will be joined later in reverse sc edging around jacket].

### FINISHING

**Edging and Button Loops:** With right side facing, join charcoal gray with a sl st in st at left neck edge, ch 1. Working from **left** to **right** in reverse sc, work one st in each st around hood and right neck edge to 3-sc group at outer corner of granny square at right neck edge. Work button loop as follows: work (sl st, ch 10, sl st) all in next sc; then sl st back across 10 chs just made, sl st in same sc [at base of button loop]. * Ch 1, continuing in reverse sc, work one st in each st to first st at joining of squares along right front trim; work button loop in next st; rep from * 3 times, ch 1; continuing in reverse sc, work one st in each st around rem edges of jacket, joining bottom edges of pocket and right front tog; join with a sl st in beg ch-1. Finish off, weave in all yarn ends. Sew on buttons; sew snap fastener to left neck edge and to joining at neck edge of right front and granny square trim.

# STRIPED T-TOP

*designed by Doris England*

| SIZES: | Small | Large |
|---|---|---|
| Body Bust: | 33″ | 37″ |
| **Garment Measurements:** | | |
| bust | 38″ | 42″ |
| length to underarm | 10″ | 11″ |

**Size Note:** Instructions are the same for both sizes; size difference is achieved by changing hook sizes. Refer to **Materials** and **Gauge** for recommended hook size and specified gauge.

**MATERIALS:** Sport weight yarn, 8(10) oz light rust and 6(8) oz off white; aluminum crochet hook size F for small size garment or size G for large size garment (or size required for gauge).

**Materials Note:** Change in yarn requirements for large size appears in parentheses.

**GAUGE:** For small size:
   with size F hook, in Stripe Patt,
      13 sts = 3″; 13 rows = 3″
   with size F hook, one Square = 2¼″
For large size:
   with size G hook, in Stripe Patt,
      12 sts = 3″; 12 rows = 3″
   with size G hook, one Square = 2½″

## INSTRUCTIONS

**Note:** Use size F hook for small size garment or size G hook for large size garment (or size required for gauge) throughout patt.

*FRONT*
*Diagonal Granny Section*
*Square (make 8)*
With rust, ch 3, join with a sl st to form a ring.

**Rnd 1 (right side):** Pull up lp on hook to measure ½″; * work cluster as follows: (YO, insert hook in ring and draw up ½″ lp) 3 times: [7 lps now on hook]; YO and draw through all 7 lps, ch 1: cluster made; rep from * 7 times more, join with a sl st in top of beg cluster = 8 clusters.

**Rnd 2:** Ch 3, work (2 dc, ch 1, 2 dc) all in next sp between clusters, * dc in top of next cluster; dc in next sp between clusters, dc in top of next cluster; work (2 dc, ch 1, 2 dc) all in next sp between clusters; rep from * twice, dc in top of next cluster, dc in last sp between clusters, join with a sl st in top of beg ch-3.

**Rnd 3:** Sl st into next sp between ch 3 and dc; ch 2, hdc in next sp between dc; * work (2 hdc, ch 2, 2 hdc) all in ch-1 corner sp, hdc in each of next 6 sps between dc along side; rep from * 3 times, ending last rep by working hdc in each of last 4 sps between dc along last side, join with a sl st in top of beg ch-2. Finish off, weave in yarn ends.

*Half Square (make 2)*
With rust, ch 3, join with a sl st to form a ring.

**Row 1 (right side):** Pull up lp on hook to measure ½″; work 4 clusters in ring.

**Row 2:** Ch 2, **turn**; 2 dc in top of first cluster, dc in next sp between clusters; 2 dc in top of next cluster, work (2 dc, ch 1, 2 dc) all in next sp between clusters for corner;

2 dc in top of next cluster, dc in next sp between clusters, 3 dc in top of last cluster.

**Row 3:** Ch 1, **turn**; 2 hdc in sp between first 2 dc, hdc in each of next 6 sps between dc; work (2 hdc, ch 2, 2 hdc) all in ch-1 corner sp, hdc in each of next 6 sps between dc, 2 hdc in Tch sp. Finish off, weave in yarn ends.

**Joining Squares:** Refer to Fig 1 for positioning of squares. Join squares by holding 2 squares with right sides tog. Carefully matching sts and working in **outer lps only**, with rust, beg in ch st at one corner and sl st LOOSELY across, ending in ch st at next corner. Weave in all loose yarn ends. Lightly steam press joinings.

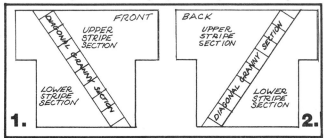

*Diagonal Stripe Sections*
Both sections are worked in the following pattern stitch.
*Stripe Pattern* With white, ch 3.

**Patt Row 1:** Work 2 hdc in 3rd ch from hook.

**Note:** You will be increasing 2 hdc on each following row.

**Patt Row 2:** Ch 1, turn; 2 hdc in sp between first 2 hdc, hdc in next sp between hdc and ch 3; hdc in same sp changing to rust as follows: work hdc until there are 3 lps on hook, drop white but do not cut [color not in use is carried along edge of garment]; with rust, YO and draw through all 3 lps = 4 hdc.

**Patt Row 3:** Continuing with rust, ch 1, turn; 2 hdc in sp between first 2 hdc, hdc in each sp between hdcs across, ending 2 hdc in Tch sp.

**Patt Row 4:** Rep Patt Row 3, changing to white in last hdc.

**Patt Row 5:** Continuing with white, ch 1, turn; 2 hdc in sp between first 2 hdc, hdc in each sp between hdcs across, ending 2 hdc in Tch sp.

**Patt Row 6:** Rep Patt Row 5, changing to rust in last hdc. [At end of first 6 rows, you should have 12 hdc.]
Rep Patt Rows 3 through 6 for stripe patt.

*Lower Stripe Section* **Note:** This section is begun as two pieces, which are then joined.

**Sleeve Piece:** Beg at lower outer edge of sleeve and work Stripe Patt until 9 stripes (18 rows) have been completed = 36 hdc. Finish off and mark last hdc worked with a small safety pin or a piece of contrasting yarn.

**Body Piece:** Beg at bottom side edge and work Stripe Patt until 13 stripes (26 rows) have been completed = 52 hdc. Do not finish off. **Joining Row:** Working across body piece and continuing with rust, ch 1, turn; 2 hdc in sp between first 2 hdc, hdc in each sp between hdcs across, ending 2 hdc in Tch sp [you should have 54 hdc]; working across sleeve piece, work 2 hdc in sp between marked hdc and next hdc, hdc in each sp between hdcs across, ending 2 hdc in Tch sp. You should now have 92 hdc. Beg with Patt Row 4 and work 7 more rows in Stripe Patt = 106 hdc.

**Shaping: Note:** Continue working in sps between sts and in Tch sps as before.

**Row 1:** Continuing with rust, ch 1, turn; 2 hdc in first sp, hdc in each sp across to last 2 sps, decrease over last 2 sps as follows: YO, insert hook in first sp and draw up a lp (3 lps now on hook); insert hook in next sp and draw up a lp (4 lps now on hook); YO and draw through all lps on hook—dec made = 106 sts. **Row 2:** Ch 1, turn; dec over first 2 sps as before, hdc in each sp across to last sp, 2 hdc in last sp changing to white = 106 sts. **Row 3:** Continuing with white, rep Row 1. **Row 4:** Rep Row 2, changing to rust in last hdc. Rep last 4 rows once more; finish off.

Refer to Fig 1 and with rust, join last row of section just worked to Diagonal Granny Section as follows. Hold sections tog with wrong side of Diagonal Granny Section facing you. Carefully match sts [on Diagonal Granny Section, use 10 sts across each square and 2 sts at each joining] and with rust sl st LOOSELY across, working in **outer lps only** of corresponding sts.

*Upper Stripe Section*
**Note:** Section is worked in one piece.

Beg at top outer edge of sleeve and work Stripe Patt until 13 stripes (26 rows) have been completed = 52 hdc. Outer edge of sleeve is completed; you will now shape bottom edge of sleeve.

**Shaping: Note:** Continue working in sps between sts and in Tch sps as before. **Row 1:** Continuing with rust, ch 1, turn; 2 hdc in first sp, hdc in each sp across to last 2 sps, dec over last 2 sps = 52 sts. **Row 2:** Ch 1, turn; dec over first 2 sps, hdc in each sp across, ending 2 hdc in Tch sp changing to white = 52 sts. **Row 3:** Continuing with white, rep Row 1. **Row 4:** Rep Row 2, changing to rust in last hdc. Rep last 4 rows, 3 times; then rep Rows 1 and 2 once more = 9 stripes (18 rows). Now beg with Patt Row 5 and work in Stripe Patt for 13 more stripes (26 rows). Side edge and bottom edge of sleeve have now been completed and you should have 104 sts. Continue with bottom edge shaping and work Rows 1 through

4 of Shaping [Upper Stripe Section]. Finish off and join to opposite edge of Diagonal Granny Section in same manner as other section omitting first and last st on Diagonal Granny Section.

*BACK*
Work sections same as for Front; refer to Fig 2 for positioning of squares and sections and join in same manner as before.

**Seams:** Join shoulder seams by holding Front and Back with right sides tog and carefully matching sts, use rust and sl st LOOSELY in **inner lps only** of corresponding sts across 15 stripes for one shoulder seam and across 5 stripes on neck side of Diagonal Granny Section, Diagonal Granny Section and 4 stripes of sleeve for other shoulder seam. Join side and sleeve seams in same manner.

**Sleeve and Neck Edgings:** With right side facing and working in sps between sts, work one rnd with rust in reverse sc (see Chapter 8) around neck and sleeve edges.

**Waistband:** With right side facing, join rust with a sl st at either side seam. **Rnd 1:** Ch 2 (counts as first hdc of rnd), work hdc in each row across stripes, 10 hdc across each Diagonal Granny Section and 2 hdc at each side seam, join with a sl st in top of beg ch-2 = 114 hdc (counting ch 2). **Rnd 2:** Ch 1, turn; work hdc in each sp between sts around, join with a sl st in beg ch-1. **Rnd 3:** Rep Rnd 2. **Rnd 4 (beading row):** Ch 2, turn; dc in first sp, ch 1, sk 1 sp; * dc in each of next 2 sps, ch 1, sk 1 sp; rep from * around, join with a sl st in top of beg ch-2. **Rnd 5:** Ch 1, turn; work hdc in each sp between dc and 2 hdc in each ch-1 sp around, join with a sl st in beg ch-1. **Rnd 6:** Rep Rnd 2. **Rnd 7:** Ch 1, turn; working from left to right in sps between hdc, work one rnd in reverse sc, join with a sl st in beg ch-1. Finish off, weave in yarn ends.

**Drawstring:** With 2 strands of white held tog, make a chain to measure approx 56(60)" or desired length. Beg at right side seam and weave drawstring through ch-1 sps in Beading Row. Fringe ends of chain if desired.

## FINISHING

**Blocking:** Place Back and Front pieces out flat on a padded surface, right sides down; lightly steam press, being careful not to stretch work. Allow to dry thoroughly before picking up.

**Front and Back Edging:** Before sewing side, sleeve and shoulder seams, work edging on both Front and Back pieces as follows. With right side facing, hold piece with side edge across top and bottom edge to your right; join rust with a sl st at upper right-hand corner, ch 1; work 3 hdc across each of first 12 stripes along side edge; across next 2 white stripes (4 rows) at underarm [do not work in rust stripe between white stripes], work hdc in each of next 2 rows, work dec in same row as last hdc and in next row, hdc in same row where dec was completed and in next row; work 3 hdc across each of next 8 stripes to lower outside corner of sleeve, 3 hdc in corner st; work 3 hdc across each of next 13 stripes to upper outer corner of sleeve, 3 hdc in corner st; across top edge, work 3 hdc across each stripe and 15 hdc across Diagonal Granny Section; then work rem edges as before, ending at bottom corner of other side edge [bottom edge is left unworked]; finish off.

# PULLOVER T-SWEATER

*designed by Doris England*

| SIZES: | Small | Medium | Large |
|---|---|---|---|
| **Body Bust:** | 32″ | 34″ | 36″ |
| **Garment Measurements:** | | | |
|   bust | 35″ | 37½″ | 40″ |
|   length from bottom | | | |
|     edge to shoulder | 25″ | 26¾″ | 28½″ |

**Size Note:** Instructions are the same for all sizes; size difference is achieved by changing hook sizes. Refer to **Materials** and **Gauge** for recommended hook size and specified gauge.

**MATERIALS: Unger's Fluffy yarn** in 1¾ oz balls, 6(8-10) rust; **Unger's Roly-Sport yarn** in 1¾ oz balls, 4(6-8) ecru; aluminum crochet hook **size G for size small garment, size H for size medium garment, or size I for size large garment** (or size required for gauge).

**GAUGE:** For small size:
    with size G hook and rust yarn,
      one Small Square = 8″
    For medium size:
    with size H hook and rust yarn,
      one Small Square = 8½″
    For large size:
    with size I hook and rust yarn,
      one Small Square = 9″

## INSTRUCTIONS

*SMALL SQUARE (make 12)*
With rust ch 6, join with a sl st to form a ring.

**Rnd 1:** Work a **beg cluster** in ring as follows: ch 2, keeping last lp of each st on hook, work 2 dc (3 lps now on hook—*Fig 1*), YO and draw through all 3 lps (beg cluster made); * ch 2, work a **cluster** in ring as follows: keeping last lp of each st on hook, work 3 dc (4 lps now on hook); YO and draw through all 4 lps (cluster made); rep from * 6 times, ch 2, join with a sl st in top of beg cluster = 8 clusters.

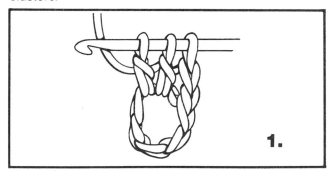

1.

**Rnd 2:** Sl st into next ch-2 sp; for first corner, work (beg cluster, ch 2, cluster) all in same sp; * for side, ch 2, 3 dc in next ch-2 sp, ch 2; for corner, work (cluster, ch 2, cluster) in next ch-2 sp; rep from * twice; for last side, ch 2, 3 dc in last ch-2 sp, **ch 1,** join with a sl st in top of beg cluster.

**Rnd 3:** Sl st into next ch-2 sp; in same sp, work beg corner as before; * for side, ch 2, 2 dc in next ch-2 sp, dc in each dc to next ch-2 sp, 2 dc in next ch-2 sp, ch 2; in next ch-2 sp, work corner as before; rep from * twice; for last side, ch 2, 2 dc in next ch-2 sp, dc in each dc to

last sp, 2 dc in last sp, **ch 1,** join with a sl st in top of beg cluster = 7 dc along each side.

**Rnd 4:** Rep Rnd 3 = 11 dc along each side.

**Rnd 5:** Rep Rnd 3 = 15 dc along each side.

**Rnd 6:** Rep Rnd 3 = 19 dc along each side. Finish off rust.

**Rnd 7:** With right side facing, join ecru with a sl st in any corner sp, ch 2 (counts as hdc); 2 hdc in same sp; * hdc in top of cluster, 2 hdc in ch-2 sp, hdc in each of next 19 dc; 2 hdc in ch-2 sp, hdc in top of cluster, 3 hdc in corner sp; rep from * 3 times, ending last rep by joining with a sl st in top of beg ch-2.

**Rnd 8:** Working in each sp between hdcs around, sl st into next sp, ch 2, * 2 hdc in next sp, hdc in each sp to 3-hdc group at corner, hdc in next sp; rep from * 3 times, ending last rep by joining with a sl st in top of beg ch-2. Finish off, weave in yarn ends.

**Joining Squares:** Join squares for two sleeve/yoke sections. Each section is 2 squares wide by 3 squares long. To join squares, hold 2 squares with right sides tog. Carefully matching sts, with ecru, beg in one ch st of corner and sl st LOOSELY across, working in **inner lps only** across corresponding sts, ending in ch st at next corner.

*LARGE SQUARE (make 2)*
Follow instructions for Small Square and work Rnds 1 through 6; at end of last rnd, do not finish off.

**Rnds 7 through 11:** Rep Rnd 3 (in Small Square instructions) five times. At end of last rnd, you should have 39 dc along each side. Finish off, weave in yarn ends. Now work triangular piece in rows across each side of square as follows. Hold square with right side facing and join ecru with a sl st in any corner sp.

**Row 1:** Ch 2, hdc in top of cluster, hdc in ch-2 sp, hdc in each of next 39 dc; hdc in ch-2 sp, hdc in top of cluster, hdc in corner sp = 45 hdc (counting ch 2).

**Row 2:** Ch 1, **turn**; working in each sp between hdcs across, decrease (dec) over first 2 sps as follows: YO, insert hook in first sp and draw up a lp, insert hook in next sp and draw up a lp (4 lps now on hook), YO and draw through all 4 lps (dec made); hdc in each sp across to last 2 sps, work a dec as before = 42 sts.

**Row 3:** Ch 1, **turn**; working in each sp between sts across and in Tch sp, dec over first 2 sps, hdc in each sp across to last 2 sps, dec over last 2 sps = 40 sts.

**Rows 4 through 21:** Rep Row 3, eighteen times. At end of last row, you should have 4 sts (you will be decreasing 2 sts each row).

**Row 22:** Ch 1, **turn**; (dec over 2 sps) twice = 2 sts.

**Row 23:** Ch 1, **turn**; dec over rem 2 sps, finish off.

Work rem 3 sides of square in same manner. At end of last side, do not finish off; work edging on right side.

**Edging: Rnd 1:** Ch 2 (counts as hdc), * work 28 hdc evenly spaced to corner sp of rust square, 2 hdc in corner sp; work 28 hdc evenly spaced to corner, work 3 hdc in st at corner; rep from * 3 times, ending last rep by working 2 hdc in st at last corner, join with a sl st in top of beg ch-2. **Rnd 2:** Working in each sp between hdcs, sl st into next sp, ch 2; * hdc in each sp to 3-hdc corner

*(Shown in color
on the book jacket.)*

group, hdc in next sp, 2 hdc in next sp; rep from * 3 times, join with a sl st in top of beg ch-2. Finish off.

**Joining Squares:** Hold squares with right sides tog; with ecru, use same joining method and join squares for body section at opposite edges (side seams) leaving 16 sts open at same end on each side for bottom slits.

*FINISHING*

**Assembling:** With same joining method and ecru, refer to Fig 2 and join sleeve/yoke section to body section aligning 2 squares on sleeve/yoke section with half of

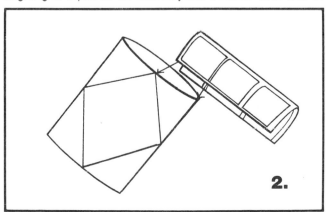

**2.**

each square on body section [on each side of side seam], leaving center st of each square on body section free. Join other sleeve/yoke section in same manner. Then join rem squares of sleeve/yoke sections for sleeve seams.

**Neck Edging:** With right side facing and working in each sp between sts, join ecru with a sl st in sp at either shoulder. **Rnd 1:** Ch 2, * work hdc in each sp to within 3 sps of center st of body (left unworked in joining), dec 3 times; rep from * once, hdc in each rem sp, join with a sl st in top of beg ch-2. **Rnd 2:** Ch 1, working from **left** to **right** in reverse sc (see Chapter 8), * work one st in each st to first dec at center neck edge, sk one st, work one st in next st, sk one st; rep from * once, work one st in each rem st, join with a sl st in beg ch-1. Finish off.

**Bottom Edging:** With right side facing, join ecru with a sl st at either side seam, ch 1; working in reverse sc, work one st in each st around, join with a sl st in beg ch-1. Finish off.

**Sleeve Edging (make 2):** With right side facing, join ecru with a sl st at seam, ch 1; working in reverse sc, work one st in each st around, join with a sl st in beg sc. Finish off, weave in all yarn ends. Lightly steam press garment on wrong side.

# TABARD

*designed by Barbara Retzke*

**SIZE: Garment measures approx 16″ wide x 26″ long**

**MATERIALS: Sport weight yarn, 10 oz medium blue; aluminum crochet hook size E (or size required for gauge).**

**GAUGE: One Motif = 4″ square**

## INSTRUCTIONS

*MOTIF (make 50)*

Ch 5, join with a sl st to form a ring.

**Rnd 1:** Make a beg cluster as follows: Ch 3, † YO, insert hook in ring and draw up ½″ lp, YO and draw through 2 lps on hook †; YO and draw through 2 lps now on hook (beg cluster made). * Ch 2, make a cluster as follows: Rep from † to † twice, YO and draw through 3 lps now on hook (cluster made); rep from * 6 times more, ch 2, join with a sl st in top of beg cluster = 8 clusters.

**Rnd 2:** Sl st into next ch-2 sp, ch 1; in same sp, work (sc, ch 9, sc); * ch 4, sc in next ch-2 sp, ch 4; in next ch-2 sp, work (sc, ch 9, sc); rep from * twice, ch 4, sc in last ch-2 sp, ch 4, join with a sl st in beg sc.

**Rnd 3:** Sl st in each of first 3 chs of ch-9 and then into ch-9 sp, ch 3; in same sp, work (4 dc, ch 2, 9 dc) for petal; * sc in next ch-4 sp, ch 9, sc in next ch-4 sp; in next ch-9 sp, work (9 dc, ch 2, 9 dc) for petal; rep from * twice, sc in next ch-4 sp, ch 9, sc in next ch-4 sp; in beg ch-9 sp, work 4 dc over beg sl sts, join with a sl st in top of beg ch-3.

**Rnd 4:** * Ch 4, work (sc, ch 3, sc) in ch-2 sp at tip of petal; ch 4, sl st in 5th dc from tip; ch 3, sl st in 5th ch of ch-9; ch 3, sl st in 5th dc of next petal; rep from * 3 times, ending last rep by joining with a sl st in first ch of beg ch-4.

**Rnd 5:** Sl st into next ch-4 sp, ch 3, work 3 more dc in same sp; * work (2 dc, ch 3, 2 dc) in ch-3 sp at tip of petal; work 4 dc in each of next four ch sps; rep from * 3 times, ending last rep by working 4 dc in each of last three ch sps, join with a sl st in top of beg ch-3. Finish off, weave in yarn ends.

### ASSEMBLING

Arrange motifs as shown in Fig 1. Join motifs in rows; use joining method 5 in Chapter 8, beg and ending in ch st of corners leaving center corner ch sts free. With same method, join rows sewing matching center corner ch sts of motifs at each four-corner junction.

### TIE (make 2)

Make a chain to measure 24″; then work hdc in 3rd ch from hook and in each rem ch across. Finish off, weave in yarn ends. Insert one tie on each side of tabard through matching sps of motifs at waistline.

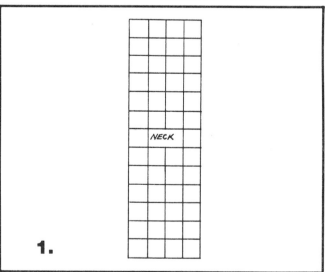

**1.**

# BEACH COVER-UP

*designed by Mary Thomas*

**SIZE:** Garment measures 21″ across front at under-arms and 26″ from bottom edge to shoulder, and will fit women's dress sizes 8-18.

**MATERIALS:** Bucilla Perlette yarn in 1¾ oz balls, 10 bright yellow; aluminum crochet hook size F (or size required for gauge).

**GAUGE:** One Square = 5¼″

## INSTRUCTIONS

*SQUARE (make 54)*
Ch 6, join with a sl st to form a ring.

**Rnd 1:** Work a **beg cluster** in ring as follows: ch 3, keeping last lp of each st on hook, work 2 dc (3 lps now on hook—*Fig 1*), YO and draw through all 3 lps (beg cluster made); * ch 3, work a **cluster** in ring as follows: keeping last lp of each st on hook, work 3 dc; YO and draw through all 4 lps (cluster made); rep from * 6 times, ch 3, join with a sl st in top of beg ch-3 = 8 clusters.

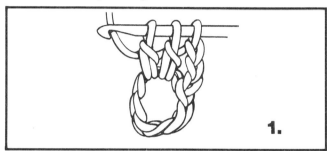

**1.**

**Rnd 2:** Sl st in top of beg cluster and into ch-3 sp; work (beg cluster, ch 4, cluster) all in same sp for beg corner; * ch 2, 2 dc in next ch-3 sp, ch 2; work (cluster, ch 4, cluster) all in next ch-3 sp for corner; rep from * twice, ch 2, 2 dc in last ch-3 sp, ch 2, join as before.

**Rnd 3:** Sl st in top of beg cluster and into corner sp; work (beg cluster, ch 4, cluster) in same sp; * ch 2, dc in next ch-2 sp; dc in each of next 2 dc, dc in next ch-2 sp; ch 2, work (cluster, ch 4, cluster) in next corner sp; rep from * twice, ch 2, dc in next ch-2 sp; dc in each of next 2 dc, dc in last ch-2 sp, ch 2, join.

**Rnd 4:** Sl st in top of beg cluster and into corner sp; work (beg cluster, ch 4, cluster) in same sp; * ch 2, work (dc, ch 1, dc) all in next ch-2 sp; dc in each of next 4 dc, work (dc, ch 1, dc) in next ch-2 sp; ch 2, work (cluster, ch 4, cluster) in next corner sp; rep from * twice, ch 2, work (dc, ch 1, dc) in next ch-2 sp; dc in each of next 4 dc, work (dc, ch 1, dc) in last ch-2 sp, ch 2, join.

**Rnd 5:** Sl st in top of beg cluster and into corner sp; work (beg cluster, ch 4, cluster) in same sp; * ch 2, work (dc in next ch sp, ch 1) twice; sk one dc, dc in each of next 4 dc; sk one dc, work (ch 1, dc in next ch sp) twice; ch 2, work (cluster, ch 4, cluster) in next corner sp; rep from * twice, ch 2, work (dc in next ch sp, ch 1) twice; sk one dc, dc in each of next 4 dc; sk one dc, work (ch 1, dc in next ch sp) twice, ch 2, join.

**Rnd 6:** Sl st in top of beg cluster and into corner sp; work (beg cluster, ch 4, cluster) in same sp; * ch 3, work (dc in next ch sp, ch 1) 3 times; sk one dc, dc in each of next 2 dc; sk one dc, work (ch 1, dc in next ch sp) 3 times; ch 3, work (cluster, ch 4, cluster) in next corner sp; rep from *

twice, ch 3, work (dc in next ch sp, ch 1) 3 times; sk one dc, dc in each of next 2 dc; sk one dc, work (ch 1, dc in next ch sp) 3 times, ch 3, join. Finish off, weave in ends.

*ASSEMBLING*
Join squares as shown in Fig 2 using joining method 5 in Chapter 8. After all squares have been joined, fold garment in half at shoulders; use same joining method and sew squares tog for side and sleeve seams.

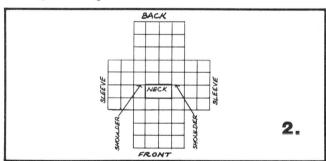

**2.**

**Neck Edging:** Hold garment with right side facing and two squares at back neck edge across top; join yarn with a sl st in right-hand corner sp. **Rnd 1:** Work a beg cluster in same sp as joining, ch 2; work (cluster, ch 2) in each sp across edges and in each of 3 corner sps at each inside corner, join with a sl st in top of beg cluster. **Rnd 2:** Ch 1, working from **left** to **right** in reverse sc (see Chapter 8), work one st in top of each cluster and in each ch-2 sp around, join with a sl st in beg sc. Finish off.

**Bottom Edging:** With right side facing, join yarn with a sl st in corner sp of any square. **Rnd 1:** Work beg cluster in same sp, ch 2; work (cluster, ch 2) in each sp around, join with a sl st in top of beg cluster. **Rnd 2:** Rep Rnd 2 of Neck Edging.

**Sleeve Edging (make 2):** Follow instructions for Bottom Edging.

**Tie:** With 2 strands of yarn held tog, make a chain to measure approx 60″. Beg at center front neck edge and weave chain through clusters around edge; knot each end of chain.

*(Shown in color on page 75.)*

# BED JACKET

*designed by Mary Thomas*

**SIZE:** Garment measures 21″ across back at underarms and will fit women's dress sizes 8-18. Sleeve and body lengths can be adjusted.

**MATERIALS:** Sport weight yarn, 16 oz white and 1 oz orange; aluminum crochet hook size D (or size required for gauge).

**GAUGE:** One Square = 3″

## INSTRUCTIONS

*SQUARE (make 10)*

**Note:** All rnds are worked on right side.

With orange, ch 5, join with a sl st to form a ring.

**Rnd 1:** Ch 3, work 15 dc in ring, join with a sl st to form a ring.

**Rnd 2:** Ch 2, work (hdc, ch 1, 2 hdc) in same st as joining; * ch 1, sk one dc, work (2 hdc, ch 1, 2 hdc) in next dc; rep from * around, ch 1, sk last dc, join with a sl st in top of beg ch-2. Finish off orange.

**Rnd 3:** With right side facing, join white with a sl st in any ch-2 sp over sk dc of prev rnd; work beg cluster in same sp as follows: Ch 3, † YO, insert hook in ch-1 sp and draw up ½″ lp, YO and draw through 2 lps on hook †; rep from † to † once more, YO and draw through 3 lps now on hook (beg cluster made). * Ch 2, make a cluster in next ch-1 sp as follows: Rep from † to † 3 times, YO and draw through 4 lps now on hook (cluster made); rep from * around, ch 2, join with a sl st in top of beg cluster = 16 clusters.

**Rnd 4:** Sl st into next ch-2 sp, ch 3; work (2 dc, ch 2, 3 dc) all in same sp for beg corner; * ch 1, (2 sc in next ch-2 sp, ch 1) 3 times; work (3 dc, ch 2, 3 dc) all in next ch-2 sp for corner; rep from * twice, ch 1, (2 sc in next ch-2 sp, ch 1) 3 times, join with a sl st in top of beg ch-3. Finish off, weave in yarn ends.

*YOKE*

See Fig 1 for positioning of squares; then join squares using joining method 5 in Chapter 8. Then hold joined squares with right side facing you and 4 squares of front across top. Beg in square to left of center opening and join white with a sl st in upper right-hand corner sp.

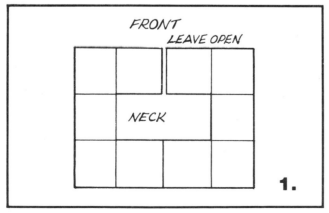

FRONT
LEAVE OPEN

NECK

**1.**

**Row 1:** Ch 3, 2 dc in same sp; * work 3 dc in each ch-1 sp and ch-2 corner sp along edge of squares to corner, work (3 dc, ch 2, 3 dc) in corner ch-2 sp; rep from * 3 times; work 3 dc in each ch-1 sp and ch-2 corner sp along last edge of squares, ending by working 3 dc in corner ch-2 sp at right front center opening.

**Row 2:** Ch 3, turn; * 3 dc between each pair of 3-dc groups along edge to corner sp, work (3 dc, ch 2, 3 dc) in corner ch-2 sp; rep from * 3 times; 3 dc between each pair of 3-dc groups along last edge, dc in top of ch-3 at center edge opening.

**Row 3:** Ch 3, turn; 2 dc in first sp (sp between last dc and 3-dc group of prev row), * 3 dc between each pair of 3-dc groups along edge to corner sp, work (3 dc, ch 2, 3 dc) in corner ch-2 sp; rep from * 3 times; 3 dc between each pair of 3-dc groups along last edge, ending 3 dc in sp under Tch at center edge opening.

**Rows 4 through 13:** Rep Rows 2 and 3, five times. At end of Row 13, do not finish off.

*BODY*

**Dividing Row:** Ch 3, turn; * 3 dc between each pair of 3-dc groups along edge to corner sp, 3 dc in corner ch-2 sp, ch 1; sk 3-dc groups along next edge to corner sp (for sleeve opening), 3 dc in corner ch-2 sp; rep from * once; 3 dc between each pair of 3-dc groups along last edge, dc in top of ch-3 at center edge opening.

**Row 1 (right side):** Ch 3, turn; 2 dc in first sp (sp between last dc and 3-dc group of prev row); * work 3 dc between each pair of 3-dc groups and each ch-1 sp at underarm across, ending 3 dc in sp under Tch at center edge opening.

**Row 2:** Ch 3, turn; 3 dc between each pair of 3-dc groups across, dc in top of ch-3 at center edge opening.

**Row 3:** Ch 3, turn; 2 dc in first sp, 3 dc between each pair of 3-dc groups across, ending 3 dc in sp under Tch at center edge opening.

Rep Rows 2 and 3 until piece measures approx 12″ from underarm or desired length. Finish off.

*SLEEVE (make 2)*

With wrong side facing you, join white with a sl st in ch-1 at underarm.

**Rnd 1:** Ch 3, 2 dc in same st, † 3 dc in ch-2 sp (same sp where 3-dc group was worked in Dividing Row of Body); † 3 dc between each pair of 3-dc groups around, rep from † to † once, join with a sl st in top of beg ch-3.

**Rnd 2:** TURN; sl st between beg and end 3 dc groups of prev rnd, ch 3; 2 dc in same sp; 3 dc between each pair of 3-dc groups around, join with a sl st in top of beg ch-3.

Rep Rnd 2 until sleeve measures approx 8″ from underarm or desired length. Finish off, weave in all yarn ends.

*FINISHING*

With orange, make a chain to measure approx 36″; weave through ch sps of last rnd of squares around neck edge. Make two 1½″ diameter orange pompons (see Pompon instructions in Chapter 8) and attach one pompon to each end of chain.

(Shown in color on page 76.)

# LACY SHAWL

*designed by Eleanor Denner*

**SIZE: Approx 70″ wide x 34″ deep before fringing**
**MATERIALS: Sport weight yarn, 10 oz white; aluminum crochet hook size H (or size required for gauge).**
**GAUGE: One Square = 3½″**

## PATTERN STITCHES

**Front Post Dc (abbreviated FPdc):** YO, insert hook from front to back around post of dc in row below (*Fig 1*); YO, draw yarn through and complete st as a dc.

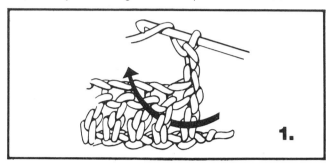

**Back Post Dc (abbreviated BPdc):** Same as FPdc, except hook is inserted from back to front (*Fig 2*).

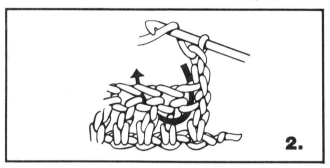

## INSTRUCTIONS

SQUARE (make 91)
Ch 4, join with a sl st to form a ring.

**Rnd 1 (wrong side):** Ch 3 (counts as first dc), work 11 dc in ring, join with a sl st in top of beg ch-3.

**Rnd 2:** Ch 3, do not turn; work FPdc around post of first dc [ch 3], * work (BPdc, FPdc) around post of next dc; rep from * 10 times, join with a sl st in top of beg ch-3.

**Rnd 3:** Ch 6, TURN; dc in same st as joining, * (ch 1, sk one st, dc in next st) twice; ch 1, sk one st, work (dc, ch 3, dc) all in next st for corner; rep from * twice; (ch 1, sk one st, dc in next st) twice; ch 1, sk last st, join with a sl st in 3rd ch of beg ch-6.

**Rnd 4:** Do not turn; sl st into ch-3 sp, ch 6, dc in same sp; * (ch 2, dc in next ch-1 sp) 3 times, ch 2, work (dc, ch 3, dc) all in next corner sp; rep from * twice; (ch 2, dc in next ch-1 sp) 3 times, ch 2, join with a sl st in 3rd ch of beg ch-6. Finish off, leaving 12″ sewing length.

HALF SQUARE (make 14)
Ch 4, join with a sl st to form a ring.

**Row 1 (wrong side):** Ch 3, work 5 dc in ring.

**Row 2:** Ch 3, **turn**; work FPdc around post of first dc, * work (FPdc, BPdc) around post of next dc; rep from * 3 times; work (FPdc, BPdc) around ch-3.

**Row 3:** Ch 4, **turn**; (dc in next st, ch 1, sk one st) twice, work (dc, ch 3, dc) all in next st for corner; (ch 1, sk one st, dc in next st) twice; ch 1, dc in top of Tch.

**Row 4:** Ch 5, **turn**; dc in first ch-1 sp, (ch 2, dc in next ch-1 sp) twice; ch 2, work (dc, ch 3, dc) in corner sp; (ch 2, dc in next ch-1 sp) twice; ch 2, dc in Tch sp, ch 2, dc in 3rd ch of Tch. Finish off, leaving 12″ sewing length.

ASSEMBLING
Use joining method 5 in Chapter 8 and join squares as shown in Fig 3, carefully matching each dc and each ch st.

EDGING
Hold shawl with right side facing and long edge across top. Join yarn with a sl st in st at upper left-hand corner, ch 1; 2 sc in same st as joining, † work (2 sc in next sp, sc in next dc) 4 times across square, sc in corner sp of same square; sc in sp at joining, sc in corner sp of next square, sc in next dc †; rep from † to † across side edge to square at tip of shawl; work (2 sc in next sp, sc in next dc) 4 times, 5 sc in next sp at tip of shawl, sc in next dc; rep from † to † across side edge to half square at long edge of shawl; work (2 sc in next sp, sc in next dc) 3 times, 2 sc in next sp, 2 sc in last st; * 2 sc in each of next 4 sps, sc in ring; 2 sc in each of next 4 sps, sc in corner sp of center square at joining; rep from * across long edge of shawl, ending last rep by joining with a sl st in beg sc. Finish off, weave in yarn ends.

FRINGING
Cut 12″ strands of yarn. Work Spaghetti Fringe as in Chapter 8 and knot one strand in each sc across each side edge of shawl.

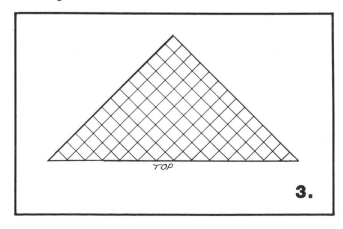

# SHAPED GRANNY STOLE

*designed by Eleanor Denner*

**MATERIALS: Worsted weight yarn, 28 oz brown, 16 oz beige, and 4 oz cream; aluminum crochet hook size I (or size required for gauge).**

**GAUGE: One Small Square (6 rnds) = 7″**
**One Large Square (18 rnds) = 21″**

## INSTRUCTIONS

### SMALL SQUARE (make 6)

With brown, ch 4, join with a sl st to form a ring.

**Rnd 1:** Ch 3, 2 dc in ring; (ch 2, 3 dc in ring) 3 times; ch 2, join with a sl st in 3rd ch of beg ch-3.

**Rnd 2:** Sl st across next 2 dc and into first ch-2 sp; ch 3, work (2 dc, ch 2, 3 dc) all in same sp; * in next ch-2 sp, work (3 dc, ch 2, 3 dc); rep from * twice, join with a sl st in 3rd ch of beg ch-3.

**Rnd 3:** Sl st across next 2 dc and into first ch-2 sp; ch 3, work (2 dc, ch 2, 3 dc) all in same sp for corner; * 3 dc between next two 3-dc groups; in next corner ch-2 sp, work (3 dc, ch 2, 3 dc); rep from * twice; 3 dc between next two 3-dc groups, join as before.

**Rnd 4:** Sl st across next 2 dc and into first ch-2 sp; ch 3, work (2 dc, ch 2, 3 dc) all in same sp for corner; * (3 dc between next two 3-dc groups) twice for side; in next corner ch-2 sp, work (3 dc, ch 2, 3 dc); rep from * twice; (3 dc between next two 3-dc groups) twice for side, join as before.

**Rnd 5:** Sl st across next 2 dc and into first ch-2 sp; ch 3, work (2 dc, ch 2, 3 dc) all in same sp for corner; * 3 dc between each 3-dc group along side; in next corner ch-2 sp, work (3 dc, ch 2, 3 dc); rep from * twice; 3 dc between each 3-dc group along side, join as before.

**Rnd 6:** Rep Rnd 5; at end, finish off yarn, weave in ends.

### LARGE SQUARE (make 3)

In this square, you will be changing colors on some rnds. For information on how to do this, see **Granny's Recipe** on page 6.

With cream, work Rnds 1, 2 and 3 same as for Small Square. Finish off cream.

Join beige and work Rnds 4 and 5 same as for Small Square. Finish off beige.

Join cream and work Rnd 6 as for Small Square. Finish off cream.

Continuing to work as for Rnd 6 of Small Square, work next rnds as follows: Rnds 7, 8 and 9, with beige; Rnds 10, 11 and 12, with brown; Rnd 13, with beige; Rnds 14 through 18, with brown. At end of Rnd 18, finish off brown, leaving a 30″ yarn end for sewing squares tog later.

### ASSEMBLING

First join Small Squares into two strips of 3 squares each. To join, hold two squares with right sides tog. Thread brown yarn into tapestry needle. Join yarn at upper right-hand corner sp, and sew with overcast st, carefully matching stitches, working in **outer lps only**. Lightly steam press joinings. Set aside.

Using same joining method and brown yarn, join large squares as shown in Fig 1. Then join strips of small squares as shown in same Fig, matching the sts on the smaller squares to the sts on the larger squares. Do not stitch too tightly.

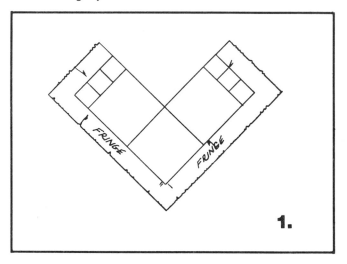

**1.**

### EDGING

Hold stole with right side of work facing you, and bottom edge of left front at top.

**Rnd 1:** Make a sl knot on hook and join cream with a sc in outer corner sp of top right square; work 2 more sc in same corner, sc in each st and joining across side, 3 sc in outer corner; continue in this manner around entire garment, always working 3 sc in outer corners; at V-shaped joining at center back of garment, adjust sts to keep work flat; join in first sc of rnd; finish off cream.

**Rnd 2:** With right side facing and beige, join yarn and sc in each sc around, working 3 sc in each outer corner sc. Finish off, weave in all yarn ends. Lightly steam press all joinings and edging.

### SPAGHETTI FRINGE

Cut brown yarn into 12″ lengths. Work Spaghetti Fringe (see Chapter 8) and tie one knot in each st around outer edges of stole.

# TEXTURED TOTEBAG

*designed by Eleanor Denner*

This striking bag is made of deeply textured squares, fashioned from popcorn stitches. You can make the shoulder-strap length, as we show it, or shorter if you desire.

**APPROX SIZE: 12″ wide by 15″ deep (without strap)**

**MATERIALS: Worsted weight yarn, 16 oz beige; aluminum crochet hook size H (or size required for gauge); pair of 12″ wooden dowel rods with wooden bead end-stops.**

**GAUGE: One Popcorn Square = 3″**
　　　　**In hdc for strap, 8 sts = 2″; 6 rows = 2″**

## INSTRUCTIONS

*POPCORN SQUARE (make 40)*

Ch 4, join with a sl st to make a ring.

**Rnd 1:** Ch 2, hdc in ring; work Popcorn (abbreviated PC) in ring as follows: work 5 dc, drop lp from hook, insert hook in top of first dc made, and then into dropped lp *(Fig 1)*; YO and draw through both lps on hook: PC made; (2 hdc in ring, PC in ring) 3 times; join with a sl st in top of beg ch-2.

**Rnd 2:** Ch 2, 2 hdc in same ch as joining; 3 hdc in next hdc, work PC in top of PC *(Fig 2)*; (3 hdc in each of next 2 hdc, work PC in top of PC) 3 times; join with a sl st in top of beg ch-2.

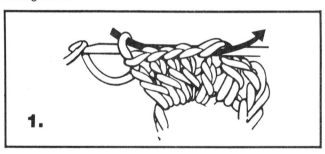

**1.**

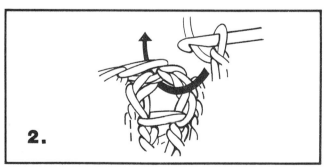

**2.**

**Rnd 3:** Ch 2, 2 hdc in next hdc; (hdc in next hdc, 2 hdc in next hdc) twice; work PC in top of PC; * (hdc in next hdc, 2 hdc in next hdc) 3 times; work PC in top of next PC; rep from * twice, join with a sl st in top of beg ch-2. Finish off, leaving an 8″ yarn end for later joining of squares.

## ASSEMBLING

Place two squares with right sides tog, and 8″ yarn end from one square in upper right-hand corner. Thread yarn end into tapestry needle. Working in **back (outer) lps only** of each st, overcast from top of PC in right-hand corner of square across hdcs and into top of PC in left-hand corner of square, carefully matching sts. Finish off,

weave in yarn end. In same manner, join additional squares until there are 5 in a strip. Make a total of 8 strips; then in same manner, being sure to match corners and sts carefully, join 4 strips for front and 4 strips for back. You should now have two pieces, each 4 squares wide and 5 squares high. Weave in all loose yarn ends.

## GUSSET AND STRAP

Ch 10.

**Row 1:** Hdc in 3rd ch from hook and in each rem ch across = 9 hdc (counting beg 2 chs as hdc).

**Row 2:** Ch 2, turn; hdc in next hdc and in each hdc across = 9 hdc.

Rep Row 2 until piece measures 63″ for shoulder bag, or 50″ for hand bag. Finish off. Place two short ends of piece tog, and weave edges tog so that piece forms a circle.

## ASSEMBLING

Hold back of bag with wrong side facing you, and long edge across top. Place joined seam of strap at top of outer PC on square at right-hand edge. Holding strap flat across top of back piece, join the two pieces with sc, carefully matching each st in PC squares with rows on strap (adjust spacing of sc sts on strap rows as needed to keep work flat). Continue joining in same manner across this first side, across bottom and up other side of back piece; then continue working sc along strap edge only, join with a sl st in sc where you first began; finish off.

Hold front of bag with wrong side facing you, and long edge across top. Place free edge of strap against front piece and join in same manner as before, working around 3 sides; then continue sc around edge of strap only, join with a sl st in sc where you first began; finish off. Weave in yarn ends.

*ATTACHING DOWELS*
Hold bag with open edge at top. Join yarn at outer top right-hand corner. Working over rod, sc loosely in each st across tops of squares. Finish off. Work in same manner to attach rod on opposite side. Glue wooden bead end-stops to each end of each dowel rod.

# NEEDLEWORK BAG
*designed by Eleanor Denner*

**SIZE: Approx 15½″ wide x 10½″ deep without handles**

**MATERIALS: Worsted weight yarn, 10 oz ombre in shades of white/yellow/red/green, 4 oz green; aluminum crochet hook size F (or size required for gauge); approx 1 lb polyester filling for stuffing; wooden handle set, 12″ wide.**

**GAUGE: One Granny Square = 2″**

## INSTRUCTIONS
*GRANNY SQUARE (make 136)*

With ombre, ch 4, join with a sl st to form a ring.

**Rnd 1:** Ch 3, 2 dc in ring; ch 1, work (3 dc in ring, ch 1) 3 times, join with a sl st in top of beg ch-3.

**Rnd 2:** Sl st in each of next 2 dc and into ch-1 sp, ch 3; work (2 dc, ch 1, 3 dc) all in same sp; * work (3 dc, ch 1, 3 dc) all in next ch-1 sp; rep from * twice, join with a sl st in top of beg ch-3. Finish off, weave in yarn ends.

**Note:** The following Puff and Half Puff Squares are constructed from the previously made Granny Squares.

*PUFF SQUARE (make 66)*

Hold 2 squares with wrong sides tog; join green with a sl st in any ch-1 corner sp. Carefully matching sts and working in 2 lps of each st across both squares, ch 1; * work 3 sc in corner sp, sc in each dc across to next corner; rep from * twice [3 sides now joined]; stuff with polyester filling, then rep from * once more, join with a sl st in beg sc; finish off, weave in yarn ends.

*HALF PUFF SQUARE (make 4)*

Hold one square folded in half diagonally with right side facing you; beg with fold at your right. Join green with a sl st in corner sp at top of fold; ch 1, work in same manner as full square; beg stuffing when you reach next corner sp, continuing to stuff as you work across last side; finish off, weave in yarn ends.

*ASSEMBLING AND JOINING*

Arrange squares for front and back as shown in photo. To join 2 puff squares, join green with a sl st in center sc at any corner, ch 1; carefully matching sts and working in 2 lps of each st across both squares, sl st in each sc across ending in center sc of next corner. Join addi-

HALF SQUARES

tional squares to form a row in same manner; join each following row in same manner, working across all squares to end of row. The side where all joining is made will be wrong side of work. When all puff squares have been joined, hold front and back with wrong sides facing, with short end across top and half square at upper right hand corner, join green with a sl st in corner of first full square [to your left of half square]; ch 1, sc in same st; carefully matching sts and working in 2 lps of each st across both pieces, work (sc in each st across to corner; work 3 sc in corner st) twice, sc in each st across rem 4 full squares [do not work into half square]; finish off, weave in yarn ends.

*FINISHING*

Sew each handle [to front and back] with tapestry needle and green yarn, overcasting [through slot of handle] and working one overcast st in each sc across five full puff squares at top, leaving half squares unworked.

# SLIPPERS for Women

*designed by Mary Thomas*

**SIZES:**         **Small**    **Medium**    **Large**
  fits shoe sizes    5-6      7-8      9-10

**Size Note:** Instructions are written for sizes as follows: Small(Medium-Large).

**MATERIALS: Worsted weight yarn, one 4-oz skein each white and orange; aluminum crochet hook size G (or size required for gauge).**

**GAUGE: In hdc, 11 sts = 3″; 3 rows = 1″**

## INSTRUCTIONS (make 2)

### SOLE

With white, ch 21(25-29) loosely.

**Rnd 1 (right side):** Work 3 sc in 2nd ch from hook [heel], sc in each of next 9(11-13) chs; hdc in each of next 4(5-6) chs, dc in each of next 5(6-7) chs; work 5 dc in last ch [toe]. Then working along opposite side of starting ch, dc in each of next 5(6-7) chs, hdc in each of next 4(5-6) chs; sc in each of rem 9(11-13) chs, join with a sl st in beg sc.

**Rnd 2:** Ch 1, do not turn; 2 hdc in same sc as joining, 2 hdc in each of next 2 sc; hdc in each of next 9(11-13) sc, hdc in each of next 4(5-6) hdc; hdc in each of next 5(6-7) dc, work 2 dc in each of next 5 dc; hdc in each of next 5(6-7) dc, hdc in each of next 4(5-6) hdc; hdc in each of next 9(11-13) sc, join with a sl st in beg hdc.

**Rnd 3:** Ch 3, do not turn; dc in same hdc as joining, dc in next hdc; 2 dc in each of next 2 hdc, dc in next hdc, 2 dc in next hdc; dc in each of next 7(11-15) hdc, dc in next hdc and mark this st with a small safety pin or piece of yarn in contrasting color [to be used later for joining]; dc in each of next 10 hdc, work (dc in next dc, 2 dc in next dc) 5 times; dc in each of next 18(22-26) hdc, join with a sl st in top of beg ch-3. Finish off; weave in yarn ends.

### TOP SHAPING

Beg at center upper front section with orange, ch 4; join with a sl st to form a ring.

**Rnd 1 (right side):** Ch 2, work 7 hdc in ring, join with a sl st in top of beg ch-2.

**Rnd 2:** Ch 2, do not turn; hdc in same sp as joining, ch 1; work (2 hdc in next hdc, ch 1) 7 times, join with a sl st in top of ch-2. Finish off orange.

**Rnd 3:** With right side facing, join white with a sl st in any ch-1 sp; ch 2, work (hdc, ch 1, 2 hdc) in same sp as joining, ch 1; * work (2 hdc, ch 1, 2 hdc) in next ch-1 sp, ch 1; rep from * 6 times more, join with a sl st in top of beg ch-2. Finish off white.

**Rnd 4:** With right side facing, join orange with a sl st in any ch-1 sp; ch 2, hdc in same sp as joining, ch 1; * work 2 hdc in next ch-1 sp, ch 1; rep from * around, join with a sl st in top of beg ch-2. Finish off orange.

**Rnd 5:** With right side facing, join white with a sl st in any ch-1 sp; ch 4, hdc in next ch-1 sp, ch 1; † sc in next ch-1 sp, ch 1†; rep from † to † once; hdc in next ch-1 sp, ch 1; work (dc, hdc, sc) in next ch-1 sp, ch 1; rep from † to † 10 times; work (sc, hdc) in next ch-1 sp [same sp as beg ch-4], join with a sl st in 3rd ch of beg ch-4.

**Rnd 6:** Sl st into next ch-1 sp; ch 3, do not turn; work 2 dc in same sp, sc in next hdc, sc in next ch-1 sp; work (sc in next sc, sc in next ch-1 sp) twice; sc in next hdc, 3 dc in next ch-1 sp. DO NOT turn; with right side facing, ch 26(34-42) for back of slipper and attach with a sl st in top of beg ch-3, being careful not to twist ch. Do not finish off.

### SIDE SHAPING

**Rnd 1:** Ch 3, do not turn; working under 2 lps of each ch, dc in each of 26(34-42) chs just made; 2 dc in next sp under dc, dc in each of next 3 sts; † dc in next ch-1 sp, dc in next sc †; rep from † to † twice, * 2 dc in next ch-1 sp, dc in next sc; dc in next ch-1 sp, dc in next sc; rep from * twice; rep from † to † twice, dc in each of next 2 sts; 2 dc in sp under ch-3, join with a sl st in top beg ch-3.

**Rnd 2:** Ch 3, turn; dc in each dc around, join with a sl st in top of beg ch-3. Do not finish off; you will now work short rows across back of slipper as follows:

**Row 1:** Ch 1, turn; sc in each of next 4(5-6) dc, hdc in each of next 4(5-6) dc; dc in each of next 10(14-18) dc, hdc in each of next 4(5-6) dc, sc in each of next 4(5-6) dc.

**Row 2:** TURN; sl st in first sc, sc in each of next 3(4-5) sc; hdc in each of next 4(5-6) hdc, dc in each of next 10(14-18) dc; hdc in each of next 4(5-6) hdc, sc in each of next 3(4-5) sc [last sc is left unworked]. Do not finish off; you will now join top piece and sole tog.

### FINISHING

Hold both pieces with wrong sides tog and position marked st on sole with **next** st on top piece. Carefully matching sts, sc in each st of both pieces around, join with a sl st in beg sc. Finish off.

**Edging:** With right side facing, join white with a sl st in st [unworked lp of ch] at center back. Ch 1, work (sc, ch 2, sc) in same ch as joining, sk one st; * work (sc, ch 2, sc) in next st, sk one st; rep from * around, join with a sl st in beg sc. Finish off, weave in all yarn ends.

## Chapter 7

# At Granny's House

Utilizing the unlimited versatility of the granny square, we've included a collection of personal accents you can make for every room in your home—to re-create the warmth of Granny's house.

From small gift items—ruffled pillow, potholders—to unusual decorative accents—a window panel, rugs, floor pillows—our selection of designs lets you blend the charm of tradition with your contemporary lifestyle.

In this chapter, we also use a variety of materials—including crochet cotton and macrame cord—which give a whole new look to the granny motif.

# GRANNY POTHOLDER
*designed by Jean Leinhauser*

**SIZE:** Approx 6″ square

**MATERIALS:** Bedspread weight crochet cotton, one ball each blue and bright yellow; steel crochet hook size 7 (or size required for gauge); 2 pieces of blue felt for padding, each 6″ square.

**GAUGE:** One square = 6″

## INSTRUCTIONS

*SQUARE (make 2)*

**Note:** All rnds are worked on right side.

With blue, ch 5, join with a sl st to form a ring.

**Rnd 1:** Ch 3, 2 dc in ring; work (ch 2, 3 dc in ring) 3 times; ch 2, join with a sl st in top of beg ch-3.

**Rnd 2:** Sl st in each of next 2 dc and into ch-2 sp; ch 3, work (2 dc, ch 2, 3 dc) all in same sp, * work (3 dc, ch 2, 3 dc) in next ch-2 sp; rep from * twice, join with a sl st in top of beg ch-3; finish off.

**Rnd 3:** Join yellow with a sl st in any ch-2 sp; ch 3, work (2 dc, ch 2, 3 dc) all in same sp for beg corner; * 3 dc in sp between next two 3-dc groups for side, work (3 dc, ch 2, 3 dc) in next ch-2 sp for corner; rep from * twice, 3 dc in sp between next two 3-dc groups for last side, join with a sl st in top of beg ch-3; finish off.

**Rnd 4:** Join blue with a sl st in any corner sp; ch 3, work (2 dc, ch 2, 3 dc) all in same sp; * work 3 dc in each sp between pairs of 3-dc groups along side, work (3 dc, ch 2, 3 dc) in next corner sp; rep from * twice, work 3 dc in each sp between pairs of 3-dc groups along last side, join with a sl st in top of beg ch-3; finish off.

**Rnd 5:** With yellow, rep Rnd 4.

**Rnd 6:** With blue, rep Rnd 4.

**Rnd 7:** With yellow, rep Rnd 4.

**Rnd 8:** With blue, rep Rnd 4.

**Rnd 9:** With yellow, rep Rnd 4.

**Rnd 10:** With blue, rep Rnd 4; at end of rnd, do not finish off.

**Rnds 11 through 13:** Continuing with blue, sl st in each of next 2 dc and into corner sp; ch 3, work (2 dc, ch 2, 3 dc) in same sp; * work 3 dc in each sp between pairs of 3-dc groups along side, work (3 dc, ch 2, 3 dc) in next corner sp; rep from * twice, work 3 dc in each sp between pairs of 3-dc groups along last side, join with a sl st in top of beg ch-3. At end of last rnd, finish off and weave in all ends.

*FINISHING*

Hold 2 squares with wrong sides tog. Working in corresponding sts and corner sps of both squares, join blue with a sl st in any corner sp; ch 1, work sc in each dc across sides and 4 sc in each corner sp to last side; insert felt between squares for padding, sc in each dc across last side; work (2 sc, ch 12 [hanger], 2 sc) in last corner sp, join with a sl st in beg sc; TURN, sl st in each st of corner just made (2 sc, 12 chs, 2 sc). Finish off and weave in all ends.

# POPCORN STITCH POTHOLDER
*designed by Jean Leinhauser*

**SIZE:** Approx 6″ square

**MATERIALS:** Bedspread weight crochet cotton, one ball each green and light yellow; steel crochet hook size 7 (or size required for gauge); 2 pieces of green felt for padding, each 6″ square.

**GAUGE:** One square = 6″

## INSTRUCTIONS

*SQUARE (make 2)*

Following Popcorn Diamond Square instructions for Popcorn Diamonds Afghan in Chapter 1, work **Rnd 1** with green, **Rnds 2 through 4** with yellow and **Rnds 5 through 9** with green. At end of last rnd, do not finish off; continue with green as follows.

**Rnd 10:** Sl st into ch-2 sp, work beg corner as before; * ch 1, dc in next sp, dc in each of next 3 dc, ch 1, PC in next dc; work (dc in next dc, dc in ch at back of next PC, dc in next dc, ch 1, PC in next dc) 5 times, dc in each of next 3 dc, dc in next sp, ch 1, work corner as before; rep from * 3 times, ending in same manner as before. You should have 6 PC along each side.

**Rnd 11:** Sl st into ch-2 sp, work beg corner as before; * ch 1, 2 dc in next sp, dc in each of next 2 dc, ch 1, PC in next dc; work (dc in next dc, dc in ch at back of next PC, dc in next dc, ch 1, PC in next dc) 6 times, dc in each of next 2 dc, 2 dc in next sp, ch 1, work corner as before; rep from * 3 times, ending in same manner as before. You should have 7 PC along each side; finish off, weave in all ends.

*FINISHING*

Hold 2 squares with wrong sides tog. Working in corresponding sts and corner sps of both squares, join green with a sl st in any corner sp; ch 1, work sc in each st across sides and 4 sc in each corner sp to last side; insert felt between squares for padding, sc in each st across last side; work (2 sc, ch 12 [hanger], 2 sc) in last corner sp, join with a sl st in beg sc; TURN, sl st in each st of corner just made (2 sc, 12 chs, 2 sc). Finish off and weave in all ends.

# GIANT CHECKERBOARD GAME

*designed by Anis Duncan and Barbara Luoma*

**SIZE: Checkerboard measures approx 24″ square**
**Checker measures approx 2¼″ diameter**

**MATERIALS: Worsted weight yarn, 7 oz each black and red; aluminum crochet hooks sizes E and G (or size required for gauge).**

**GAUGE: With larger size hook, one square = 3″**

## INSTRUCTIONS
*CHECKERBOARD*

**Square (make 32 black and 32 red):** With larger size hook, ch 4, join with a sl st to form a ring.

**Rnd 1 (right side):** Ch 3, 2 dc in ring; work (ch 2, 3 dc in ring) 3 times, ch 2, join with a sl st in top of beg ch-3.

**Rnd 2 (wrong side):** TURN; sk joining sl st just made, sl st in next ch st and into ch-2 sp; ch 3, 2 dc in same sp, ch 1; * work (3 dc, ch 2, 3 dc) all in next ch-2 sp for corner, ch 1; rep from * twice, work 3 dc in beg sp, ch 2, join with a sl st in top of beg ch-3 [beg corner completed].

**Rnd 3:** TURN; sk joining sl st just made, sl st in next ch st and into beg corner sp; ch 3, 2 dc in same sp, ch 1; * work 3 dc in next ch-1 sp between two 3-dc groups, ch 1; work (3 dc, ch 2, 3 dc) in next corner sp, ch 1; rep from * twice, work 3 dc in last ch-1 sp between two 3-dc groups, ch 1; work 3 dc in beg corner sp, ch 2, join with a sl st in top of beg ch-3. Finish off, leaving 12″ yarn length for joining.

**Assembling:** Checkerboard is 8 squares wide by 8 squares long. Using joining method 5 in Chapter 8, join one row of squares, alternating black and red. Then join squares for each following row, having first square of row in opposite color of first square in prev row. Then join rows in same manner, having each 4-corner intersection firmly joined.

*CHECKER (make 12 black and 12 red)*

**Top:** With smaller size hook, ch 4. **Rnd 1:** Work 10 dc in 4th ch from hook, join with a sl st in top of beg ch. **Rnd 2:** Ch 3, 2 dc in same sp as joining, work 3 dc in each dc around, join with a sl st in top of beg ch-3; finish off.

**Bottom:** Work same as Top; at end of Rnd 2, do not finish off. Join top to bottom with wrong sides tog; matching sts carefully and inserting hook into **both lps** of corresponding sts, sl st loosely in each st around. Finish off and weave in all yarn ends.

# FOLDING FLOOR PILLOWS

*designed by Anis Duncan*

**SIZE: Each pillow measures approx 18″ square x 3″ deep**

**MATERIALS: Worsted weight yarn, 16 oz each yellow, medium green and dark green; aluminum crochet hook size G (or size required for gauge); 3 pieces of foam rubber, each 18″ square x 3″ deep.**

**GAUGE: First 6 rnds of Granny Square = 6″**

## GRANNY SQUARE

With color A, ch 4, join with a sl st to form a ring.

**Rnd 1:** Ch 3, 2 dc in ring; drop color A, pick up color B and draw through lp on hook [one ch made]; with color B work 3 dc in ring, drop color B, pick up color C and draw through lp on hook [one ch made]; with color C work (3 dc, ch 1, 3 dc) in ring, ch 1, join with a sl st in top of beg ch-3.

**Rnd 2:** TURN; continuing with color C, work 2 sl sts in ch-1 sp; ch 3, 2 dc in **same** sp; work (3 dc, ch 2, 3 dc) in next ch-1 sp [for corner]; in next ch-1 corner sp, work 3 dc, ch 2; drop color C, with color B work 3 dc in same sp; 3 dc in next ch-1 corner sp; ch 2, drop color B, pick up color A and work 3 dc in same sp; work 3 dc in beg corner sp; ch 2, join with a sl st in top of beg ch-3.

**Rnd 3:** TURN; continuing with color A, work 2 sl sts in ch-2 corner sp; ch 3, 2 dc in same sp; 3 dc in sp between next two 3-dc groups [for side]; in next ch-2 corner sp, work 3 dc, ch 2; drop color A, pick up color B and work 3 dc in same sp; 3 dc in sp between next two 3-dc groups [for side]; in next ch-2 corner sp, work 3 dc, ch 2; drop color B, pick up color C and work 3 dc in same sp; 3 dc in sp between next two 3-dc groups [for side]; in next corner sp, work (3 dc, ch 2, 3 dc); 3 dc in sp between next two 3-dc groups [for side]; in beg corner sp, work 3 dc, ch 2, join with a sl st in top of beg ch-3.

**Rnd 4:** TURN; continuing with color C, work 2 sl sts in corner sp; ch 3, 2 dc in same sp; work 3 dc in sp between each pair of 3-dc groups along side; in next corner sp, work (3 dc, ch 2, 3 dc), work 3 dc in sp between each pair of 3-dc groups along side; in next corner sp, work 3 dc, ch 2; drop color C, pick up color B and work 3 dc in same sp; work 3 dc in sp between each pair of 3-dc groups along side; in next corner sp, work 3 dc, ch 2; drop color B, pick up color A and work 3 dc in same sp; work 3 dc in sp between each pair of 3-dc groups along side; in beg corner sp, work 3 dc, ch 2, join with a sl st in top of beg ch-3.

**Rnd 5:** TURN; continuing with color A, work 2 sl sts in corner sp; ch 3, 2 dc in same sp; work 3 dc in sp between each pair of 3-dc groups along side; in next corner sp, work 3 dc, ch 2; drop color A, pick up color B and work 3 dc in same sp; work 3 dc in sp between each pair of 3-dc groups along side; in next corner sp, work 3 dc, ch 2; drop color B, pick up color C and work 3 dc in same sp; work 3 dc in sp between each pair of 3-dc groups along side; in next corner sp, work (3 dc, ch 2, 3 dc), work 3 dc in sp between each pair of 3-dc groups

along last side; in beg corner sp, work 3 dc, ch 2, join with a sl st in top of beg ch-3.

**Rnds 6 through 19:** Rep Rnds 4 and 5, 7 times. At end of last rnd, finish off and weave in all yarn ends.

## INSTRUCTIONS

### FIRST PILLOW

**Top/Bottom:** Follow Granny Square instructions and make 2 squares in the following color combination:
- Color A—Yellow
- Color B—Med Green
- Color C—Dk Green

**Side Strip:** With dk green, ch 14. **Row 1:** Dc in 4th ch from hook and in each rem ch across = 12 dc (counting ch 3). **Row 2:** Ch 3, turn; dc in each sp between dc across, ending dc in sp between last dc and ch-3 = 12 dc (counting ch 3). Rep Row 2 until strip measures approx 72″. Then join beg and last rows tog; sl st loosely across, carefully matching sts. Finish off and weave in yarn ends. **Note:** When assembling pillow, row of joining sl sts should be on the inside.

**Assembling:** With wrong sides tog, pin long edge of side strip around edges of top piece, aligning joining row of strip with one corner of top. With side strip facing you, use dk green and join edges tog in sc. Then join opposite edge of side strip to bottom piece in same manner, joining edges around 3 sides being careful to have colors of top and bottom pieces in same position. Insert foam rubber piece and then join edges of last side. Weave in all yarn ends.

### SECOND PILLOW

**Top/Bottom:** Follow Granny Square instructions and make 2 squares in the following color combination:
- Color A—Dk Green
- Color B—Med Green
- Color C—Yellow

**Side Strip and Assembling:** With yellow, follow instructions for Side Strip and Assembling of First Pillow.

### THIRD PILLOW

**Top/Bottom:** Follow Granny Square instructions and make 2 squares in the following color combination:
- Color A—Dk Green
- Color B—Yellow
- Color C—Med Green

**Side Strip and Assembling:** With med green, follow instructions for Side Strip and Assembling of First Pillow.

### JOINING PILLOWS

Join edge of First Pillow to edge of Second Pillow *(see Fig 1)*; use dk green and sl st loosely in corresponding sc across (sts used in pillow assembly). Turn joined pillows over and then join edge of Second Pillow to edge of Third Pillow *(see Fig 1)*; use med green and work in same manner. Your pillows should now fold one upon the other.

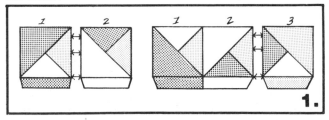

**1.**

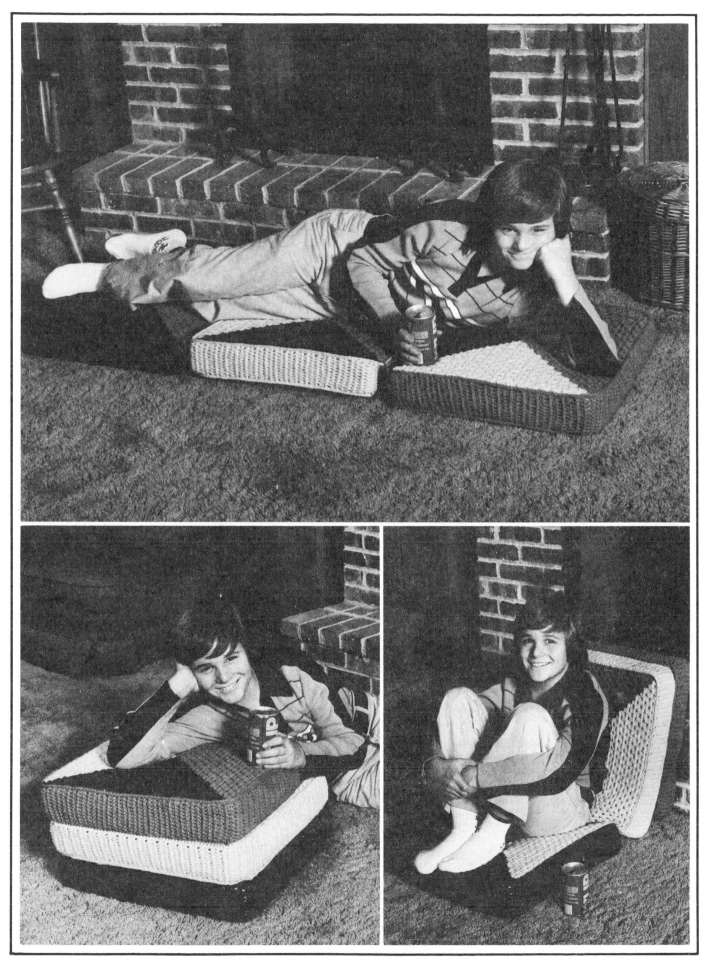

(Shown in color on page 73.)

# AZTEC-TILE MAT

*designed by Anis Duncan*

**SIZE: Approx 24" × 40"**

**MATERIALS: 3-Ply Acrylic Indoor-Outdoor Macrame Cord in 55-yd spools, 15 spools gold; aluminum crochet hook size J (or size required for gauge).**

**GAUGE: One square = 8"**

## INSTRUCTIONS

*SQUARE (make 15)*

**Note:** All rnds are worked on right side.

Ch 8, join with a sl st to form a ring.

**Rnd 1:** Ch 3, work 15 dc in ring, join with a sl st in top of beg ch-3.

**Rnd 2:** Ch 7, * sk next dc, hdc in next dc, ch 5; rep from * 6 times, sk last dc, join with a sl st in 2nd ch of beg ch-7.

**Rnd 3:** Ch 5, * sc in next sp, ch 2; work (4 dc, ch 4, 4 dc) all in next sp for corner, ch 2; rep from * twice, sc in next sp, ch 2, work (4 dc, ch 4, 3 dc) all in last sp, join with a sl st in 3rd ch of beg ch-5 [last corner made].

**Rnd 4:** Ch 6, * sk next sc, dc in **back lp only** (abbreviated BLO) in each of next 4 dc; work (2 dc, ch 4, 2 dc) in corner sp, dc in BLO in each of next 4 dc, ch 3; rep from * 3 times, ending last rep by working dc in BLO in each of last 3 dc, join with a sl st in 3rd ch of beg ch-6.

**Rnd 5:** Ch 3, * 3 dc in next sp, dc in BLO in each of next 6 dc; work (2 dc, ch 4, 2 dc) in corner sp, dc in BLO in each of next 6 dc; rep from * 3 times, ending last rep by working dc in BLO in each of last 5 dc, join with a sl st in top of beg ch-3. Finish off and weave in all ends.

*ASSEMBLING*

Mat is 3 squares wide by 5 squares long. To join, hold two squares with right sides tog; thread approx 32" length of macrame cord into yarn needle and carefully matching sts, sew with overcast st in **outer lps only** in each st across side, beg and ending with 2nd corner ch st. When joining rows of squares, be sure that each four-corner junction is firmly joined. Weave in all ends.

# SCATTER RUG

*designed by Anis Duncan*

**SIZE: Approx 30" × 40" before fringing**

**MATERIALS: Rug yarn in 70-yd skeins, 13 skeins cream, 2 skeins beige and 4 skeins rust; aluminum crochet hook size H (or size required for gauge).**

**GAUGE: One square = 5"**

## ONE-COLOR GRANNY SQUARE

Ch 4, join with a sl st to form a ring.

**Rnd 1 (wrong side):** Ch 3, 2 dc in ring, ch 2; work (3 dc in ring, ch 2) 3 times, join with a sl st in top of beg ch-3.

**Rnd 2 (right side):** TURN; sk joining sl st just made, sl st in next ch st and into ch-2 sp; ch 3, 2 dc in same sp, ch 1; * work (3 dc, ch 2, 3 dc) all in next ch-2 sp for corner, ch 1; rep from * twice; complete beg corner by working 3 dc over 2 sl sts in beg sp, ch 2, join with a sl st in top of beg ch-3.

**Rnd 3:** TURN; sk joining sl st as before, sl st in next ch st and into ch-2 corner sp; ch 3, 2 dc in same sp, ch 1; * 3 dc in ch-1 sp between next two 3-dc groups for side, ch 1; work (3 dc, ch 2, 3 dc) all in next ch-2 corner sp, ch 1; rep from * twice, 3 dc in ch-1 sp between next two 3-dc groups for last side, ch 1; complete beg corner by working 3 dc in beg sp, ch 2, join with a sl st in top of beg ch-3.

**Rnd 4:** TURN; sk joining sl st as before, sl st in next ch st and into corner sp; ch 3, 2 dc in same sp, ch 1; * work (3 dc, ch 1) in each sp between pairs of 3-dc groups along side, work (3 dc, ch 2, 3 dc) all in next corner sp, ch 1; rep from * twice; work (3 dc, ch 1) in each sp between pairs of 3-dc groups along last side; complete beg corner by working 3 dc in beg sp, ch 2, join with a sl st in top of beg ch-3. Finish off, leaving approx 12" sewing length.

## DIAGONAL TWO-COLOR GRANNY SQUARE

With color A, ch 4, join with a sl st to form a ring.

**Rnd 1 (wrong side):** Ch 3, 2 dc in ring, ch 2; 3 dc in ring, drop color A but do not cut; draw color B through lp on hook (one ch made); continuing with color B, ch 1, 3 dc in ring; ch 2, 3 dc in ring; ch 2, join with a sl st in top of beg ch-3 of color A.

**Rnd 2 (right side):** TURN; sk joining sl st just made, sl st in next ch st and into ch-2 sp; ch 3, 2 dc in same sp, ch 1; work (3 dc, ch 2, 3 dc) all in next ch-2 sp for corner; ch 1, 3 dc in next ch-2 sp; ch 2, drop color B; with color A, work 3 dc in same sp [corner made], ch 1; work (3 dc, ch 2, 3 dc) all in next ch-2 sp for corner, ch 1; complete beg corner by working 3 dc over 2 sl sts of color B in beg sp, ch 2, join with a sl st in top of beg ch-3 of color B.

**Rnd 3:** TURN; sk joining sl st as before, sl st in next ch st and into corner sp; ch 3, 2 dc in same sp, ch 1; 3 dc in ch-1 sp between next two 3-dc groups for side, ch 1; work (3 dc, ch 2, 3 dc) all in next corner sp, ch 1; 3 dc in ch-1 sp between next two 3-dc groups for side, ch 1; work 3 dc in next corner sp, ch 2, drop color A; with color B, work 3 dc in same sp, ch 1; 3 dc in ch-1 sp between next two 3-dc groups for side, ch 1; work (3 dc, ch 2, 3 dc) all in next corner sp, ch 1; 3 dc in ch-1 sp between next two 3-dc groups for last side, ch 1; complete beg corner by working 3 dc over 2 sl sts of color A in beg sp, ch 2, join with a sl st in top of beg ch-3 of color A.

**Rnd 4:** TURN; sk joining sl st as before, sl st in next ch st and into corner sp; ch 3, 2 dc in same sp, ch 1; work (3 dc, ch 1) in each sp between pairs of 3-dc groups along side; work (3 dc, ch 2, 3 dc) all in next corner sp, ch 1; work (3 dc, ch 1) in each sp between pairs of 3-dc groups along side; work 3 dc in next corner sp, ch 2, drop color B; with color A, work 3 dc in same sp, ch 1; work (3 dc, ch 1) in each sp between pairs of 3-dc groups along side; work (3 dc, ch 2, 3 dc) all in next corner sp, ch 1; work (3 dc, ch 1) in each sp between pairs of 3-dc groups along last side; complete beg corner by working 3 dc over 2 sl sts of color B in beg sp, ch 2, join with a sl st in top of beg ch-3 of color B. Finish off, leaving approx 12" sewing lengths.

## INSTRUCTIONS

Following One-Color Granny Square instructions above, make 20 squares with cream.

*(Shown in color on page 72.)*

Then following Diagonal Two-Color Granny Square instructions, make:

| COLOR A | | COLOR B | |
|---|---|---|---|
| 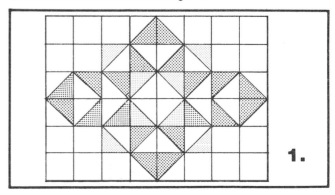 | cream | beige | 8 squares |
| | cream | rust | 20 squares |

### ASSEMBLING

See Fig 1 for placement of squares. To join, hold two squares with right sides tog; thread yarn end into tapestry needle and carefully matching sts, sew with overcast st in **outer lps only** of each st across side, beg and ending with one corner st. When joining rows of squares, be sure that each four-corner junction is firmly joined. Weave in all yarn ends.

### FRINGE

Following Basic Fringe Instructions in Chapter 8, cut 10″ strands of cream. With wrong side of rug facing you, work Single Knot Fringe and tie one strand in each st around all four sides of rug.

**1.**

# DECORATIVE WINDOW PANEL

*designed by Anis Duncan*

**SIZE:** Approx 42″ wide × adaptable length
**MATERIALS:** Speed Cro-Sheen in 100-yd balls, 11 balls white; aluminum crochet hook size E (or size required for gauge); ½″ diameter curtain rod.
**GAUGE:** One square = 5″

## INSTRUCTIONS

### SQUARE (make 19)

**Note:** All rnds are worked on right side.

Ch 8, join with a sl st to form a ring.

**Rnd 1:** Make a **beg cluster** in ring as follows: ch 3 [one lp now on hook], keeping last lp of each of next 2 sts on hook, work 2 dc [3 lps now on hook—*Fig 1*]; YO and draw through all 3 lps—beg cluster made. Ch 2, * make a **cluster** in ring as follows: keeping last lp of each st on hook, work 3 dc [4 lps now on hook]; YO and draw through all 4 lps—cluster made. Ch 2, rep from * 6 times, join with a sl st in top of beg cluster = 8 clusters.

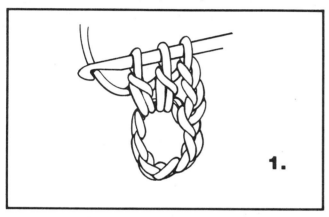

**1.**

**Rnd 2:** Sl st into ch-2 sp, work (beg cluster, ch 3, cluster) in same sp for beg corner; * ch 3, dc in next ch-2 sp, ch 3; work (cluster, ch 3, cluster) all in next ch-2 sp for corner; rep from * twice, ch 3, dc in last ch-2 sp, ch 3, join with a sl st in top of beg cluster.

**Rnd 3:** Sl st into beg corner sp, work (beg cluster, ch 3, cluster) in same sp; * ch 4, dc in next ch-3 sp; dc in next dc, dc in next ch-3 sp, ch 4; work (cluster, ch 3, cluster) in next corner sp; rep from * twice, ch 4, dc in next ch-3 sp; dc in next dc, dc in last ch-3 sp, ch 4, join with a sl st in top of beg cluster.

**Rnd 4:** Sl st into beg corner sp, work (beg cluster, ch 3, cluster) in same sp; * ch 5, dc in next ch-4 sp, dc in each of next 3 dc; dc in next ch-4 sp, ch 5; work (cluster, ch 3, cluster) in next corner sp; rep from * twice, ch 5, dc in next ch-4 sp, dc in each of next 3 dc; dc in last ch-4 sp, ch 5, join with a sl st in top of beg cluster.

**Rnd 5:** Sl st into beg corner sp, work (beg cluster, ch 3, cluster) in same sp; * ch 6, dc in next ch-5 sp, dc in each of next 5 dc; dc in next ch-5 sp, ch 6; work (cluster, ch 3, cluster) in next corner sp; rep from * twice, ch 6, dc in next ch-5 sp, dc in each of next 5 dc; dc in last ch-5 sp, ch 6, join with a sl st in top of beg cluster. Finish off and weave in all ends.

### JOINING SQUARES

Arrange squares as shown in Fig 2; then join squares using joining method 5 in Chapter 8, beg in center ch st of one corner and end in center ch st of next corner.

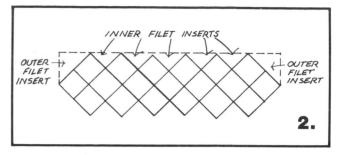

**2.**

### INNER FILET INSERT (make 5)

You will be working in open V-shape area between 2 squares (*see Fig 2*).

**Row 1:** With right side facing, beg in center of V-shape opening and counting to your right, sk corner cluster and next ch st on right-hand square; join with a sl st in next ch st, ch 1, sc in same st; ch 2, dc in sp at joining between squares, ch 2; on left-hand square, sk corner cluster and next ch st, sc in next ch st; sl st in each of next 2 ch sts, sc in next ch st.

**Row 2:** Ch 1, TURN; sk last sc and 2 sl sts just made; dc in next sc, ch 2; dc in dc of prev row, ch 2; on left-hand square, dc in ch st [same ch where joining sl st was made at beg of Row 1], ch 1; sc in 5th ch of ch-6; sl st in next ch, sl st in first dc, sc in next dc.

**Row 3:** Ch 1, TURN; sk last sc and sl sts just made, dc in next sc; work (ch 2, dc in next dc) 3 times, ch 2; on left-hand square, dc in 5th ch [same st where last sc of Row 1 was worked], ch 1; sc in 3rd dc of 7-dc group, sl st in each of next 2 dc, sc in next dc.

**Row 4:** Ch 1, TURN; sk last sc and sl sts just made, dc in next sc; work (ch 2, dc in next dc) 5 times, ch 2; on left-hand square, dc in dc [where last sc of Row 2 was worked], ch 1; sc in 6th dc of 7-dc group, sl st in next dc and in next ch, sc in next ch.

**Row 5:** Ch 1, TURN; sk last sc and sl sts, dc in next sc; work (ch 2, dc in next dc) 7 times, ch 2; on left-hand square, dc in dc [where last sc of Row 3 was worked], ch 1, sc in 3rd ch of ch-6, sl st in each of next 2 chs, sc in next ch.

**Row 6:** Ch 1, TURN; sk last sc and sl sts, dc in next sc; work (ch 2, dc in next dc) 9 times, ch 2; on left-hand square, dc in ch [where last sc of Row 4 was worked], ch 1; sc in 6th ch of ch-6. Finish off and weave in all ends.

### OUTER FILET INSERT (make 2)

**For first insert:** hold piece with **wrong** side facing and inserts just worked across top. **For 2nd insert:** hold piece with **right** side facing and inserts just worked across top.

**Row 1:** Beg in corner at right-hand edge and join with a sl st in center ch between clusters, ch 1, sc in same st; ch 5, sk cluster, sc in next ch, sl st in each of next 2 chs, sc in next ch.

**Row 2:** Ch 1, TURN; sk sc and sl sts, dc in next sc [first sc of prev row]; ch 2, dc in 3rd ch of beg ch-5 of Row 1.

**Row 3:** Ch 5, TURN; dc in next dc, ch 2; dc in ch st [where last sc of Row 1 was worked], ch 1; sc in 2nd dc of 7-dc group, sl st in each of next 2 dc, sc in next dc.

**Row 4:** Ch 1, TURN; sk sc and sl sts, dc in next sc; work (ch 2, dc in next dc) twice, ch 2, dc in 3rd ch of ch-5.

**Row 5:** Ch 5, TURN; dc in next dc, work (ch 2, dc in next dc) twice, ch 2; dc in dc [where last sc of Row 3 was worked], ch 1; sk 2 dc, sc in next ch, sl st in each of next 2 chs, sc in next ch.

**Row 6:** Ch 1, TURN; sk sc and sl sts, dc in next sc; work (ch 2, dc in next dc) 4 times, ch 2, dc in 3rd ch of ch-5.

**Row 7:** Ch 5, TURN; dc in next dc, work (ch 2, dc in next dc) 4 times, ch 2; dc in ch st [where last sc of Row 5 was worked], ch 1; sc in cluster st, sl st in corner ch of same square and in corner ch of next square (sk joining), sc in cluster.

**Row 8:** Ch 1, TURN; sk sc and sl sts, dc in next sc; work (ch 2, dc in next dc) 6 times, ch 2, dc in 3rd ch of ch-5.

**Row 9:** Ch 5, TURN; dc in next dc, work (ch 2, dc in next dc) 6 times, ch 2; dc in cluster [where last sc of Row 7 was worked], ch 1; sk 2 chs, sc in next ch, sl st in each of next 2 chs, sc in next ch.

**Row 10:** Ch 1, TURN; sk sc and sl sts, dc in next sc; work (ch 2, dc in next dc) 8 times, ch 2, dc in 3rd ch of ch-5.

**Row 11:** Ch 5, TURN; dc in next dc, work (ch 2, dc in next dc) 8 times, ch 2; dc in ch st [where last sc of Row 9 was worked], ch 1; sc in 3rd dc of 7-dc group, sl st in each of next 2 dc, sc in next dc.

**Row 12:** Ch 1, TURN; sk sc and sl sts, dc in next sc; work (ch 2, dc in next dc) 10 times, ch 2, dc in 3rd ch of ch-5.

**Row 13:** Ch 5, TURN; dc in next dc, work (ch 2, dc in next dc) 10 times, ch 2; dc in dc [where last sc of Row 11 was worked], ch 1; sk 2 chs, sc in next ch, sl st in each of next 2 chs, sc in next ch.

**Row 14:** Ch 1, TURN; sk sc and sl sts, dc in next sc; work (ch 2, dc in next dc) 12 times, ch 2, dc in 3rd ch of ch-5. **For first insert:** finish off, weave in all ends. **For 2nd insert:** do not finish off, continue with same thread and work Filet Body.

*FILET BODY*

**Row 1 (right side):** Ch 5, TURN; work (dc in next dc, ch 2) 13 times, * dc in ch before cluster [same st where sc was worked in last row of insert]; ch 2, dc in center ch of corner [between clusters], ch 2, sk cluster, dc in next ch [same st where sc was worked in last row of insert]; ch 2, work (dc in next dc, ch 2) 11 times; rep from * across, ending last rep by working (dc in next dc, ch 2) 13 times, dc in last dc.

**Row 2:** Ch 5, TURN; * dc in next dc, ch 2; rep from * across, ending dc in 3rd ch of ch-5. Rep Row 2 until panel measures desired length. The panel in our photo measures approx 27"long.

**Last Row:** Ch 8, TURN; * sc in next dc, ch 8; rep from * across, ending sc in 3rd ch of ch-5. Finish off and weave in all ends.

*FINISHING*

Place panel on a flat padded surface covered with a clean white sheet. Keeping edges straight, insert rust-proof pins in sts around panel. Then spray with a commercial spray starch until wet. Let dry thoroughly (this may take several days in muggy weather) before removing pins. Insert curtain rod through ch-8 lps at top of panel.

# GIANT FLOOR BALL

*designed by Kathie Schroeder*

This giant ball is many things: a conversation piece, a decorative accessory, a hassock, something to lean against while watching TV and a fascinating sampler of textured stitches. We chose an interesting blending of Indian type colors; you can substitute as you desire to match your own decor.

**SIZE: Approx 30″ diameter**

**MATERIALS: Aunt Lydia's Heavy Rug Yarn in 70-yd skeins, 16 skeins Peacock, 8 skeins each White and Yellow, 7 skeins each Grass Green and Spring Green, and 5 skeins Rust; aluminum crochet hook size G (or size required for gauge); approx 20 lbs polyester filling for stuffing.**

**GAUGE: In dc, 11 sts = 3″; 4 rows = 2″**

## PATTERN STITCHES

This project uses several stitches that may be new to you. Among them are:

*DOUBLE DOUBLE CROCHET*
*(abbreviated ddc)*
YO hook twice as for a tr; insert hook into st, hook yarn and draw through st [4 lps now on hook]; YO and pull through 2 lps, YO and pull through 3 lps.

*EXTENDED SINGLE CROCHET*
*(abbreviated esc)*
Insert hook in st, hook yarn and draw through st [2 lps now on hook]; YO and pull through one lp; YO and pull through 2 lps.

**Pattern Stitches Note:** Instructions and diagrams for other pattern stitches are given in the instructions, where they first occur. Be on the alert for the abbreviations "ddc" and "esc" so you don't inadvertently work regular dc or sc instead.

## INSTRUCTIONS

PENTAGON (make 12)
With White, ch 2.

**Rnd 1 (right side):** Work 5 sc in 2nd ch from hook, join with a sl st in beg sc.

**Rnd 2:** Ch 2 [counts as first hdc of rnd], 2 hdc in same st as joining; work 3 hdc in each rem sc around, join with a sl st in top of beg ch-2 = 15 hdc. Finish off White.

**Rnd 3:** With right side facing, join Yellow with a sl st in center hdc of any 3-hdc group; ch 3 [counts as first ddc of rnd], work (ddc, ch 1, 2 ddc) all in same st as joining for beg corner; * ddc in each of next 2 sts, work (2 ddc, ch 1, 2 ddc) all in next st [center hdc of 3-hdc group] for corner; rep from * 3 times, ddc in each of last 2 sts, join with a sl st in top of beg ch-3. You should have five sides and five ch-1 corner sps. Finish off Yellow.

**Rnd 4:** With right side facing, make a slip knot on hook with Spring Green and join with sc in any ch-1 corner sp; ch 1, sc in same sp; * sk one ddc, sc in each of next 5 ddc along side; work (sc, ch 1, sc) all in next ch-1 corner sp; rep from * around, ending last rep without working corner, join with a sl st in beg sc.

**Rnd 5:** Sl st into ch-1 corner sp; ch 4 [first 3 chs count as beg ddc of rnd], ddc in same sp; * work ddc in **back lp**

only (lp away from you) in each of 7 sc along side, work (ddc, ch 1, ddc) all in next ch-1 corner sp; rep from * around, ending last rep without working corner, join with a sl st in 3rd ch of beg ch-4.

**Rnd 6 (wrong side):** Ch 2 [counts as first st of rnd], TURN; working in **front lp only** (lp toward you) in each st around, sc in each of next 8 sts along first side; * work (sc, ch 1, sc) all in next ch-1 corner sp, sc in each of next 9 sts along side; rep from * around to last ch-1 corner sp, work (sc, ch 1, sc) all in corner sp, join with a sl st in top of beg ch-2. Finish off Spring Green.

**Note:** Now continue by working in **both lps** of sts.

**Rnd 7:** TURN; with right side facing, make a slip knot on hook with Grass Green and join with sc in any ch-1 corner sp; ch 1, sc in same sp; * sc in each of 11 sc along side, work (sc, ch 1, sc) all in ch-1 corner sp; rep from * around, ending last rep without working corner, join with a sl st in beg sc. Finish off Grass Green.

**Rnd 8:** With right side facing, make a slip knot on hook with White and join with sc in any ch-1 corner sp; ch 1, sc in same sp; * sc in next st, work long sc over next st [to work long sc: insert hook in st (sc) in 2nd row below *(Fig 1)* and complete st as sc—long sc made]; sc in next st, work (long sc over next st, sc in next st) 5 times; work (sc, ch 1, sc) in ch-1 corner sp; rep from * around, ending last rep without working corner, join with a sl st in beg sc. Finish off White.

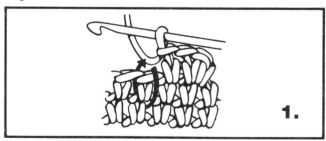

**1.**

**Rnd 9:** With right side facing, join Peacock with a sl st in any ch-1 corner sp; ch 4 [first 3 chs count as beg dc of rnd], dc in same sp; * sk one st, dc in each of next 2 sts; work popcorn (abbreviated PC) in next st [to make PC: work 5 dc in st, remove hook and insert in first dc of 5-dc group, hook dropped lp *(Fig 2)* and pull through st, ch 1 —PC made]; work (dc in next st, PC in next st) 4 times, dc in each of next 2 sts, sk one st; work (dc, ch 1, dc) all in ch-1 corner sp; rep from * around, ending last rep without working corner, join with a sl st in 3rd ch of beg ch-4. You should have 5 PC along each side. Finish off Peacock.

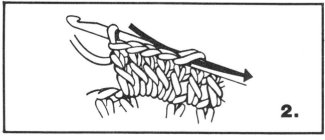

**2.**

**Rnd 10:** With right side facing, make a slip knot on hook with White and join with sc in any ch-1 corner sp; ch 1, sc in same sp; * sk one dc, sc in each of next 2 dc; work (sc in ch-1 at top of next PC, sc in next dc) 5 times, sc in

next dc; sk one dc, work (sc, ch 1, sc) all in ch-1 corner sp; rep from * around, ending last rep without working corner, join with a sl st in beg sc. You should have 15 sc along each side between ch-1 corner sps. Finish off White.

**Rnd 11:** With right side facing, make a slip knot on hook with Rust and join with esc in any ch-1 corner sp; ch 1, esc in same sp; * work esc in each of next 15 sc, work (esc, ch 1, esc) all in ch-1 corner sp; rep from * around, ending last rep without working corner, join with a sl st in beg esc. Finish off Rust.

**Rnd 12:** With right side facing, make a slip knot on hook with Spring Green and join with sc in any ch-1 corner sp; ch 1, sc in same sp; * sk one st, † work (sc, dc) in next st, sk one st †; rep from † to † 7 times; work (sc, ch 1, sc) all in ch-1 corner sp; rep from * around, ending last rep without working corner, join with a sl st in beg sc.

**Rnd 13 (wrong side):** Ch 1, TURN; * † work (sc, dc) in next **dc,** sk sc †; rep from † to † 7 times; work (sc, dc) in **sc** before corner sp, work (sc, ch 1, sc) all in ch-1 corner sp; rep from * around, join with a sl st in beg sc. Finish off Spring Green.

**Rnd 14:** With right side facing, join Yellow with a sl st in any ch-1 corner sp; ch 4, dc in same sp; * sk one st, dc in next st, work one wrap st [to make wrap st: dc in next st, (YO, insert hook in sp between last 2 dc worked—see Fig 3; hook yarn and draw lp through) 5 times—you should now have 11 lps on hook; YO and draw through all lps on hook—see Fig 4; ch 1: wrap st made]; work (dc in each of next 2 sts, make one wrap st) 5 times, dc in

next st; sk one st, work (dc, ch 1, dc) all in ch-1 corner sp; rep from * around, ending last rep without working corner, join with a sl st in 3rd ch of beg ch-4. You should have 6 wrap sts along each side.

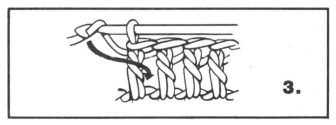

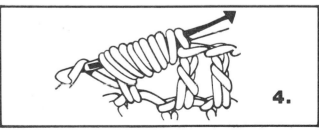

**Rnd 15:** Ch 1, sc in same st as joining; * work (sc, ch 1, sc) in ch-1 corner sp; work (sc in each of next 2 dc, sc in top of wrap st) 6 times, sc in each of next 2 dc; rep from * around, ending last rep by working sc in last dc, join with a sl st in beg sc. You should have 22 sc along each side between ch-1 corner sps. Finish off Yellow.

**Rnd 16:** With right side facing, make a slip knot on hook with Grass Green and join with sc in any ch-1 corner sp; ch 1, sc in same sp; * sk one st, sc in next st, work long

*(Shown in color on page 67.)*

sc over next st [to make long sc: insert hook in sp between 2 dc in 2nd row below (*Fig 5*) and complete st as sc—long sc made]; work (sc in each of next 2 sts, long sc over next st) 6 times, sc in next st; work (sc, ch 1, sc) in ch-1 corner sp; rep from * around, ending last rep without working corner, join with a sl st in beg sc. You should have 7 long sc across each side. Finish off Grass Green.

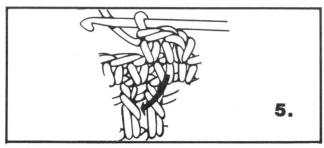

**5.**

**Rnd 17:** With right side facing, make a slip knot on hook with White and join with esc in any ch-1 corner sp; ch 1, esc in same sp; * work esc in each of next 23 sts, work (esc, ch 1, esc) in ch-1 corner sp; rep from * around, ending last rep without working corner, join with a sl st in beg esc. Finish off White.

**Rnd 18:** With right side facing, join Peacock with a sl st in any ch-1 corner sp; ch 4, dc in same sp; * sk one st, dc in each of next 2 sts, work (PC in next st, dc in each of next 2 sts) 7 times; sk one st, work (dc, ch 1, dc) all in ch-1 corner sp; rep from * around, ending last rep without working corner, join with a sl st in 3rd ch of beg ch-4. You should have 7 PC along each side.

**Rnd 19:** Ch 1, sc in same st as joining; * work (sc, ch 1, sc) in ch-1 corner sp; work sc in each dc and in ch-1 at top of each PC along side; rep from * around, join with a sl st in beg sc. You should have 27 sc along each side between ch-1 corner sps. Finish off Peacock.

**Rnd 20:** With right side facing, make a slip knot on hook with White and join with esc in any ch-1 corner sp; ch 1, esc in same sp; * sk one st, work esc in each of next 25 sc, sk one st, work (esc, ch 1, esc) in ch-1 corner sp; rep

from * around, ending last rep without working corner, join with a sl st in beg esc. Finish off White.

**Rnd 21:** With right side facing, join Grass Green with a sl st in any ch-1 corner sp; work 2 sc in **front lp only** of each esc around (omitting ch-1 corner sps), join with a sl st in beg sc. Finish off and weave in all yarn ends.

*JOINING*

Hold two pentagons with wrong sides tog. Working in **back lp only** of sts in Rnd 20 (lps left unworked in prev rnd—see *Fig 6*) and carefully matching sts across side, join rust with a sl st in corner st, ch 1; work 2 sc in same st as joining and in each st across, ending in st at next corner. Join rem pentagons in same manner, so that you have six pairs of joined pentagons. Then use same joining method and join pairs as shown in Fig 7, leaving one final side open for stuffing. Stuff firmly with polyester filling; ball should be firm, not squashy. As stuffing has a tendency to settle a bit, we suggest you let your stuffed ball rest a day or two before joining last side. Add more stuffing if desired, join last side as before.

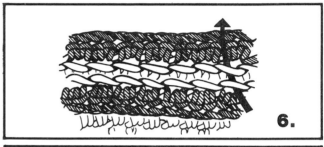

**6.**

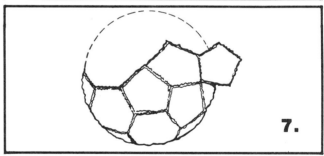

**7.**

# *RUFFLED PILLOW*

*designed by Jean Leinhauser*

**SIZE: Approx 16″ square before ruffle**

**MATERIALS: Sport weight yarn, 6 oz white; aluminum crochet hook size F (or size required for gauge); 16″ knife-edge pillow form, covered in satin fabric in color of your choice.**

**GAUGE: In dc, 8 sts = 2″; 5 rows = 2″**

## *INSTRUCTIONS*

*FLORAL-CENTER SQUARE*

Ch 5, join with a sl st to form a ring.

**Rnd 1:** * Ch 2, work 3 dc in ring; ch 2, sc in ring; rep from * 5 times = 6 petals.

**Rnd 2:** * Ch 4, holding petal forward and working behind it, sc in **back lp only** (abbreviated BLO) of next sc; rep from * 5 times = 6 ch lps.

**Rnd 3:** * Ch 2, work 5 dc in next ch lp; ch 2, sc in BLO of next sc; rep from * 5 times = 6 petals.

**Rnd 4:** * Ch 6, holding petal forward and working behind it, sc in BLO of next sc; rep from * 5 times.

**Rnd 5:** * Ch 2, work 7 dc in next ch lp; ch 2, sc in BLO of next sc; rep from * 5 times.

**Rnd 6:** * Ch 4, work back post sc around post of 4th dc of next 7-dc group [to work back post sc: insert hook from back to front around post of dc *(Fig 1)*, hook yarn and draw through, completing st as a sc—back post sc made]; ch 3, sc in **both lps** of next sc; rep from * 5 times = 12 ch lps.

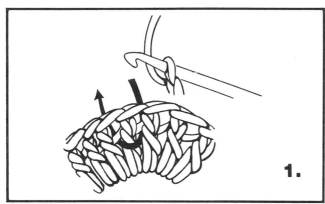

**Note:** On following rnds, work in **both lps** of each sc.

**Rnd 7:** * Ch 1, work 5 dc in next ch lp; ch 1, sc in next sc; rep from * 11 times = 12 petals.

**Rnd 8:** * Ch 5, working behind petal as before, sc in next sc; rep from * 11 times.

**Rnd 9:** * Ch 1, work 6 dc in next ch lp; ch 1, sc in next sc; rep from * 11 times.

**Rnd 10:** * Ch 6, working behind petal, sc in next sc; rep from * 11 times.

**Rnd 11:** * Ch 1, work 7 dc in next ch lp; ch 1, sc in next sc; rep from * 11 times.

**Rnd 12:** * Ch 7, working behind petal, sc in next sc; rep from * 11 times.

**Rnd 13:** * Ch 1, work 8 dc in next ch lp; ch 1, sc in next sc; rep from * 11 times.

**Rnd 14:** * Ch 8, working behind petal, sc in next sc; rep from * 11 times.

**Rnd 15:** * Work (hdc, 9 dc, hdc) all in next ch lp for corner; work 8 sc in next ch lp, sc in next sc, 8 sc in next ch lp; rep from * 3 times, join with a sl st in beg hdc. Floral center is now completed.

**Rnd 16:** Ch 3, * dc in each of next 4 dc; work (dc, ch 2, dc) all in next dc for corner, dc in each of next 4 dc and in hdc; work (ch 1, sk one sc, dc in next sc) 8 times; ch 1, sk one sc, dc in hdc; rep from * 3 times, ending last rep by working ch 1, sk last sc, join with a sl st in top of beg ch-3.

**Rnd 17:** Ch 3, dc in each of next 5 dc; * work (dc, ch 3, dc) all in corner sp, dc in each of next 6 dc; work (ch 1, dc in next dc) 8 times, ch 1, dc in each of next 6 dc; rep from * 3 times, ending last rep by working ch 1, join with a sl st in top of beg ch-3.

**Rnd 18:** Ch 3, dc in each of next 6 dc; * work (2 dc, ch 3, 2 dc) all in corner sp, dc in each of next 7 dc; work (ch 1, dc in next dc) 8 times, ch 1, dc in each of next 7 dc; rep from * 3 times, ending last rep by working ch 1, join with a sl st in top of beg ch-3.

**Rnd 19:** Ch 4, * sk one dc, dc in each of next 7 dc; work (2 dc, ch 3, 2 dc) all in corner sp, dc in each of next 7 dc; ch 1, sk one dc, work (dc in next dc, ch 1) 10 times; rep from * 3 times, ending last rep by working (dc in next dc, ch 1) 9 times, join with a sl st in 3rd ch of beg ch-4.

**Rnd 20:** Ch 4, * dc in each of next 9 dc; work (2 dc, ch 3, 2 dc) all in corner sp, dc in each of next 9 dc; ch 1, work (dc in next dc, ch 1) 10 times; rep from * 3 times, ending last rep by working (dc in next dc, ch 1) 9 times, join with a sl st in 3rd ch of beg ch-4.

**Rnd 21:** Ch 4, * dc in each of next 11 dc; work (2 dc, ch 3, 2 dc) all in corner sp, dc in each of next 11 dc; ch 1, work (dc in next dc, ch 1) 10 times; rep from * 3 times, ending last rep by working (dc in next dc, ch 1) 9 times, join with a sl st in 3rd ch of beg ch-4.

**Rnd 22:** Ch 4, dc in next dc, ch 1; * sk one dc, dc in each of next 11 dc; work (2 dc, ch 3, 2 dc) all in corner sp, dc in each of next 11 dc; ch 1, sk one dc; work (dc in next dc, ch 1) 12 times; rep from * 3 times, ending last rep by working (dc in next dc, ch 1) 10 times, join with a sl st in 3rd ch of beg ch-4.

**Rnd 23:** Ch 4, dc in next dc, ch 1; * dc in each of next 13 dc; work (2 dc, ch 3, 2 dc) all in corner sp, dc in each of next 13 dc; ch 1, work (dc in next dc, ch 1) 12 times; rep from * 3 times, ending last rep by working (dc in next dc, ch 1) 10 times, join with a sl st in 3rd ch of beg ch-4.

**Rnd 24:** Ch 4, dc in next dc, ch 1; * dc in each of next 15 dc; work (2 dc, ch 3, 2 dc) all in corner sp, dc in each of next 15 dc; ch 1, work (dc in next dc, ch 1) 12 times; rep from * 3 times, ending last rep by working (dc in next dc, ch 1) 10 times, join with a sl st in 3rd ch of beg ch-4. Do not finish off; you will now begin working a ruffled edging around square.

*RUFFLE*

**Rnd 1:** Ch 1, sc in same st as joining; work sc in **front lp only** (lp toward you) of each dc and each ch st around all four sides, join with a sl st in beg sc.

**Note:** On following rnds, work in **both lps** of sts.

**Rnd 2:** Ch 4, * dc in next sc, ch 1; rep from * around, join with a sl st in 3rd ch of beg ch-4.

**Rnd 3:** Ch 4, dc in same st as joining [beg shell made]; ch 2, * work (dc, ch 1, dc) all in next dc [shell made], ch 2; rep from * around, join with a sl st in 3rd ch of beg ch-4.

**Rnd 4:** Sl st in ch-1 sp of beg shell, ch 1, sc in same sp; * ch 5, sc in ch-1 sp of next shell; rep from * around to ch-1 sp of last shell, ch 5, join with a sl st in beg sc.

**Rnd 5:** Ch 1, sc in same st as joining; * work (3 dc, tr, 3 dc) all in next ch-5 sp, sc in next sc; rep from * around, ending last rep by joining with a sl st in beg sc. Finish off, weave in all yarn ends.

*FINISHING*

With right side facing, use sewing thread and sew Floral-Center Square to front of satin-covered pillow form, working in back lps of sts and chs in last rnd of square [unworked lps in Rnd 1 of Ruffle].

## Chapter 8

# Special Techniques

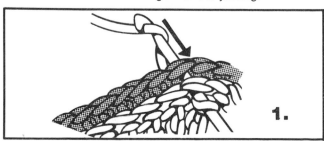

This chapter contains instructions and diagrams for many of the techniques required to finish the projects in this book. No matter how well a project is made, if the finishing is not well done, the whole project can be disappointing.

Use these special techniques, and you'll be delighted with your granny designs.

## JOINING METHODS

There are several different methods that can be used to join granny squares or garment seams. Each of our patterns tells you which method to use for that particular project.

This joining must be done correctly so that the seams are neat and lie flat. When joining seams, be careful to match sts whenever possible.

### METHOD 1

Hold squares or pieces with right sides tog. With crochet hook, join yarn and sl st through **both lps** of the matching sts on both pieces to be joined (Fig 1). Crochet LOOSELY so that seams do not pucker. You may wish to use a hook one size larger for the joining.

**1.**

### METHOD 2

Hold squares or pieces with right sides tog. With crochet hook, join yarn and sl st through **front lps only** (sometimes called **inner lps**)—(Fig 2) of matching sts on both pieces to be joined. Again, crochet LOOSELY to keep seams from puckering.

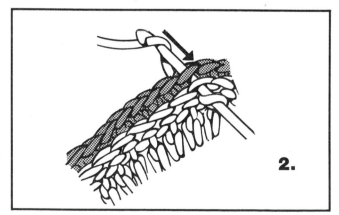

**2.**

### METHOD 3

Work same as Method 2, but work through **back lps only** (sometimes called **outer lps**)—Fig 3.

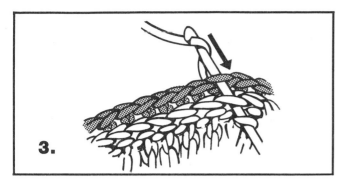

**3.**

## METHOD 4

Hold squares or pieces with right sides tog. Thread yarn into tapestry needle; with overcast st, sew through **front lps only** (Fig 4) of matching sts on both pieces to be joined.

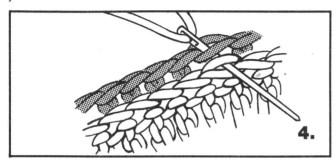

**4.**

## METHOD 5

Work same as Method 4, but work through **back lps only** (Fig 5).

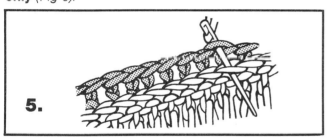

**5.**

## BASIC FRINGE INSTRUCTIONS

Cut cardboard about 6″ wide and half as long as specified in instructions for strands. Wind yarn loosely and evenly lengthwise around cardboard; when card is filled, cut yarn across one end. Do this several times; then start fringing. You can wind and cut additional strands as you need them. Unless pattern states otherwise, have wrong side of project facing you as you fringe.

### SPAGHETTI FRINGE

This fringe uses just one strand of yarn in a knot. Fold a strand in half, then use crochet hook to draw folded end through sp or st, pull loose ends through folded section (Fig 6), and draw knot up firmly. Space knots as indicated in specific project instructions. When project is completely fringed, trim ends to even off.

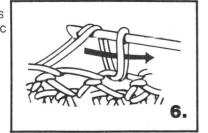

**6.**

### SINGLE KNOT FRINGE

Your pattern will tell you how many strands to use in one knot of fringe. Hold this number of strands together, then fold in half. Use crochet hook to draw folded end through space or st, pull loose ends through folded section (Fig 7), and draw knot up firmly (Fig 8). Space knots of fringe as indicated in individual project instructions. Trim ends to even off.

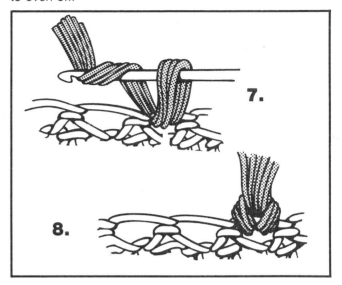

**7.**

**8.**

### TRIPLE KNOT FRINGE

Begin by working Single Knot Fringe as above completely across one end or edge of piece. Turn piece so right side is facing you. Working from left to right, take half the strands in the first knot, and half the strands in the knot next to it, and knot them together (Fig 9). Again working from left to right, tie third row of knots as in Fig 10.

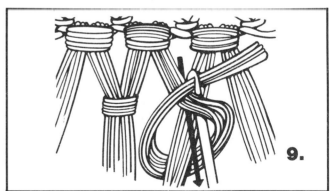

**9.**

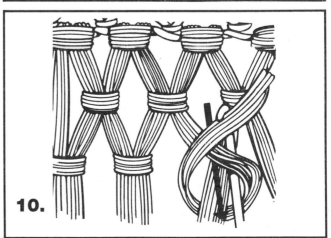

**10.**

## POMPON

To make a pompon, cut two cardboard circles, each ½″ in diameter larger than desired finished pompon size. Cut a hole in the center of each circle, approx ½″ diameter. Thread a tapestry needle with a 72″ length of yarn, doubled. Holding both circles tog, insert needle through center hole, over outside edge, through center again (Fig 11), until entire circle is covered. Thread more lengths of yarn as needed.

With very sharp scissors, cut yarn between the two circles all around the circumference (Fig 12). Using a 12″ strand of yarn doubled, slip yarn between circles, pull up tightly and tie very firmly. Remove cardboards, and fluff out pompon by rolling it between your hands. Trim evenly with scissors.

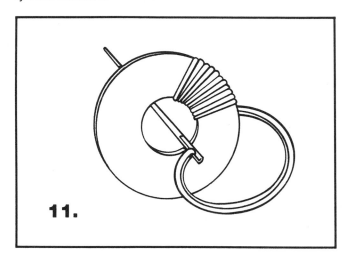

11.

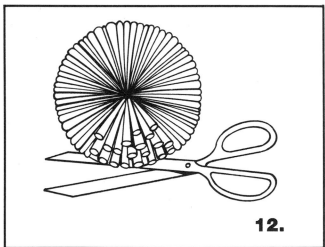

12.

## TASSEL

Cut a piece of cardboard about 6″ wide, and as long as desired length of finished tassel. Wind yarn around length of cardboard the number of times specified in pattern instructions. Cut a piece of yarn about 20″ long, and thread into tapestry needle doubled. Insert needle through all strands at top of cardboard, pull up tightly and knot securely, leaving ends for attaching to garment. Cut yarn at opposite end of cardboard (Fig 13); remove cardboard.

Cut another strand of yarn 10″ long, and wrap it tightly twice around tassel 1½″ (or less on a tiny tassel) below top knot. Knot securely and allow excess ends to fall as part of tassel.

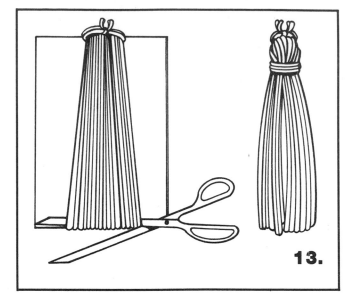

13.

## REVERSE SINGLE CROCHET

This is an attractive finishing touch worked on right side of garment as for regular single crochet, but from **left** to **right.** Join yarn at specified point, and ch 1; * insert hook in next st to your right, hook yarn and pull through in direction of arrow in Fig 14: 2 lps on hook; hook yarn and pull through both lps (Fig 15). Rep from * across edge, finish off. Take care not to work too tightly.

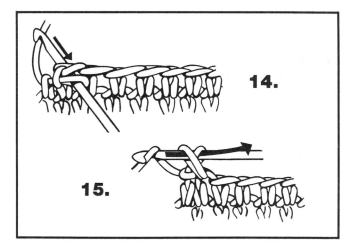

14.

15.

## BLOCKING

Most crocheted projects don't need to be completely blocked, as do most knit garments. However, a light bit of steaming along joinings and outer edges is desirable. This helps the work to lie flat. To steam, place work on a padded surface (for a large piece, a carpeted floor, covered with an old sheet, works well). Place a damp terry towel between work and iron: never let iron rest directly on the crocheted piece. Do not use pressure: let the steam do the work. Let project dry completely before lifting.